Diners of the Great Lakes
Michael Engle
Michael Engle Publishing

To the builders and operators of diners.

Library of Congress Control Number
2018908066

Copyright
Michael Engle Publishing 2018

Troy, New York

All photographs used in this book remain in the ownership of the credited person/entity.

Please note that the layout of this book is not the original intent. The original intent was 11 width x 8.5 height instead of 8.5 width x 11 height. This was forced by the fact that very few on demand printers allow 11 x 8.5 dimensions. If you are interested in purchasing this book in the original design, please contact the author directly.

Contents

Acknowledgments. 4
Introduction. 6
Geekery? 7

Lunch Wagons. 8
Closson Lunch Wagon Company. 38
Earl Richardson and Silver Creek. 62
Ward and Dickinson Dining Car Company. 88

Kuppy's Diner. 118

Others Followed in Building Diners. 132
Ohio Diners and Diner Builders. 160
Sectional Diner Construction. 180
After the War. Who was Building Diners. 204
Decline of the Diner. 228
Diners Make a Comeback. 254
Great Lakes Diner Directory. 270

Acknowledgments.

There are so many people who have helped, guided, motivated and inspired me along the way. The diner world, so to speak, is a small community, but there are many other people who are just historians, collectors of the past.

Other than the last person(s) mentioned, these are in no particular order.

To Richard J.S. Gutman for writing the best history of diners on the book shelves, *American Diner, Then and Now*. Gutman blazed a path for future diner historians and has always promoted diners in a positive way. John Baeder for helping to make people see diners as a work of art. People started seeing diners as more than just an utilitarian building. Daniel Zilka for guidance when I first got serious in researching diners. For opening up the American Diner Heritage's collection to me and this book. As I traveled for research, I can not tell you how many times I heard, "Oh, a guy named Zilka was here researching diners a couple of years ago." Also to Daniel for helping to save diners like the Kullman (Now Hullabaloo's Diner in Wellborn, Texas) in Stillwater, New York and for his time and effort helping to save the old Goodell diner from Wellington, Ohio. He also brought with him Toni Deller to assist us with the preservation of this beautiful diner. Larry Cultrera for opening up his collections of photos he took in the 1980s. He blazed a path for many people in the diner world by being part of the first wave of diner documentarians. Vince Martonis for opening up the collection of the Hanover History Center in Silver Creek, New York, home of Ward & Dickinson. The research he has put in and the resources he and the center have are a valuable resource. Marybelle Beigh for researching as many of the diners in Chautauqua County that she could. She has been very persistent in preserving their memories. Glenn

Wells for going on so many road trips to visit diners neither of us had seen before. Spencer Stewart for his diner sleuthing and the ability to find things no one else had yet found. David Hebb for being open with his collection that he amassed. Wesli Dymoke for helping to flesh out grammar, spelling errors and other issues that often plague my books. Ron Dylewski for opening up his own collection of photographs and his expertise on design concerns. Steve Boksenbaum for opening up his collection of photographs from western Pennsylvania. Brian Butko for his research in western Pennsylvania and for his work with Kevin Patrick and Kyle Weaver in the inspirational Diners of Pennsylvania book. Many people don't realize how much Brian has done in helping to uncover the history of western Pennsylvania. I wish Pittsburgh was closer so I could get together at a diner with Ron, Steve and Brian. Randy Garbin for his work on getting the message out to the masses when it comes to diners and the whole roadside scene. Dean Smith for helping to preserve the last Richardson built diner in Penn Yan, New York. He helped to make sure it was passed on to the more than capable hands of the current owners. Kathy Stribley for helping to preserve diner history in Syracuse, New York. All of the Pennsylvania Prothonotaries and Historian offices that see the benefit in preserving obscure records like Conditional Sales Dockets. To everyone who has saved photographs of diners and the history of their relative's or their town's diners. All the employees who have put in long hours, especially in the old time twenty-four hour diners. And the people who keep these relics of the past alive today. Another thank you to everyone who has been a member of my facebook group that guided me in the process of putting this book together. And finally to Gordon Tindall and his wife Val, for being friends and to Gordon for helping to restore three diners and for having the heart of a dreamer.

I know I have missed people, so to everyone else who helped along the way, I thank you and I hope you do not give me too much grief for omitting your name.

Introduction.

Richard J.S. Gutman wrote the authoritative book on diners: *American Diner, Then and Now,* but even this book left many stories uncovered. He gave a scant few pages to the history of diners in the Great Lake states.

For people unfamiliar with the history of diners, most people associate diners with the east coast. New Jersey and Long Island were practically littered with diners from the 1920s on. Few people know just how popular diners were in the Great Lakes region in the 1920s and 1930s, especially the eastern Great Lakes. While Great Lakes diners were not as popular as they were along the east coast, a diner could still be found in most cities and villages. Nor do people know how many lunch wagons plied their trade in Minneapolis-St. Paul around the first decade of the 1900s.

My goal for this book is to begin to remedy some of these omissions. Even though, this book will still have an immeasurable number of omissions. This book is meant as a first attempt. It is intended to build upon the story told in *American Diner, Then and Now* and continue it with more information on the builders who were located mostly near the shores of the Great Lakes or had some connection to that region. Most people do not know that in the 1930s practically any village with over a thousand people along the shores of Lakes Erie and Ontario had a diner doing business there. One by one, starting around World War II, these diners started to vanish, and unlike the east coast where these old diners were replaced with shiny new and larger diners, in the Great Lakes they just disappeared.

Lunch wagons were once hugely popular in more than a number of places in the Great Lakes and mid-west. They went from novelty to becoming a status symbol for a locality, to a place for late night citizens. More often than not, the numbers of wagons did not correspond to the numbers of diners from the 1920s on. But this did not stop diner builders from making valiant attempts to place diners into Midwestern and Great Lake towns.

What started as work to document the Ward & Dickinson Dining Car Company grew into this book. This book is my attempt to focus on the story of builders along Lake Erie from 1912 up to 1949 and then accompany that with more builders of diners in the Great Lakes. I hope that you learn something from this book, and if you have ancestors who ran diners in the past, I hope you find your photos and stories and share them with the rest of the world.

Geekery?

Each chapter is finished off with a section called "Geekery." What does Geekery mean? The Cambridge Dictionary defines the word as: "a great interest in and knowledge of a particular subject." The Geekery section is reserved for minutiae that many people may not be interested in, but still important enough to tell the story about diners and the researching of diners.

Chapter 1: Gardner & Gorman's Lunch Wagon Patent.

Chapter 2: Albert Closson's Lunch Wagon Patent.

Chapter 3: Listing of known diners between Silver Creek, New York and Geneva, Ohio.

Chapter 4: List of known Ward and Dickinson diners.

Chapter 5: Chattels and Bankruptcy Sales.

Chapter 6: Menus over the Years.

Chapter 7: Coffee Prices around the 1950s.

Chapter 8: Other Portable Restaurant builders.

Chapter 9: Conditional Sales Dockets.

Instead of Chapter 10 having a geekery section, Chapter 10 is followed by a directory of current diners in nine states that roughly surround the Great Lakes. The directory will include an address, maker and some very basic information about each diner. I make no guarantees for the accuracy of the information in the directory. If you want to visit a diner, I highly suggest that you contact the diner as even on-line information has been found to be wrong at times.

Chapter 1

Lunch Wagons

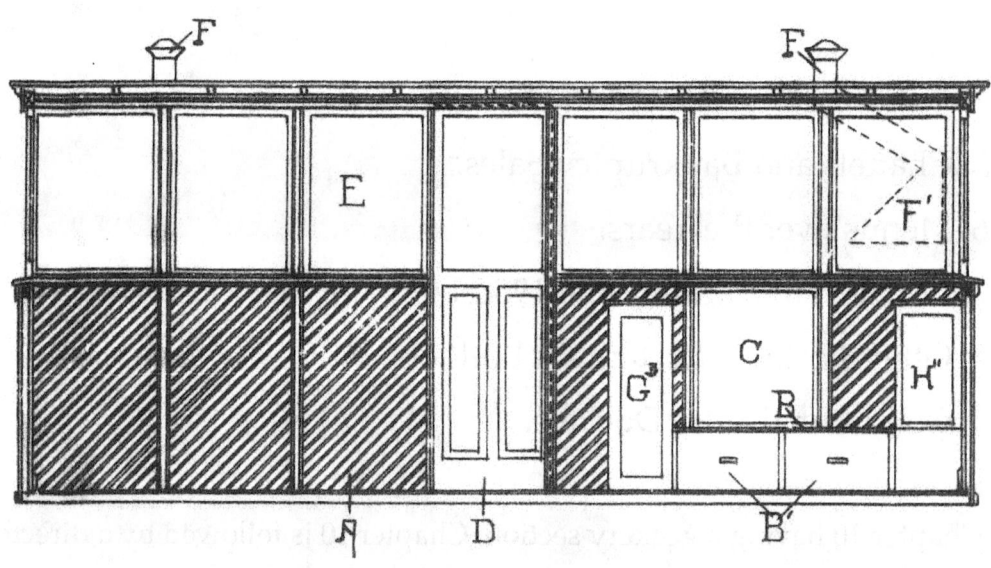

Cortland is becoming more citified everyday and especially this year, with the electric road, sewers, etc. But the latest is a night cafe that will be on the street all night to furnish everything that can be found in a first-class restaurant. The name of it is the White House Cafe, and is in charge of Mr. Bert Bosworth. For
the present it will be located at the corner of Court and Main streets near the National Bank and will be open for business Saturday night. The patronage of the public is solicited, and the manager assures all that everything used will be the best of its kind and served neatly and quickly.

The bill of fare for the present will consist of chicken, ham, sardine and cheese sandwiches, hot frankfort sausages with rolls, apple, mince, custard and pumpkin pies, milk and hot coffee with cream, choice cigars. the prices will be reasonable. Try it on your way from the club or theater when in want of a lunch.

-Cortland Standard

Richard Gutman's *American Diner, Then and Now* tells an in-depth story about the first lunch wagon builders and why the lunch wagon came to be. What were the conditions that allowed for the lunch wagon to become a profitable business for both proprietor and builder alike? Simply put, New England was in the midst of the Industrial Revolution. With the introduction of water powered machinery that could run round the clock, the American workforce was introduced to the "graveyard shift." And it became apparent to one man, Walter Scott, that he could profit from feeding these nighttime employees.[1]

The vehicle that the food was delivered in quickly evolved. What started as a push cart developed into a wagon, where at first the proprietor could stand inside, to one that customers could also use to get out of the elements.

Newspapermen would often half joke that the arrival of a lunch wagon meant that they had "arrived." In many towns, the younger class enjoyed the novel idea of a lunch wagon. The *Silver Springs [New York] Signal* on December 5, 1901 said, "Perry [New York] takes more of an appearance of a city. Waldo Coburn purchased a handsome night lunch wagon…."[2]

Articles from two of Elmira's [New York] newspapers told the basic story.
>An Elmira gentleman who attended the Lizzie Borden trial at New Bedford, Mass., said yesterday to a TELEGRAM reporter: "When I was at New Bedford I noticed an innovation called night lunch carts. These are big covered wagons something like a photographer's outfit that was occasionally seen in this country, only the lunch carts are gotten up more gorgeously with stained glass windows and a dining-room and kitchen inside where hot coffee, chicken, ham and frankfurtter sandwiches are served at five cents each. These wagons perambulate through the streets taking a position for an hour or two at one street corner, then going to another until about midnight when they become stationary for the remainder of the night. I am told that they are the fad

TYPICAL ST. PAUL LUNCH WAGON.

Above:

A newspaper drawing of a lunch wagon that could be seen on the streets of St. Paul, Minnesota around 1900. Besides Andrew Low, who had three lunch wagons, there were many more on the streets of St. Paul.

all through the manufacturing towns of New England and that the proprietors make a nice thing out of the venture. They are well patronized, and now that Elmira is showing pretensions to being a manufacturing city I think a night lunch cart would pay here." – *Telegraph*, August 20, 1893[3]

Since that time [June, 1895] they have been an ever present blessing to those who have cause to perambulate the sidewalks of Elmira after nightfall. The lunch wagon in Elmira might be called an evolution. Years ago when Joe Benjamin started a candy wagon, he also sold sandwiches to hungry pedestrians and made many a dime thereby. Next came the man who trudged through the streets at the lonely hour of midnight with a steaming basket on his arm, crying out in the night air, "Hot frankforts!" He soon disappeared, however, and then Dutch Charley, with his waffle cart, came to town. Charley made the most of his sales during the day, until the sound of "Hot waffles" became as familiar to the ears of Elmirans as does the clang of the bells on the electric cars, to which it bore a remarkable resemblance. Charley, after a time, became tired of the town and turned the weary footsteps of his horse to new pastures. The present lunch wagons, however, have come to stay. They have become a fad in many cities of the United States and can be found in nearly all of the eastern cities. – *Daily Gazette*

Left:
In the Midwest, the typical New England lunch wagon was not alone on the streets. Smaller lunch cars along with popcorn and peanut wagons were also typically seen on the streets of many Midwestern locations.

and Free Press, September 24, 1895[4]

The Midwest was maybe five or ten years behind the east coast in the lunch wagon "fad." But food wagons had made their presence known in various shapes and forms all across the country in the second half of the nineteenth century. In the quarter century after the Civil War, The *St. Paul Globe* on February 19, 1899 noticed that food wagons made their presence known.

> The "red hot" man, the tamale peddler, the cigarette and all-night lunch wagons are evolutions of the past twenty-five years in the northern portions of this country. In the Southern states all of them, with the possible exception of night lunch wagons, have nourished profitably a much longer period than is spanned by a quarter of a century. To this list the South adds the chili con carni man, one seldom met in Northern cities, and who deals in a pungent, highly-spiced concoction, of which black beans form the body and red pepper the stimulating condiment.[5]

By 1902, there were twelve wagons in St. Paul, and Andrew Low, who was credited with bringing the lunch wagon to St. Paul in 1890, owned three of them. A *St. Paul Globe* article dated, March 23, 1902 noted that the sandwich was a hit in cities like St. Paul.

> There may be many devotees that worship at the shrine of the apple and custard, but the new cult of sandwich has had an unparalleled growth, as can be seen by watching the pilgrims that nightly adjourn to their Mecca, the lunch wagon.[6]

Pies would never lose their place on the menu of most lunch wagons, but both the lunch wagon and sandwich came onto the scene of American culture right around the same time. They were a perfect fit for each other. Sandwiches were easy to make and didn't require a plate to eat. This meant one could eat a sandwich while standing around or even moving from place to place. They could even be delivered to hungry customers with relative ease.

There was also a social, as well as gastronomical, aspect to the popularity of the lunch wagon. From a March 3, 1898 blurb from The *Tioga County Record*: "... For a long time, the residents of Owego, especially the younger class, have felt the loss caused by the removal of the one [lunch wagon] which was located here some two years ago."[7]

These rather new inventions were popular with the younger generation. They were a place for them to go to for nutrition while out having a good time. But the younger generation was not the only group who enjoyed the presence of the lunch wagon.

The same *St. Paul Globe* article from March 23, 1902 also explained what a typical night looked like for the lunch wagon man. The article especially told about the different customers one would expect to see at a lunch wagon.

> About 7 o'clock every night, each lunch wagon Is surrounded by a crowd of newsboys and bootblacks, who long ago learned that their nickel or dime cannot be expended to any better purpose than in purchase of a sandwich. The tastes of the gamins are simple, rising to no higher flights than a ham and egg.... As the theater hour draws near the class of trade that patronizes the lunch wagon changes. The newsboys have all slipped away to wherever they sleep, and the theater-goer begins to appear with his hunger for a sandwich.... When the curtain rises in the theater, there is a lull for a short time, during which the lunch wagon man begins cooking his chicken for the after theater patrons. There is no place on earth where a half chicken can be purchased for 10 cents that tastes so good as in a lunch wagon, and

Above:

Even though this lunch wagon had a door where patrons could enter, the proprietor preferred to do business through the up and down sliding service window. Many lunch wagons were built where the proprietor had the option of conducting his business the most efficient way to serve his customers and his particular location.

(Don Rittner)

the romantic idea of devouring fowl on the street corner utterly oblivious to the passing throng adds an unexplainable zest to the appetite. When the crowds surge out of the opera houses, there is a line drawn up in front of the narrow window of the lunch wagon, like at a country post office.... About midnight the "night owl" begin to flutter around for the bite. These arc all old friends of the lunch wagon man and they discuss every topic under the sun, the choice being left entirely to the customer. Hackdrivers from nearby stands slide up, glad of an opportunity of getting inside a cozy place, for the St. Paul lunch wagons have accommodation for those who wish to eat inside. There is a stove and two short benches at the disposal of those who wish to use them.... This class of trade lasts into the early hours of the morning. Most of it is regular, but there is enough variety in the shape of belated roisterers to keep away all thoughts of monotony. The callow youth who has imbibed more than his per capita share of beer, comes careening up for a sandwich of sobering properties and the ancient "rounders" knows the medicinal value of this diet from long years of experience.[6]

Walter Scott was the first to operate one, but Thomas Buckley was the man who would spread the lunch wagon far and wide. At the time of his death in 1903, he had wagons in at least 275 locations.[8] One way or another, Mr. Buckley found Ogdensburg, New York, a village to the west of the Adirondack Mountains on the St. Lawrence River.

Here in Ogdensburg, Buckley built strong attachments to the village, vacationing here and even donating money to one of the local churches. In 1898 when he replaced an older wagon with a newly built one, the local newspaper noted that he had 78 wagons located. Buckley would place wagons all over the nearby villages like Watertown, Carthage, Plattsburgh, Malone, and Saranac Lake in the mid to late 1890s.[9]

Ephraim Hamel was actually the first lunch wagon builder to hit Central New York. Hamel and Buckley both built wagons known as White House Lunch Wagons. To help sell their wagons, they would place them in a town and hire someone to run them, normally leasing it to them for three years. Hopefully, after the agreement ran out, that person would buy the wagon. In 1894, Hamel had a wagon in Auburn and planned to place one in Oswego.[10] In 1896, Hamel had plans to put three lunch wagons in St. Louis, and would put a Mr. B. H. Bosworth of Cortland, New York in charge. Bosworth's brother, Arthur brought the first lunch wagon to Geneva, New York.[11]

Not everything was perfect. Mr. Hamel ran into a disagreement in Ithaca with a customer who first rented and then bought one of his lunch wagons. First and foremost, this was a serious business, and reducing competition was important.

> CONTRACT OF SALE OF A LUNCH WAGON.— Robert M. Love and Amanda Love, vendees in a written "contract for the sale of a lunch wagon," contended that the sale was made upon condition that the vendor, Ephraim Hamel, - would not maintain a lunch wagon in the City of Ithaca or sell one to anybody else to be operated there. They at first forgot, however, to mention that provision to the attorney who drew the written contract, and when they did call his attention to it he said he would draw a new contract or interline the omitted provision in the contract already drawn. Hamel said it was not necessary, that he was in a hurry, that the Loves had always done as they agreed by him, and he certainly would by them. The lawyer said it would be better to have the entire agreement in writing, but it was not redrawn or changed. In an action brought by the Loves against Hamel to recover

Below: **The inside of a typical lunch wagon. Based upon the stained glass window, this was probably a Buckley lunch wagon. This wagon was located by the Ontario and Western Railway station in Norwich, New York.** (Chenango County Historical Society)

> damages for alleged breach of the agreement not to put another lunch wagon in Ithaca....[12]

The Loves brought one of their wagons onto the Campus of Cornell University near Sibley Hall. Cornell University has a long and storied history with the lunch wagon, and a variation of one even operates on the campus today. Louis Zounakos ran Louie's Lunch Wagon across from Risley Dorm from 1916 to 1956. Zounakos was perhaps the best known lunch wagon proprietor on the campus of Cornell. In 1938, the wagon was threatened when the President of Cornell intended to ban it, but with 3000 students planning to march on his office, Louie's was again safe.[13]

In 1901, Thomas Buckley won the right to supply lunch wagons and kiosks for the World's Fair in New York the next year. He ran wagons at all the entrances and the kiosks inside the fair. The Ogdensburg News reported on March 23, 1901,

> In addition to the exposition privilege, he has secured for his company the right to operate lunch wagons on the streets of Buffalo during the exposition season, also on the streets of Niagara Falls, Lockport, Tonawanda and other towns within a radius of 10 miles of the exposition grounds.[14]

Later that same week, it would be written that 17 large lunch wagons and fifteen kiosks were being readied to be sent to Buffalo from Buckley's factory in Worcester, Massachusetts.[15]

Who would watch over the food operations? He needed a good manager. While it is not known whom he finally chose, his first choice was Mr. R.H. Hanna of Plattsburgh, whom he offered a "tempting salary of $100 a week."[16] Mr. Hanna had won over Buckley and his customers in the four or five years he had been running his White House Cafe. As typical with Buckley's wagons, he rented the wagon for the first three years, before buying the wagon outright.

At the end of the fair, instead of hauling all the wagons back to Worcester, Buckley decided to sell them all. One of the wagons was sold to "Crab" Miles of Olean, New

York. Crab's lunch wagon was publicized in Ripley's Believe It or Not! cartoon series as, "the oldest lunch wagon in the country drawn by horses." "The Midnight Mayor," as he became known, bought the original wagon from Will Austin in 1899, replaced that one in 1902, and ran it until Christmas Eve in 1937. Typical of many towns, the night lunch wagon was the only place to get a snack or meal after dark for many years. For the entire time, except for the last year, horses were used to bring the wagon, nightly, to the front of Olean's City Building.[17] One horse was so well trained that it could be harnessed at the stable and then make its way to "Crab" Miles' house on its own. This horse could even make its way back to the stable after bringing the lunch wagon downtown. "The horse would then be unhitched, amble over to the watering trough at the City Hall for a drink of water and then make its own way back to the stables," stated the *Olean Times Herald* in 1937.

> Parking the wagon nightly in front of the City building brought consternation to some residents. They occasionally complained that the Midnight Mayor was getting special privileges of being able to park his wagon in front of a public building, every night. The Olean Evening Times on February 25, 1927 published an editorial,
> "I think Olean is a most orderly city, and I consider the city officials deserve great credit for this condition. But I do think that great laxity is shown in some things. Why, even a lunch wagon is permitted to park every night right at the corner of North Union and North Street…."[18]

The editorial went on to point out that a state law prohibits parking within ten feet of an intersection.

It is a highly dangerous business driving

Right:
The lunch wagon in Norwich, New York was placed off the streets. Some cities and towns banned lunch wagons from being parked on streets during business hours. This was especially true on streets with trolley car tracks. Many lunch wagons were forced onto front lawns, side lots or even alleyways on occasion.
(Chenango County Historical Society)

Right:
Nearly every Midwestern city had a lunch wagon. They were typically such a small part of many cities that their memory faded into oblivion. In Danville, Illinois, though, the lunch wagon snuck into this street scene due to its presence on a major street corner.

Vermillion Street, looking North, Danville, Ill.

out of North Street into North Union Street at night in the summer,
for the lunch wagon is at one corner and a peanut and candy wagon
is at the opposite corner. It is virtually impossible to see cars or the
condition of traffic on North Union Street until the crossing has been
reached and passed, no matter whether the driver of the car stops or
not. There is not the slightest objection to either the lunch wagon or the
peanut stand. They are patronized and appreciated by a large number
of people.[18]

Although Crab Miles' wagon was never forced to move, this editorial shows that the New York state law was passed for safety's concern. In many other cities, though, safety was the farthest thing from people's minds when prohibiting lunch wagons from city streets.

Lunch wagons started as movable wagons, brought to a site each night by horses, or occasionally moved from factory to factory, mostly at night. Eugene Barbour had Rome, New York's first wagon and for a five dollar yearly fee was allowed to keep his wagon open from 5:30 p.m. to 4 a.m. daily.[19] In 1898, Albert Closson's Crystal Palace in Glens Falls was open from 6 p.m. to 2:30 a.m. daily. He located the first wagon in Glens Falls at Monument Square.[20] Soon enough, cities began to outlaw the placement of wagons on city streets. Springfield, Massachusetts was one of the first cities to do this, in 1896. Other cities followed. Action in one city would often invigorate action in another. But perhaps the most significant example was in Chicago, Illinois.

THE LUNCH CAR GOES POLICE ORDER NOMAD RESTAURANTS
TO MOVE ON.
A Feature of Night life in the Western Metropolis. They Fed the
Hungry and made a Pleasant Sight. Story of Change.
The story of the decline and fall of the lunch wagon is a story of city life
and changes, says the Chicago News. No one seems able to recall just
when the sandwich car first sprang into existence with its array of good

things looming up in tempting neatness at the street corner, its white-aproned proprietor, its bright lights and tiny cooking apparatus, and, above all, the inviting aroma that gradually grew to be associated with the lunch car.

From an humble start it grew to be a recognized institution, in some cases outfits have been built that represented comparatively large investments. The lunch car was primarily a creature of darkness. During the day it was concealed from sight, but when the shades of night fell it was carefully drawn by horses to the spot where it was destined to radiate good cheer. There, safely anchored, it did a land office business in pleasant weather or foul, a haven of refuge to the hungry and weary nighthawk.

Every class and every grade became at once patrons of the lunch car to a greater or less degree. The rounder doing the town in a fine equipage drew up alongside to take solid refreshment. The belated person going home waiting for a night car at a lonely corner forgot his discomfort in munching at an egg sandwich well primed with thin slices of pickle, while good natured pleasure seekers returning from the ball laughed immoderately over the fun derived from wrestling with its hot, palate-tickling products.

What was sold at the lunch car was clean and pure—therefore its popularity. It was cooked before the very eyes of the purchaser and was served in a style that left no room for petty distinctions such as are sometimes experienced in a cafe or restaurant. It mattered not to the man in charge whether his patron was attired in the latest style or in tatters, whether tipsy or sober, respectable or an outcast, the service was the same to all who thrust the price through the little aperture where he presided over his gasoline fires. And so the lunch van became popular with all—that is, all except restaurant proprietors. The latter saw hundreds and thousands of persons being fed whose

Kennel Club I. C. E. Reamer, Mgr. 415 State St.

Upper Left:
This fancy lunch wagon was located in Madison, Wisconsin. Probably not allowed on the streets, the lunch wagon found a nice location to show off the artwork on the front of the wagon. The cook is even dressed in white to portray cleanliness.

(Image Courtesy of the UW-Madison Archives - Series No. 23/17 WER0571)

patronage might otherwise be theirs. Some went into the business themselves, others protested. Those who chose the latter course maintained that they had a right to be heard against men who paid no rent, but rather usurped the people's rights to the streets and who took business from established restaurant keepers, whose places in many instances had formed landmarks for years. The restaurant keepers were joined by saloon keepers with lunch-counter attachments to their bars.

Other business men with grievances of other varieties were enlisted to raise their voice against the sandwich car. There were too many in the opposition to be ignored, and one day an order came forth, from police headquarters to make the lunch vender's "move on." It brought forth a storm of counter protest, but the opposition had won the day. The lunch-car owners were violating the law every time they settled down upon a corner and they found their day had come. Some secured sites inside the building line, dismantled their cars from the wheels and settled down as permanent business men instead of nomads. Others put their outfits in storage and quit the business, while some few possessing political pull continued to adhere to the old line by changing the base of operations from time to time.

But the lunch car as a thriving institution has ceased to exist on its old lines and the nocturnal hours have lost one of their most picturesque features. – Racine Daily Journal. January 7, 1901.[21]

Even before Chicago or Springfield, Massachusetts tackled this issue, a feud against the lunch wagon men was carried out in Rochester, New York by the restaurateurs and

Lower Left:
Quite possibly an interior photo of the Madison, Wisconsin lunch wagon above. The extra monitor windows gave more opportunity for light to come inside. Along with the white clothes of the cook and the white tiles, the place intended to have a more inviting appearance.

(American Diner Heritage)

saloon men. The local newspaper, The Democrat and Chronicle, carried the action, blow by blow, during 1896.

Charles Whitney came to Rochester, New York from Worcester, Massachusetts in 1894, bringing his lunch wagon with him. As night workers caught wind of this operation, which took about a year, business prospered and other wagons began to spring up. These wagons were proving so popular that some people were quickly buying up old horse-drawn trolleys as a cheaper alternative to the lunch wagon builder's offerings. By January 1896, The Democrat and Chronicle was calling the Flower City, the "City of Lunch Wagons", stating that a traveler from New England would feel at home here in Rochester, a city that had six wagons, and "expected to increase daily." O.W. Brigham had moved to Columbus, Ohio in 1894 with a lunch cart, and heard about how the lunch wagon was being received in Rochester. By the end of 1896, he had three wagons in Rochester.[22]

In August of the same year, A.B. Sanderl, a proprietor of a restaurant and saloon on Main Street, began to distribute a petition outlawing the lunch wagons from the streets of Rochester. He considered Main Street one of the prettiest thoroughfares in the country and claimed that the lunch carts marred its beauty.[23] Sanderl also knew that while he and the brick and mortar restaurant operators paid rent, the lunch wagon owners merely paid a comparably small fee to the city for permission to operate in the city. Tack on the Raines Law fee, and Sanderl saw a bigger monetary gap between the lunch wagons owners and himself.

> Then, as has been done in my case, some fellow comes along and by paying $50 – less than $1 a week – to the city, receives permission to conduct the same kind of a business that this man is trying to make a living at ... I maintain it is a rank injustice to the restaurant keepers of the city.[24]

Mr. A.B. Sanderl's petition highlighted a grudge against the lunch wagons on two levels. The aldermen worried about vehicles like fire trucks having to maneuver around the lunch wagons in emergencies. Mr. Sanderl piggybacked on the alderman's concern, although this was not Mr. Sanderl and the other saloon men's motivation in the least.

First was the Raines Law, passed in March of 1896, which intended to hurt the saloon business via a large license fee, but also prohibited saloon keepers from giving a free lunch with the purchase of an alcoholic beverage. The free lunch part of the law was rescinded the next year. One lunch wagon mocked the saloon keepers with a sign that said, "Raines Dry House, Come in When it Raines." Mr. Sanderl knew that many people were in favor of lunch wagons due to the temperance movement. A Reverend even took up the cause of the lunch wagon in a sermon. He talked about the need to feed people without subjecting them to the evils of alcohol found in saloons.

Second was the fact that business at his restaurant was being hurt by the abundant lunch wagons in Rochester. This reasoning is typical of any business, and even goes on today. Mr Sanderl proclaimed, "If the lunch carts will come out at 12 O'Clock and stay until 6 AM in the morning, I will withdraw my protest." This type of resolution was passed, but did not allow lunch wagons at all on the busiest parts of the two main thoroughfares. The lunch wagon men commented to the aldermen that they could not possibly survive without the business before midnight, which was often their best business period.[24]

When the resolution was first passed against the lunch wagon men, a second petition was established by the friends of the lunch wagon, which was expected to be signed by 2000 men in just a single day. This second petition was signed by every editor and reporter of the two morning newspapers in Rochester, stating that the lunch wagon was a convenience and a necessity. Other professions that found the wagons important included policemen, telephone and telegraph operators, and other workers of the night. These employees, especially ones that objected to patronizing saloons, saw the wagons—typically the only establishment open after midnight—as a godsend.[24] Fortunately, lunch wagons did survive in Rochester.

Lunch wagons in Syracuse, New York took a hiatus for a few years after an ordinance was passed in 1893. Lunch wagons first appeared there in 1892 and Alderman Matty, who ran a saloon and cafe, thought that the wagons were "coming in too thick" and might injure his business. So Alderman Matty introduced a resolution to revoke the licenses of the proprietors of the wagons, which was then adopted.[25] Only a few years later, lunch wagons would reappear in Syracuse.

Lunch wagons in Buffalo would have an on again, off again relationship with the city supervisors. In a 1916 article, it was mentioned that the last lunch wagon in Buffalo was closing up. The city grew so fast that it caused storefront restaurants to open up during late hours, the typical lunch wagon hours. This, along with the various protests, caused the lunch wagon business to practically dry up in the first decade of the twentieth century in Buffalo.[26]

A different problem affected Wilbur Boyd, a lunch wagon man in Champaign, Illinois. Boyd was arrested for obstructing traffic, after a complaint was filed by the Champaign High School authorities. "They declared that he was attracting the trade of the high school cafeteria which is not run on a profit basis but at cost." Boyd was an ex-soldier and was given a soldier's permit that allowed him to operate in any city in Illinois. Fortunately for him, the American Legion was "backing Boyd to the limit," and the case was soon dismissed.[27]

One would think that a city like Detroit would have had an incredible number of lunch wagons. Although the city was ripe with possibilities due to the auto manufacturing business, the "lunch industry" had a competitor to the lunch wagon in the distribution of food. These were known as lunch box companies. The companies would make prepackaged lunches that the auto workers could take to work with them. Like any business, the lunch wagon did not catch on everywhere, and in some places, especially with the car factories in Detroit, they were replaced with more automated choices.[28]

Detroit did have lunch wagons though, as the town still had a vibrant downtown and many

Right:
Some proprietors went all out to portray their little lunch wagon as an extravagant operation. Chas Morenus did not bother calling his place a lunch wagon, instead calling it the Queen Lunch Parlor. the Queen Lunch Parlor was located in the gritty lumbering and tanning city of Gloversville, New York.

newspaper men to feed. In fact, it was not until 1926—far later than most other cities—that Detroit's city council outlawed horse-drawn lunch wagons downtown. Probably the best-known proprietor of a Detroit wagon was Andrew Scrimger, who ran his wagon at the corner of Michigan and Griswold from 1903 to 1926. The Associated Press recounted one of his favorite stories, upon the announcement of his death in June of 1931:

> He often told of the night when Woodrow Wilson was elected president, a night on which he sold 2,500 "hot dog" sandwiches, 100 loaves of bread, 30 gallons of coffee, and "so many pies I couldn't count 'em.

Two of Mr. Scrimger's most famous customers were not famous when they first came to know him and his lunch wagon. Judge Edward Command was just a newsboy then and Henry Ford was merely an employee of the Detroit Edison Company. In Richard Gutman's book on page 218-9, he notes that Henry Ford bought John Colquhoun's Owl Night Lunch in 1927, which set up near Detroit's City Hall on Fort Street West at the Bagley Fountain.[29] Colquhoun was called Detroit's "Hot Dog King" in his obituary. Colquhoun had a wagon in Detroit since 1895. It seems that Henry Ford was quite familiar with many of the lunch wagons located in the heart of Detroit. When Ford was an engineman with the Edison Company here thirty years ago he frequently ate at Colquhoun's wagon and drew in pencil on the counter designs of his "horseless

carriage" he was trying to invent."[30]

Richard Gutman begins Chapter 7 of his book with the title, ' "Ladies Invited" Or Were They?' His main thesis is that diner owners in the mid 1920s started to recognize the importance of getting the fairer sex to become their customers. He talked about booth service, new menu items which included full meals, and attempts at making the lunch car more inviting for the opposite sex. But around the turn of the twentieth century, the people of Syracuse were already receptive to the idea of ladies visiting or even owning lunch wagons. A 1907 menu for a lunch wagon in Walton, New York consisted mostly of sandwiches and pies with the highest price being ten cents;[31] and the lunch wagons in Rochester were known as beaneries, often with each wagon selling over five pounds of Boston baked beans a day. The Democrat and Chronicle commented, "Beans are to the lunch cart what the eagle is to the United States."[24] But Syracuse lunch wagons were starting to have full dinners on some days of the week. More than the food options aimed at attracting women, the most progressive act coming out of Syracuse was that three wagons were operated by women.

The August 27, 1901 edition of the Oswego Palladium interviewed one of these female proprietors and commented,

> The average number of customers for each from nine in the evening until seven in the morning is 200, and often 800 are served with coffee, pie and sandwiches. "What made me think of going into the business," said the proprietor of one of them the other night in reply to a Herald reporter, "Merely the fact that I knew it was paying other people fairly well and thought that I might be as lucky as they were. And I really have done better than I expected. I had to borrow money to start with, but I had it paid off and a little nest egg into the bargain at the end of six months."[32]

It's hard to having any restaurant paid off in just six months, but here were some women who were doing such in what was viewed a man's domain at the time.

Although T.J. Buckley worked tirelessly to gain recognition for his lunch wagon

Right:

Many lunch wagon builders in New England were supplying lunch wagons for all over the country. Some carriage builders would build a lunch wagon or two. But there were other options to a factory built lunch wagon. Some prospective owners might remodel a used wagon themselves. Others would take an old horse drawn street-car as they were being replaced by electric powered trolley cars.

(Marybelle Beigh)

outside of New England, many people decided to build their own, or hire a carriage maker to build one just as nice. Some people even reconfigured wagons to suit their purpose. John Colquhoun had his lunch wagon built by a local wagon maker in Detroit. In many cases, very little is known about these men who used the entrepreneurship of America to get ahead. And sometimes, history has skewed the facts.

Thomas Buckley's first wagon is said to have gone to Denver and introduced the lunch wagon to the west. It was not the only wagon to head west. Three gentlemen from Watertown, New York decided to go to Utah in 1902.[33] Harvey Bickerton and Thomas Burns moved out to Salt Lake City with Sherman Abbott to open night lunch wagons in the western city. Bickerton sold his restaurant that had run for only two months for $20,000 in 1909, and headed back to Watertown.[34] Clearly the lunch wagon business was very good for him.

Joseph Basloe of Herkimer, New York died in 1928, and in his obituary was credited with the invention of the lunch wagon. He would not be the last person to be mistakenly credited for the invention. Newspaper reporters misrepresented the fact that what he did was to buy old horse-drawn trolley cars and convert them into lunch wagons, which he set up in Herkimer. While there was a barrel-roofed lunch wagon also doing business in Herkimer, the newspaper men most fondly remembered Basloe, probably due to his success in the venture.[35] In Rochester, New York, lunch wagons were becoming so popular in 1895 that people were buying old horse drawn trolley cars

Below:

A less ornate lunch wagon also in Madison, Wisconsin. While this wagon gives the customer the option of going to the service window or heading indoors, customers in the winter probably chose to place their order while out of the cold of Wisconsin's winters.

(Image Courtesy of the UW-Madison Archives - Album 7.31 WER0478)

in an attempt to get in on the booming business.[22] The Miller Blum Lunch Company would set up a lunch wagon empire in Rochester, numbering well over a dozen wagons—although the wagons were actually mostly trolley car conversions. One man moved up from Binghamton and constructed a lunch cart out of one of these old trolleys, and placed it at the corner of State and Main Streets. Business was so good that he talked about adding a second story to his structure.

In Ogdensburg, New York, Walter Wells converted a milk wagon into a lunch wagon. In other places, actual carriage builders dabbled with building lunch wagons. Carriage Monthly documented the Ellis Omnibus and Cab Company venture in 1896. This Cortland, New York company was known for building trolley cars. Carriage Monthly described the interior: "One end of the car is finished with a counter, shelves, drawers, and cupboard, and is veneered throughout." The exterior was similar to those built in New England and had the wheels upon which it was drawn completely located below the body of the lunch wagon. Cortland was also home to two other locally manufactured lunch wagons. These two though were built by their operators.[36][37]

Ilion, New York was home to the Cheney and Brown Carriage Works. In 1899, they built what was called a fire-proof night lunch wagon for Louis Halbritter, a local lunch wagon operator.[38] Halbritter would go on to run two lunch wagons in Ilion.

As well built as most of these carriage works lunch wagons were, the homemade and trolley conversions could prove to be on the low side of appearances. Many people blame the poorly done horse-drawn trolley car conversions to be the main reason for the decline of the lunch wagon. This is probably an overstated opinion, but these conversions could not have helped. The lunch wagon gained popularity in the larger Midwest cities around 1890 and were associated with the rise in popularity of the sandwich and the Bohemian movement. The lunch wagons also filled a void by being the only restaurant open up during the overnight hours. At the time of the first lunch wagons, only bars and saloons were open at night. Over time, there would become more options for mid-night snackers, but for the time being, the lunch wagon had very little competition after dark. Although lunch wagons became less popular, they still survived—mostly in now permanent locations, often in formerly empty lots off of the main commercial business avenues.

Canada has been an unknown land to the history of lunch wagons. We know that they existed, especially with newspaper blurbs mentioning wagons in cities like Edmonton, Ottawa, and Montreal. Wilson Goodrich, lunch wagon builder in Springfield, Massachusetts, did bring lunch wagons up to Montreal. But the most important piece of information may just be Canadian patent #58672. William J. Gardner and Wildridge H. Gorman were two men from Ogdensburg, New York who moved just across the St. Lawrence River to Prescott, Ontario. Here, according to the Gouverneur Free Press of February 3, 1898, they were constructing ten lunch wagons for a Montreal firm, and intended to place cars, "in thirty cities of Canada on the percentage plan."[39] Although this partnership did not seem to last long at all, both participants were in Canada running lunch wagons not too soon after this mention was printed in the newspaper. William Gardner was operating a lunch wagon in Montreal, Quebec in August of the same year.[40] Wildridge Gorman joined James F. Akin and placed a lunch wagon in Brockville, Ontario in July of 1899.[41]

Another company, the Guedelhoffer Company of Indianapolis, Indiana advertised a lunch car for sale. Guedelhoffer was a well-known carriage and wagon builder in the Midwest. As the Closson Lunch Wagon Co. had placed one of their lunch wagons in

Indianapolis, it's entirely possible that this act inspired Guedelhoffer to consider getting into the business themselves. Also, lunch wagons had patrolled the Indianapolis streets at night since the mid 1890s. As researchers delve into old newspapers and various other research options, we have found that many more carriage and wagon builders throughout the country dabbled with the idea of building and selling lunch wagons over the years than we once assumed.

1 Gutman, Richard J.S., *American Diner, Then and Now* (Harper Perennial, 1993).
2 Silver Springs Signal, Silver Springs, New York December 5, 1901
3 Elmira Telegraph, Elmira, New York August 20, 1893
4 Elmira Daily Gazette and Free Press, Elmira, New York September 24, 1895
5 St Paul Globe, St. Paul, Minnesota February 19, 1899
6 St Paul (Minn.) Globe, St. Paul, Minnesota March 23, 1902
7 Tioga County Record, Owego, New York March 3, 1898
8 Gutman, *American Diner, Then and Now*.
9 The Daily Journal, Ogdensburg, New York November 17, 1898
10 Oswego Palladium, Oswego, New York, originally in Auburn Advertiser September 14, 1894
11 Cortland Democrat, Cortland, New York October 16, 1896
12 The New York Times, New York City, New York May 21, 1901
13 Louis Zounakas obituary, Cornell Daily Sun, Ithaca, New York February 6, 1956
14 Ogdensburg News, Ogdensburg, New York March 23, 1901
15 Ogdensburg News, Ogdensburg, New York March 28, 1901
16 Plattsburgh Daily Press, Plattsburgh, New York November 9, 1900
17 Sent to Author by Walter J. Hastrich. Genealogist whose wife is granddaughter of Crab Miles.
18 Olean Evening Times, Olean, New York February 25, 1937
19 Roman Citizen, Rome, New York April 24, 1896
20 Glens Falls Morning Star, Glens Falls, New York April 23, 1895
21 Racine Daily Journal, Racine, Wisconsin January 7, 1901
22 Rochester Democrat and Chronicle, Rochester, New York January 12, 1896
23 Rochester Democrat and Chronicle, Rochester, New York August 21, 1896
24 Rochester Democrat and Chronicle, Rochester, New York August 29, 1896
25 Buffalo Express, Buffalo, New York October 29, 1893
26 Buffalo Courier, Buffalo, New York June 8, 1914
27 Daily Illini, Champaign, Illinois March 22, 1921

28 various Detroit City Directories.
29 Journal of Common Council of Detroit, Michigan 1901
30 Cortland Standard, Cortland, New York November 1, 1927
31 Walton Reporter, Walton, New York August 17, 1907
32 Oswego Palladium, Oswego, New York August 27, 1901
33 Watertown Herald, Watertown, New York April 29, 1902
34 Syracuse Post Standard, Syracuse, New York July 28, 1909
35 Utica Daily Press, Utica, New York October 13, 1928
36 Cortland Democrat, Cortland, New York August 10, 1899
37 Cortland Standard, Cortland, New York February 10, 1899
38 Utica Daily Press, Utica, New York October 11, 1899
39 Gouverneur Free Press, Gouverneur, New York February 3, 1898
40 Ogdensburg Journal, Ogdensburg, New York August 11, 1898
41 Ogdensburg Advance, Ogdensburg, New York July 10, 1899,

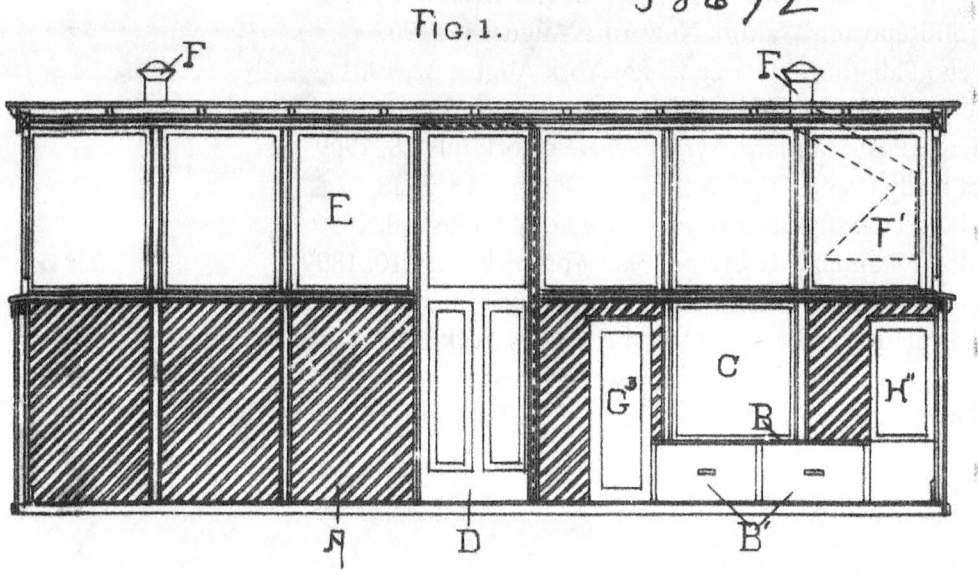

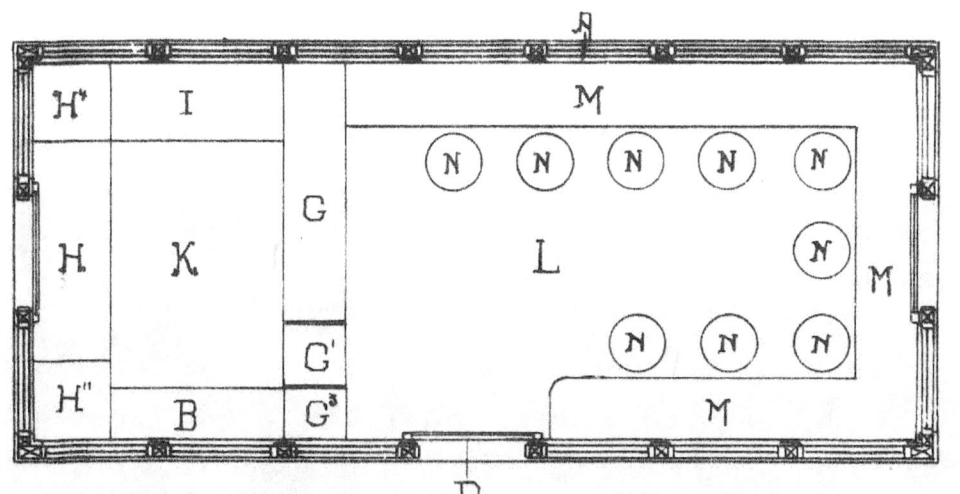

Each chapter will end in a section dedicated to a specific topic related to lunch wagons or diners. These sections may be dryer in scope to the general public, but they help tell a story. This first chapter will include a lunch wagon patent filed in Canada for a lunch wagon.

SPECIFICATION

To all it may concern: -

Be it known that we, William J. Gardner of Ogdensburg, in the County of St. Lawrence and State of New York, caterer, and Wildridge H. Gorman of the same place, bankers clerk, have jointly invented a new and useful improvement in LUNCH-WAGON BODIES, and we do hereby declare that the following is a full, clear and exact description of the same.

Reference being made to the accompanying drawings, in which, Figure 1. is an elevation of the interior of the side of a lunch-wagon body showing a portion of our invention.

Fig. 2. is a floor plan of such lunch-wagon body.

Fig. 3. is an elevation of the sideboard I, looking from K, in Fig. 2.

Fig. 4. is an elevation of the counter G, as seen from in front of the same.

Fig. 5. is a rear view of said counter, as seen from K, in fig. 2.

Fig. 6. is an elevation of the rear end of our lunch-wagon body from the interior thereof

Our invention relates to that class of lunch-wagon in which cold food can be conveniently kept and warm food prepared, and a limited number of customers can be housed and fed; and its object is to do so without discomfort or undue cost or labor, and in an appetizing manner.

Like letters refer to similar parts throughout said drawings, in which A, represents the usual frame and outer casing of a lunch-wagon body, having a series of windows E, around the upper portion thereof and a door D, in one side thereof, for entrance to and exit from the interior of said wagon. These windows may be arranged to slide downward in the usual manner and to promote ventilation the metallic ventilators F,F, are placed in the roof so as to open from interior of said wagon to the outer air; the rearmost ventilator F, is connected with the smoke-hood F', for the purpose of conveying the smoke and fumes, incident to cooking foods, to the outer air.

As shown in Figs. 1, and 2, a grill-room K, is partitioned from the main body of said wagon, and in the rear portion thereof, by serving counter G, having a swinging top portion G', and door G", for access to the grill-room. Within this counter G, is a space for the reception of a wash-sing, with access thereto from the rear, and at G^3 is a wardrobe for containing the attendant superfluous clothing.

In one side of said lunch-wagon body and opening into the grill-room, is the lower sliding sash-window C, for serving outside customers, and beneath this is a serving-shelf B, covering

GARDNER AND GORMAN'S
LUNCH-WAGON BODY.

58672

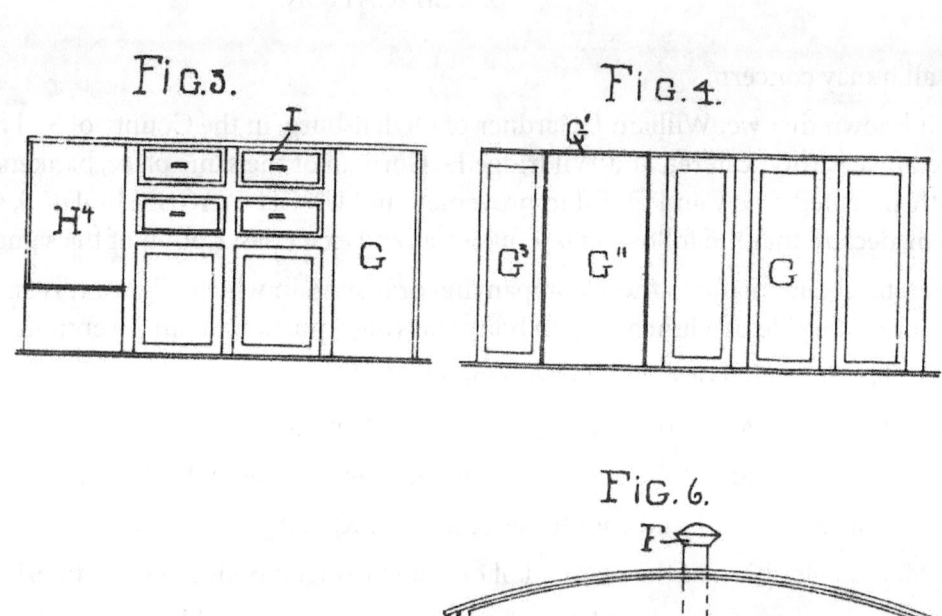

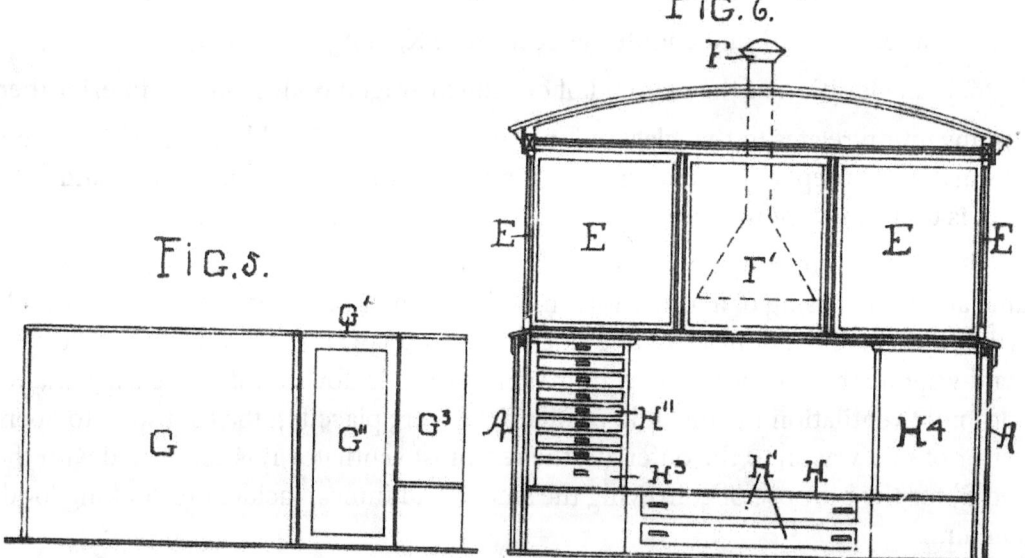

CERTIFIED TO BE THE DRAWINGS REFERED TO IN THE SPECIFICATIONS HEREUNTO ANNEXED. OGDENSBURG, NEW YORK. DECEMBER 17th 1897.

WITNESSES.
R. Porter Johnston
Herbert Howard

INVENTORS
William J. Gardner
Wildrider H. Gorman
per George B. Shepard, Atty

two bread drawers B'.

At the rear end of said wagon-body, and of said grill—room, is the grill-shelf H, for supporting the cooking apparatus, and above this is the smoke-Hood F' hereinbefore described; There is also an elevated case of drawers H", and H³, for containing pies and table knives and forks respectively; the long drawers H' for food receptacles, and the enclosure H⁴, which may be provided with a separable cover and used for a store closet.

On the remaining side of said grill-room is placed a side-board containing in its upper portion a set of drawers for containing the usual small supplies, such as eggs, &c., and underneath them closets for larger supplies, such as coffee, ham, &c

The eating-room L, in the main portion of said wagon, is provided with a lunch shelf M, secured to the side walls of same, and the customers seats M, conveniently arranged with reference thereto.

From the foregoing it will be seen that we have produced a lunch-wagon body which is more conveniently arranged for the purpose than anything heretofore made, and which can be constructed strongly and without undue expense for its purposes; and which can be kept clean and free from smoke and smell of cooking, and is both comfortably and conveniently arranged to serve the purposes of both customers and attendants.

Having thus described our said improved lunch-wagon body, what we claim as new and desire to secure by Letters Patent, is:-

1. A lunch-wagon body comprising an eating-room and a grill-room; a range of windows around the upper portion thereof a sliding sash in the lower portion of one side of said body, opening from the grill-room, over a low serving-shelf, into the outer air; a grill-shelf at the rear end of said wagon-body with elevated cabinets on each side thereof and a smoke-hood suspended over such shelf and having a conduit to the outer air; an elevated sideboard contiguous to said grill-shelf; a serving-counter partitioning the grill-room from the eating-room; and one or more elevated ventilators in the roof of said wagon-body.

2. In a lunch-wagon body, the combination of an eating-room L, a grill-room K, the windows E, a sliding sash C, over a serving-shelf B, the deep drawers B', B', thereunder; a cabinet of elevated drawers H"; a grill-shelf H, long drawers H' thereunder; the elevated sideboard I, the serving-counter G, the smoke-hood F', and ventilators F, all arranged substantially as, and for the purposes, described.

Chapter 2
Closson Lunch Wagon Company

James Sutphen was recommended by two detectives as being a sort of "king bee" among the lunch-wagon men of the city, and as detectives have a wide acquaintance and are night birds anyways, they surely should know...

"You see, I know how to put the stuff up," he explained. "There's a young fellow in the business up on Pennsylvania street and a man out on West Washington street and an old fellow on South Illinois street that mean all right and do the best they know how, but they haven't learned the finer-points of the business yet. There's three other fellows with wagons drawn by horses in the down-town district..."

"I don't know how many of the pushcart men there are-the kind that sell wieners and such small fry, but I guess about several hundred.
"Every man with a lunch wagon has his particular stand and never infringes on the territory of his brothers..."

"Oh, the time of year cuts no ice. Summer's just as good as winter and winter's just as good as summer; but, say, there's going to be a Harvest Fair week. There'll be about three times as much business done as ordinary. Sunday's a good time too. So many people go out to the parks and come back in the evening as hungry as wolves-only they wouldn't eat their own babies, like wolves do. They want sandwiches and such things."

9/13/1901 - Indianapolis News

CRYSTAL PALACE LUNCH WAGON,
ALBERT H. CLOSSON, Proprietor,
On Fountain Square.

Open from 6:00 p. m. until 2:30 a. m. The very best Home-Made Bread and Pastry served. Chops and Steaks a specialty. Oysters in season.

THE PROPRIETOR IS A GENIAL FELLOW AND PARTS HIS HAIR IN THE MIDDLE.

Above:
Albert Closson's advertisement in a Glens Falls city directory. Lunch wagons were open only at night in the beginning. Note he was attempting to promote a wholesome atmosphere at the wagon.

Most people who built lunch wagons got their start by running one. Some of the names include T.J. Buckley, Walter Scott, Pop Tierney, Jerry O'Mahoney and Albert Closson. These and others, had great ambition and recognized that they could make more money building lunch wagons. Other companies that built carriages and trolleys also built a few lunch wagons, but knowledge of these companies is sparse. Cheney and Brown of Ilion, New York built a lunch wagon in 1900. Known as The Waldorf, the wagon was 7 feet wide by 22 feet with stained glass windows, just like most New England wagons of the time.[1] The Ellis Omnibus and Cab Company built one in 1896 that caught the eye of Carriage Monthly in 1896. In 1914, another lunch wagon caught the eye of this magazine: The Closson Lunch Wagon Company had recently moved to Westfield, New York from Glens Falls, New York and intended to build lunch wagons on a large scale. They were the only known prolific builder outside of New England or Metro New York City.

Albert Closson was the first person to operate a lunch wagon in Glens Falls, a city located on the Hudson River about 200 miles north of New York City and 50 miles north of Albany. From just south of Glens Falls, the Champlain Canal leaves the Hudson Valley and heads to Lake Champlain. Glens Falls is also just outside of the Adirondacks, and is historically known for its paper industry and other lumber related concerns, with the lumber coming down the Hudson from the mountains.

Albert Closson's lunch wagon was located on Fountain Square from 1896 to 1903. Closson called this wagon the "Crystal Palace." In an advertisement, he stated, "The owner is a genial fellow and parts his hair in the middle."[2] Like any typical wagon of the time, the hours of operation were in the nighttime, 6 p.m. to 2:30 a.m. Although many wagons had such stately names, this did not stop one reporter in the local

Left:

Samuel Rivette is shown in front of one of his Closson lunch wagons. This one replaced a similar Closson wagon. Note the closed up space above the front wheels, probably used for more storage space.

(Tom Prebble)

newspaper, The Glens Falls Times, from showing little respect for what was quickly becoming a New England institution by 1904. "The night lunch wagon has just made its appearance in London and is regarded with great novelty. The night lunch wagon has been an established dyspepsia breeder in Glens Falls for many years, and it is strange that it has not been introduced in London before."[3] Perhaps every proprietor did not live up to these names with their quality of food that they served. Ironically, Charley Fuller once ran a lunch wagon under the London Bridge before moving to Massena, New York to work for the local newspaper.

No one knows where Albert Closson got the idea to start building the wagons himself, but his design did not look like Buckley's White House Lunch Wagon or Hamel's Columbia Cafe. Instead Closson's wagon more resembled a trolley car. It is possible that being a staunch temperate, Closson saw what the Women's Temperance movement was doing in New York City with their wagons and wanted to have the same influence. The Womens Temperance movement were running lunch wagons in the heart of New York City offering lunches to night time workers. Prior to their appearance in the city, one of the only places to get lunches overnight was at a bar or saloon. Obviously, this bothered the Temperates. Therefore, the lunch wagon had a friend in the Temperates.

By 1903, Closson filed for a patent to build his own lunch wagons. He also filed a patent in Canada in 1905. His design did not have a barrel roof. Instead it had a monitor roof similar to trolley cars. His patent did a good job of explaining what his lunch wagon consisted of:

> The object of the present invention is to provide an improved
> commodious kitchen and dining room which is mounted on wheels to
> permit of easy transportation and which may be easily and conveniently

entered by pedestrians from the street, as well as to furnish a booth from which persons standing on the outside may be readily served with lunches. Another object is to provide a vehicle of this character in which the facilities for preparing and serving lunches are greatly increased by the peculiar arrangement and aggroupment of the furnishings, which enables a maximum number of persons to be served with a minimum amount of labor and trouble, the tables and seats being so arranged in the dining-space as to afford easy access by the waiter to each seated person without crowding each other or obstructing the passage for the admission and exit of other guests and of the waiter and at the same time permit standing persons to be served from a counter in front of the kitchen, which is separated from the dining-space by such counter.

A further object is to arrange the furnishings so as not to obstruct the light through the windows and at the same time obviate the use of floor space for cupboards, closets, shelves, &c., and, in fact, everything except that which is necessary for the comfort of the customers, and to these ends the kitchen is located at the front of the wagon, and the entire front wall, where there are no windows, is equipped with necessary closets, shelves, cupboards, and sink, while the projecting front end of the ventilated car-roof, which is

Above Left:

Albert Closson would include a scenic painting on the end of his wagons and also had his company's information painted along a metal band below the picture. The wagon was placed in Malone, New York which had a population of 10,000 in 1900 and supported a couple of lunch wagons.

(Patrick Tatro)

Above Right:

This Closson lunch wagon was located in Saratoga Springs, New York near a trolley station. Trolleys, the railroads and horses were the main modes of transportation at the time.

(Saratoga Springs (New York) Public Library)

Right:
A 1910 advertisement in a Glens Falls city directory. Closson had a moderate but respectable business while located in Glens Falls.

usually of no practical utility, may conveniently accommodate a tank for supplying water to the sink.[4]

Albert Closson was definitely building a top-notch lunch wagon in 1903. He was probably the first person to introduce electricity to his wagons. Closson also gave the operator the opportunity to have running water. For the time period, there was very comfortable seating for as many as eleven people. Although by today's standards the entryway to the lunch wagon was quite small, at the time, Closson's lunch wagon was quite roomy. And being able to get out of the elements to partake in a midnight lunch and the opportunity to sit down was well worth it. Most other wagons at the time had minimal interior room for customers and none are known to have had as many as eleven seats at such an early juncture.

Albert spent the next nine years building lunch wagons in a residential part of Glens Falls on a small scale. Closson's unique wagons had distinctive name and number plates attached on the outside of each wagon, which made them even more recognizable. To the left of the door was the name of the wagon, placed inside a fancy dark olive green frame, and on the right was the number of the wagon, in a smaller fancy frame. Like lunch wagons of the time, many of his wagons were given catchy names such as "Try Me" or "The Grand Isle", or Native American names such as "Ondawa Lunch."

Many of the villages near Glens Falls had Closson lunch wagons. Glens Falls actually only had one non-Closson wagon, with at least five Clossons doing business within the city. While the village of Corinth instead had an older White House Lunch Wagon, other places like Schuylerville, Gloversville and Ballston Spa all sported Closson lunch wagons. Whitehall, Saratoga Springs, and Glens Falls were the big winners of the Closson trade. Saratoga had three wagons, two of which were definitely built by Closson. Whitehall, a Champlain Canal village of about 4000 people, had four wagons at one time, at least three being Closson wagons. At one time, all four were on the same street, all alongside the Canal—two above the bridge and two below.

Dawson Feeds 'Em — Whitehall N.Y.

Top Left:

Art Dawson ran his Closson lunch wagon in the canal village of Whitehall, New York. Canals were still an important method of moving goods, and even though the population of Whitehall was roughly 5000 in 1900, there were four lunch wagons along the canal for a time. Three of those wagons are verified to have been built by Closson.

(Whitehall Historical Society)

While some Closson lunch wagons surely went to the greater Adirondacks, in places such as Watertown and Malone, many villages already had a White House Cafe such as that in Corinth. This fact, along with the decline of the logging towns by the start of the twenieth century, meant less chances in the nearby Adirondacks for Closson by 1903. Mineville, a small village near Port Henry, named for the Republic Steel iron mines that employed the residents, had two wagons at one time around 1914. Although logging dominated the Adirondack economy, pockets of other natural resources did exist here and there.

In 1912, something happened that would allow for the company to start building wagons in a new location, and at a higher rate. Dr. Charles Welch of Westfield, New York decided to invest in the Closson Lunch Wagon Company. He bought the company, moved it to Westfield, and started offering stock for sale to the residents of Westfield. The reason is unknown, except that Dr. Welch liked to dabble in investing at the time. However, he would have been well aware of the lunch wagon business from his time in New Jersey.

Diner historian Daniel Zilka figured out that Dr. Welch had a house in a New Jersey town where Jerry O'Mahony vacationed. Dr. Welch would have known about the great lunch wagon business in New Jersey and might have believed that the unique Closson model would fill a nice niche.

When the news hit the Westfield Republican on August 28, 1912, it was such a new story that Closson's name was misspelled in large type font as "CLAWSON".

> For the last two weeks, Mr. Edward L. Tiffany has been in Westfield seeking to organize a stock company and secure a site for a factory, all of which has been completed, and work will begin as soon as the certificate of incorporation can be gotten out. The Company will manufacture a high

Bottom Left:

Marion's was in Glens Falls, Closson's home town. In fact, only one lunch wagon that plyed its trade in Glens Falls was not built by Closson. In Marion's, the front section was covered over into an even bigger area than Rivette's wagon, allowing for a little extra precious storage space.

(John Baeder)

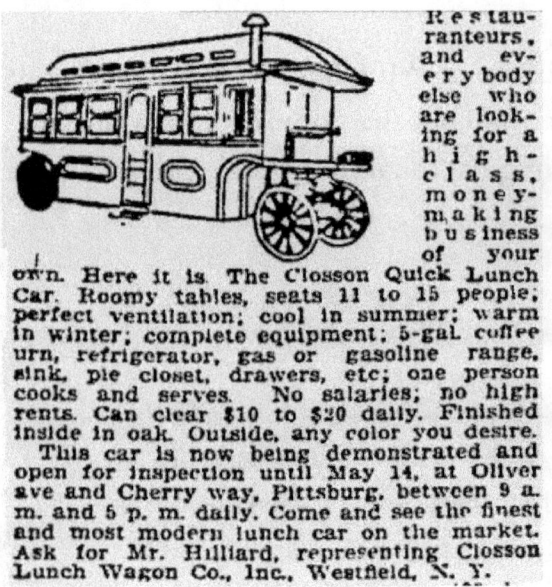

Restauranteurs, and everybody else who are looking for a high-class, money-making business of your own. Here it is. The Closson Quick Lunch Car. Roomy tables, seats 11 to 15 people; perfect ventilation; cool in summer; warm in winter; complete equipment; 5-gal. coffee urn, refrigerator, gas or gasoline range, sink, pie closet, drawers, etc; one person cooks and serves. No salaries; no high rents. Can clear $10 to $20 daily. Finished inside in oak. Outside, any color you desire.

This car is now being demonstrated and open for inspection until May 14, at Oliver ave and Cherry way, Pittsburg, between 9 a. m. and 5 p. m. daily. Come and see the finest and most modern lunch car on the market. Ask for Mr. Hilliard, representing Closson Lunch Wagon Co., Inc., Westfield, N. Y.

grade lunch wagon, such are beginning to be extensively used in cities all over the country. The lot formerly occupied by John Fay as a coal office on East Pearl Street has been secured and the plan is to erect at least one building yet this fall, in the meantime, the Company are considering the advisability of beginning work in one of the buildings of the canning factory now owned by the Welches.

Mr. Tiffany asked for a site and that the people of Westfield take $5000 stock in the company. The stock has all been subscribed and the money for the site is coming right along. About $300 more is needed to complete the whole matter. Let our people take hold of the matter in earnest, for from letters we have received from people in the home town of this concern it is an all right proposition. Common stock can still be had at $100 per share. If interested see Mr. Delaplain at once, who is in a position to tell you about it and has investigated the matter so as to be able to speak with assurance.[5]

The company started out much slower than they had hoped. Some of the difficulties can be gleaned from the second paragraph above. When the company was incorporated in October and held its first meeting of directors in late October, one could read between the lines. The idea of building their own factory had fallen through. Instead, they decided to use the old canning factory in town. The second problem being the lack of a manager through the winter months, as reported in The Westfield Republican. The company would not finish their fifth wagon until mid-April of 1913.[6] The Westfield Republican reported that their first wagon built in Westfield was sold to a company

Above:

This type of advertisement appeared in many papers during 1913-1914. This specific ad was in a Pittsburg newspaper and announced that potential owners could view a Closson lunch wagon in person. Note that by 1914, Closson figured a way to get a refrigerator inside his lunch wagons. While the company was in Westfield, New York, they employed a number of salesmen who would go on the road drumming up business. The company even had a part-time salesman in Canada.

Bottom:

A larger Closson wagon appeared on the streets of Fredonia, New York in 1918. The wagon stands in front of the ruins of the Columbia Hotel which burnt down in January of 1918.

(Vincent P. Martonis)

in Jamestown, possibly known as the Chautauqua Lunch Car Company. Coincidentally, the newspaper announced that the Closson Lunch Wagon Company's motto was, "Not how fast, but how good."[7] Closson would not catch the eye of the lunch wagon trade until The Westfield Republican reported on May 21, 1913, that the operation were now in full swing.

> A Model No. 1 Closson Lunch Car was on exhibition in front of the Citizens bank Saturday afternoon and evening and created a very favorable impression. Folks who had not seen the cars in the process of making had little idea of the high class outfit that is being made in our town.
> Dr. E. L. Tiffany is no longer connected with the company, and his place as president and manager has not been filled. Edgar T. Welch is the Vice President. If a competent manager had been in charge of the company's interests from the start, a much better showing would have been made by this time in the number of cars sold.
> The company has been doing a little advertising and they have received so far over 200 inquiries from men located in nearly every State of the Union.

The mail last Monday brought in over fifty inquiries from the two-inch advertisement in last week's Saturday Evening Post. The local men who are interested in the Closson Lunch Wagon Co. thoroughly believe that the proposition will prove a success.

Model No. 1 is the standard wagon, is 22 feet long, 7 1/2 feet wide and 10 1/2 feet high. The height of the wagon body from ground is 16 inches and it will seat eleven people.

It is made on honor. The material, pine and oak, is the best obtainable. Doors and sash are of oak. Windows extra large; lower sash colonial (translucent); upper sash clear glass. Doors fitted with easily interchangeable sash and screen for summer use. Ventilator windows in patented monitor top, flashed ruby and white ribbed alternating; the interior finish is golden oak. The exterior finish: Body, five coats Modern Red and Valentine Varnish. Beautifully paneled in dark olive green for name and serial number; exposed edges, at base, rear-wheel cut-in, over front wheels, etc, are banded with iron, finished in aluminum bronze; this, together with the bronzed panel molding adds much to the rich finish of the modern wagon. The gear

Above:

One of Closson's larger wagons. George Greene bought this wagon for use in Glens Falls. Closson kept placing the scenic paintings on the end of his wagons. The Glenwood stayed in business from 1908 into the late 1920s.

(American Diner Heritage)

Above:

Interior of Art Dawson's wagon gives us a rare glimpse inside a Closson lunch wagon. Note the upper ceiling studs are fully visible while the lower ceiling studs are behind wainscotting.

(Whitehall Historical Society)

(ironed extra heavy, in excess of reasonable strain) is painted a light canary color. The company furnish either electric or gas equipment as desired. The kitchenette is supplied with every convenience that ingenuity and practical experience can devise. The three-burner modern gasoline range (they can furnish plate for natural or artificial gas, if desired) is made exclusively for this wagon. A close fitting hood over the stove carries off heat and odors from cooking. The five gallon coffee urn is the best obtainable. Ice chest, pie closet, sink, cash drawer, closets and drawers for utensils and supplies - all are there at your hand. That portion intended for the serving of customers is furnished with sanitary tables. These, and the neat oak stools, are handsomely set off with nickel bands. The floor is covered with battleship linoleum. The price of this wagon is $1,000.[8]

The second half of 1913 saw much promise come to the company. D.J. Morey, a Brocton resident who represented the Closson Lunch Wagon Company, was sent out to garner orders for the wagons.[9] By October, The Westfield Republican was reporting sales of two cars to F.T. Boyles and F.C. Moyer, of Meadville, Pennsylvania. (This was a short-lived venture for Boyles and Moyer, with the pair selling both wagons within a year. Short-lived concerns would be a constant in the world of food operations.) The article also mentioned a car going to Erie, Pennsylvania and three "large ones" being built for New York City customers.[10] Around this time, the company hired a representative in Ontario, Canada. C.B. Dickinson of Smethport, Pennsylvania had been sent to Canada by the Luzier Gas Engine Company, where he also accepted a part time position pushing Closson lunch wagons.[11]

A February 18, 1914 Westfield Republican article reiterated the dilemma with building

Above:

A Gloversville, New York wagon was dressed up for a city wide celebration. Closson wagons were small enough to be placed in front of businesses.

(American Diner Heritage)

Below:
Portsmouth, New Hampshire is home to Gilley's PM Lunch. Gilley had a Closson lunch wagon from 1912 to 1940. This photo shows a close up of the lunch wagon is it appears in a mural located behind the current "diner." The almost thirty foot long Closson wagon was drawn by horse each day to its stand.

a new factory, though pushed to the bottom of an otherwise positive article. The Closson Lunch Wagon Company's prospects were very high.

> There is evidence of considerable activity at the plant of Closson Lunch Wagon Co. Orders for two cars have been received within the past week and there are excellent prospects of closing with several other men within the next few weeks. A car has been shipped to F.A. Hall, who is in Indianapolis representing the company. What is probably one of the largest portable lunch cars ever built has just been shipped to a point on the Hudson River. [Believed to be Peekskill, New York.] It is 10 feet wide and 28 feet long. It could not be any wider and be shipped on a railroad. The company finds that the cars that have been shipped and put in operation are bringing new purchasers.
>
> Mr. E.V.D. Phoenix, who has held a responsible position in the office of the Welch Grape Juice Co. for some months, is now giving his entire time to the Closson business and is in charge of the office and sales end. Miss Lucile Colburn is employed as stenographer and office assistant. C.W. Burnham is proving to be a very capable factory superintendent, as the splendid workmanship in the cars testify. About ten persons are employed at the present time and if the business of the company increases within the next three months as it has in the last three, the erection of their own plant will be a necessity.[12]

As well as everything was going, they only had ten employees at this time. Fortunately, this number would increase in 1914,

Below:
Mr. & Mrs. William Todd took their photograph in front of a Closson lunch wagon around 1927. A for sale sign is on the wagon and the Todds were perhaps more curious about the appearance of a lunch wagon in 1927 than anything else!

but only with five more employees by September. An interesting fact is that these fifteen men were making a little over a combined $1,000 a month. At this same time, some notable monthly salaries were about $60 a month for train porters and over $100 for beginning workers in Ford's auto plants.

That September a Westfield Republican article stated, "After about 18 months of operation the company is rushed with orders and we understand they can not now accept an order for a car to be shipped before the first of the year." The Closson Lunch Wagon Company also had plans to send an elaborate wagon to the Panama Pacific Exposition, "This car will be finished in white and gold and will be open to view for people of this vicinity before being shipped." Unfortunately, it is not known if this act was ever followed through.[13]

One of the orders that was being processed at the time was for a wagon to be sent to St. Petersburg, Florida. The company was starting to make a dent outside of New York State, especially with their next sales manager, Mr. E.V.D. Phoenix. The Westfield Republican noted Mr. Phoenix being in many cities and regions over the next year, including Racine, Wisconsin and Wilkes Barre, Pennsylvania, and other places in the Midwest and Northeast.

By October of 1915, The Westfield Republican noted Mr. Phoenix was storing his personal belongings and heading for Bound Brook, New Jersey. This act probably marked the beginning of the end for the company, at least as far as newspaper coverage went. The company lost yet another sales manager.[14] The United States was also getting heated up in World War I, and able-bodied help was becoming difficult to find. The company was probably also having a difficult time finding new purchasers for their lunch wagons. The company was likely also overextended.

On Sept 21, 1916, the Hon. John R. Hazel deemed the company bankrupt. The company was still listed in the 1917 Westfield city directory, but no

mention of any happenings in the company occurred after the date of bankruptcy.[15] By 1918, Albert Closson was again back in the Glens Falls city directory, listed as the proprietor of a lunch wagon for a few more years, before retiring. He would pass away ten years later on August 2, 1928. The headline in The Glens Falls Post-Star read, "Lunch Wagon Maker Realized Fortune in Business." While Mr. Closson did not enjoy a long retirement, that did not stop him and his wife from doing things that many people of the time were not able to do. "Mr. Closson retired from business a few years ago and he and Mrs. Closson traveled for many years. They crossed the continent six times and spent several winters in Florida and summers at Schroon Lake."[16] Perhaps he saw some of his wagons in business throughout the country.

1 Utica Daily Times, Utica, New York March 3, 1900
2 Glens Falls, New York city directory
3 Glens Falls Times, Glens Falls, New York, January 9, 1904
4 Patent #780,265 January 17, 1905
5 Westfield Republican, Westfield, New York August 28, 1912
6 Westfield Republican, Westfield, New York November 6, 1912
7 Westfield Republican, Westfield, New York April 23, 1913
8 Westfield Republican, Westfield, New York May 21, 1913
9 Westfield Republican, Westfield, New York September 17, 1913
10 Westfield Republican, Westfield, New York October 1, 1913
11 McKean Democrat, Smethport, Pennsylvania October 23, 1913
12 Westfield Republican, Westfield, New York February 18, 1914
13 Westfield Republican, Westfield, New York September 23, 1914
14 Westfield Republican, Westfield, New York October 13, 1915
15 Westfield Republican, Westfield, New York September 27, 1916
16 Glens Falls Post Star, Glens Falls, New York August 2, 1918

Next Page Above:

The Bancroft Dining Car in Westfield, New York. Westfield was the home town of the Closson Lunch Wagon Company at the time of the photograph. (American Diner Heritage)

Next Page Below:

This Closson lunch wagon appeared in a Madison, Wisconsin newspaper on April 16, 1923. Even roughly ten years after the wagon was probably built, it was considered an eyesore to some residents of Madison.

Below:

This longer Closson lunch wagon was sent to Peekskill, New York which is fifty miles north of New York City. It would seem that later in the building of Closson lunch wagons that the door was located on the end of the wagons instead of on the side as originally intended.

(Frank Goderre)

Why Should This Eye Sore Be Permitted For Next Two Years

Geekery

Specification forming part of Letters Patent No. 780,265, dated January 17, 1905.
Application filed March 30, 1904. Serial No. 200,814

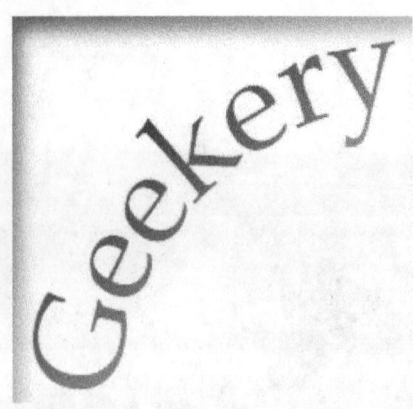

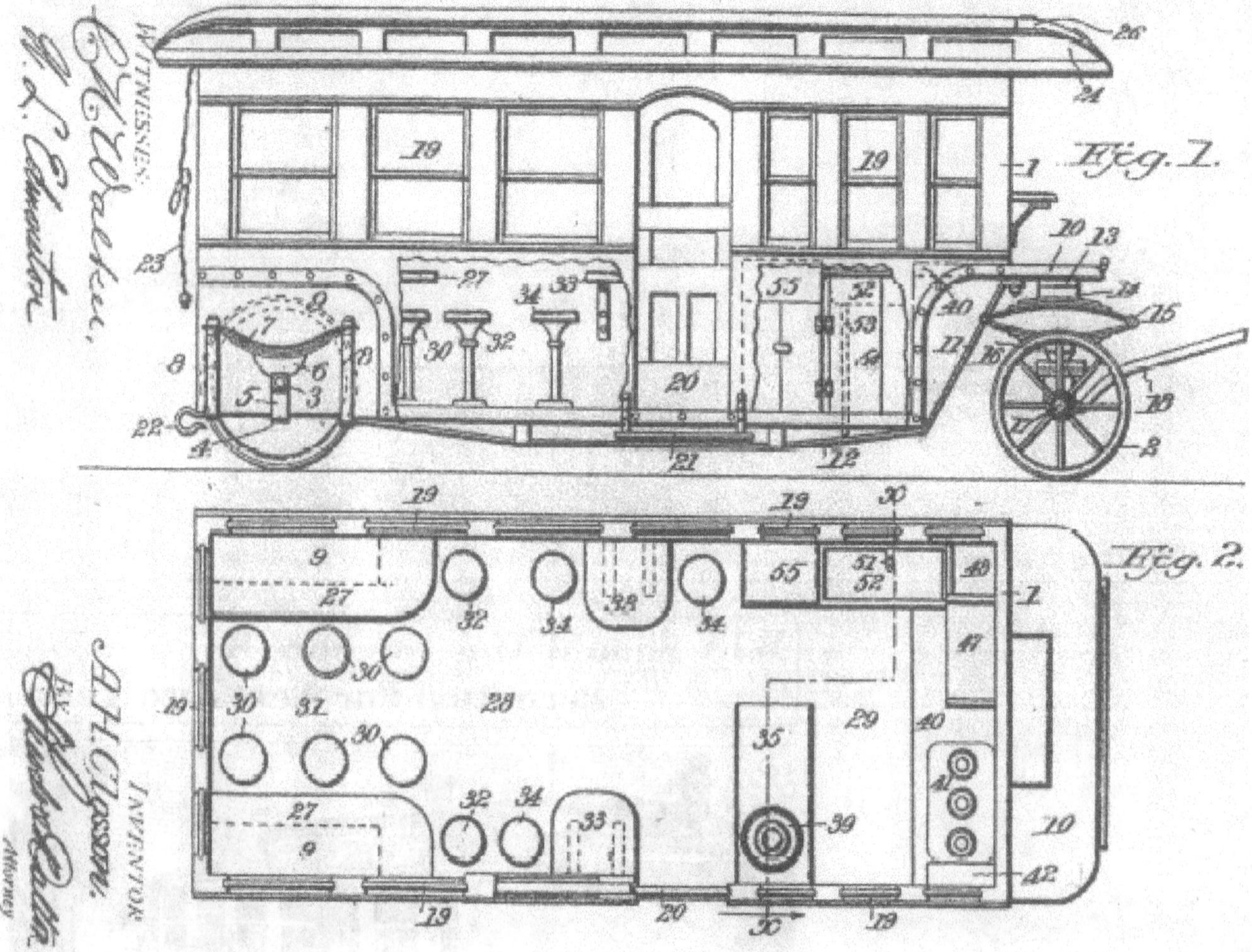

To all it may concern,

Be it known that I, Albert H. Closson, a citizen of the United States, residing at Glens Falls, in the county of Warren and State of New York, have invented new and useful Improvements in Night Lunch-Wagons, of which the following is a specification.

This invention relates to a lunch-wagon adapted for preparing and serving lunches on streets and other places, as desired.

The object of the present invention is to provide an improved commodious kitchen and dining room which is mounted on wheels to permit of easy transportation and which may be easily and conveniently entered by pedestrians from the street, as well as to furnish a booth from which persons standing on the outside may be readily served with lunches.

Another object is to provide a vehicle of this character in which the facilities for preparing and serving lunches are greatly increased by the pecular arrangement and aggroupment of the furnishings, which enables a maximum number of persons to be served with a minimum amount of labor and trouble, the tables and seats being so arranged in the dining-space as to afford easy access by the waitor to each seated person without crouding eachother or obstructing the passage for the admission and exit of other guests and of the waitor and at the same time permit standing persons to be served from a counter in front of the kitchen, which is seperated from the dining-space by such counter.

A further object is to arrange the furnishings so as not to obstruct the light through the windows and at the same time obviate the use of floor space for cupboards, closets, shelves, &c., and, in fact, everything except that which is necessary for the comfort of the customers, and to these ends the kitchen is located at the front of the wagon, and the entire front wall, where there are no windows, is equipped with necessary closets, shelves, cupboards, and sink, while the projecting front end of the ventilated car-roof, which is usually of no practical utility, may conveniently accommodate a tank for supplying water to the sink.

For a full understanding of the merits and advantages of my invention reference is to be had to the following description and the accompanying drawings, in which--

Figure 1 is a side elevation of my improved night lunch-wagon with parts of the sides broken away to expose the interior furnishings thereof. Fig 2 is a plan view with the roof removed, showing the floor-space and the arrangement of the furnishings. Fig 3 is a transverse section on the line x x of Fig 2, showing the front or kitchen end of the wagon; and Fig 4 is a rear elevation with the lowr portion of the wall broken away.

In carrying out the invention I mount the body 1 of the vehicle on suitable carrying wheels 2, which are arranged at each end thereof and confined within the space occupied by the width of the body, so as not to project beyond the sides thereof. The

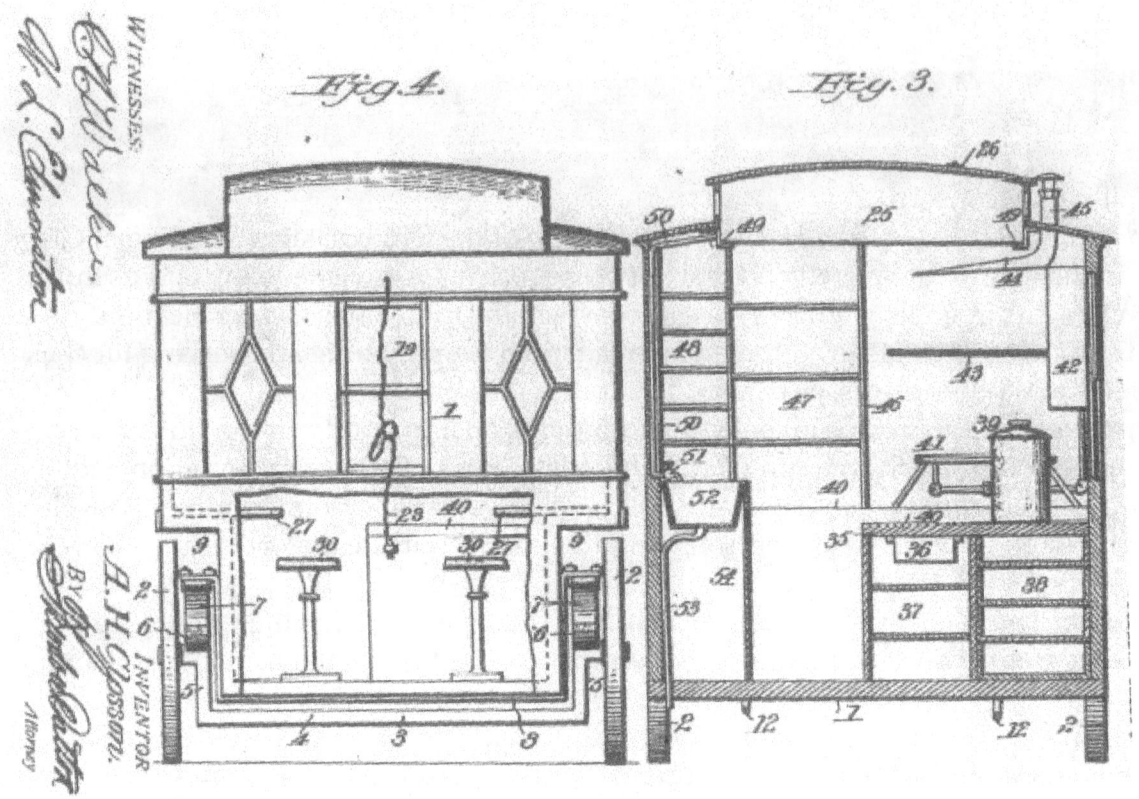

gear for the wheels is particularly adapted for my improved lunch wagon, so that the body of the same will be as low down as possible to facilitate the entrance to and exit from the wagon. The rear axle 3 is U-shaped, with an intermediate portion 4, which extends beneath the body, and the vertical upright arms 5 thereof terminate in oppositely-extending spindles, on which the wheels are mounted. On the tops of the vertical upright arms of the axle are mounted bearing-blocks 6, which are secured by suitable clips to the truck leaf-springs 7, the ends of which are looped and engaged with straps 8, extending down and beneath the vehicle-body and secured thereto, as shown in Figs 1 and 4. The vehicle-body at the rear is recessed laterally, as at 9, and the springs and wheels are confined within this recess, which does not necessitate a wider gage than usual for vehicles and at the same time permits the sides of the vehicle to be brought into close proximity to the sidewalk, with the floor substantially in the same horizontal plane therewith, thus enabling patrons to easily gain access to the door of the wagon without mounting several steps.

At the front, the vehicle-body is recessed or displaced entirely across the same at its bottom, and the running-gear is confined within this recess and beneath the front platform or footboard 10, which extends rearwardly and is connected at its rear end with the drop portions 11 of the truss-rods 12. These truss-rods extend from the rear strap 8 to the front platform, as shown in Fig 1, thereby preventing sagging of the body. Beneath the front platform is a transverse strip 13, which furnishes a bearing for the blocks 14 of the elliptical springs 15, to the under portion of which is secured the bolster 16, which is pierced by a king-bolt that enters the axle 17, on which the front wheels are mounted. Suitable thills 18 extend from the front axle. The sides and back of the body may be provided with windows 19, the sills of which are about midway between the floor and roof of the body, so that the lower portion thereof is inclosed to insure privacy. The front of the body is entirely closed, there being no windows, and about midway of the ends, upon one side thereof, is a sliding door, beneath which is an adjustable step 21. When the vehicle can not readily be backed, the horses may be hitched to a hook 22 at the rear end. The windows are preferably of the usual construction, with an upper and lower sash, the lower sash containing a colored or frosted glass, and by opening the windows lunches may be easily served therefrom to persons standing on the outside of the vehicle. A suitable electric conductor 23, with an attaching-nozzle, extends from the rear of the vehicle and furnishes an electrical connection for the electric lights on the interior thereof.

The roof of my improved lunch-wagon is of the monitor type, with the transom-windows in the sides thereof, so that the wagon may be well ventilated and an increased height obtained, as well as permitting light. At the ends this roof extends or projects beyond the front and rear of the wagon-body proper, and in the front extension 24 thereof is a water tank 25, which may be filled by a hose from the outside, access being gained thereto through the hinged door 26, as shown in Figs 1 and 3.

From the description thus far given it will be seen that the running-gear of the wagon is confined beneath the body and that by the pecular manner of mounting the rear runing-gear the floor-space between the wheels may be utilized, while that portion displaced by forming recesses for the reception of the springs and wheels furnishes shelves or tables 27 on the interior, and that the floor of the body is permitted to drop comparatively low, thus affording an increased floor-space on the interior of the same, while the recess at the floor does not remove any of the floor space to any appreciable extent, since the sides and front of the body abovethe same are utilized to good advantage, as will be hereinafter described. This manner of mounting the running-gear permits the employment of comparatively large wheels, which insures a light or easy draft.

Referring now to the interior furnishings, it will be seen that the dining-space 28 is located at the rear and center of the wagon, while the kitchen 29 is comprised within a relatively smaller space at the front of the same.   The lateral displacements or recesses at the rear do not destroy any of the floorspace for the dining room, since the tables 27 are mounted above said recesses, and in front of the tables are arranged a row of stools 30, leaving an aisle 31 therebetween, whereby all the customers may be conveniently served. At the ends of these tables 27 are stools 32, and near the center upon each side are smaller tables 33, each having stools 34 at the sides thereof. This arrangement provides a comparatively large space between the stools, which enables the waiter to gain access to each seated person and which prevents obstructing the passage for the admission and exit of other customers and of the waiter, and each customer has ample room, wherefore a great number of persons may be served in a comparatively small space. The tables 33 are preferably bracket supported and detachable, so that they may be dispensed with, if desired, and the table adjacent to the door preferably has one stool only upon one side thereof, so that the passsage to and from the door will not be obstructed.

The kitchen 29 is seperated from the dining-space by a transverse counter 35, beneath which is a money drawer, shelves 37, and drawers 38, the last of which may be utilized for storing table-linen, knives and forks, and the like, and on top of this counter is the coffee-tank 39. The rear end of the platform 10 provides a shelf 40, which extends entirely acrooss the front of the body and on which may be mounted a gas-stove 41, which is supplied with a hydrocarbon from the tank 42, and above the gas-stove is a warming-shelf 43, which may be made of heavy reticulated material, whereby some food may be kept warm while other food is being cooked, and above the warming-shelf is arranged a hood 44, which has a spout 45 projecting through the roof and by means of which the odor and steam arising from the cooking is carried off. A vertical partition 46, seperates the heating apparatus from a china-closet 47, and in the corner opposite the oil-tank is a pie cabinet 48. It will thus be seen that the entire front wall of the vehicle-body above the recess is utilized to good advantage. the water tank 25, may be supported in the projecting end of the monitor-roof by means of hangers 49, and from one end of this tank extends a supply-pipe 50, which leads to a faucet 51, above the sink 52, the discharge-pipe 53, of the sink extending down through a closet 54, therebeneath and terminating beneath the floor of the wagon-body. Adjacent to the sink at one side of the body is an ice-box or refrigerator 55.

By the arrangement above described it will be seen that all the articles necessary for a complete kitchen are provided and aggrouped in such a manner as to be within easy access of the cook, who may stand behind the counter in front of the gas-stove and easily reach the pie-case, china-closet, sink, ice-box thereby enhancing the facilities for preparing and serving lunches.

While the specific construction and arrangement of parts as above set forth are preferable, it is to be understood that changes in the form, proportions, and minor details of the several parts may be made with departing from the principle or sacrificing any of the advantages of my invention.

Having thus described my invention, that I claim, and desire to secure by Letters Patent is--

1. In a lunch-wagon of the class described, the combination of a body having lateral recesses at the lower rear ends thereof and a transverse recess at the lower front end thereof, running-gear confined within said recesses, a dining-space at the rear and central portion of the body, tables in each of the rear corners above the recesses thereof, a table upon opposite sides at about the center of the body, seats arranged in front of and at

the sides of the tables with an aisle or passage therebetween, a kitchen located at the front of said body, a transverse counter seperating the kitchen from the dining-space, a sink upon one side adjacent to the counter, a cooking and heating apparatus located in front of the body above the transverse recess, a china-closet adjacent to the cooking and heating apparatus, a pie-case, the china-closet and the pie-case also being disposed above the transverse recess, an ice-box mounted on the floor adjacent to the sink, a closet beneath the sink, and a water-supply tank for the sink mounted in top of the body at the front thereof, substantially as specified.

2. In a lunch-wagon of the class described, the combination of a body having lateral recesses at the lower rear ends thereof and a transverse recess at the lower front end thereof, running-gears confined within said recesses, a dining-space at the rear and central portion of said body, a monitor-roof for the body, having its ends projecting beyond the front and rear thereof, a water-tank mounted in the projecting front end of the roof, a sink upon one side of the body having a supply connection with said tank and also having a discharge beneath the floor, a cooking and heating apparatus located in front of the body, above the transverse recess, a china-closet adjacent to the cooking and heating apparatus, a pie case in the corner opposite the cooking apparatus, the china-closet and pie-case also being disposed above the transverse recess, an ice-box mounted on the floor adjacent to the sink, a closet beneath the sink, and a transverse counter extending from the side opposite the ice-box and having shelves and drawers therebeneath and dividing the kitchen from the dining-space, all substantially as set forth.

In testimony whereof I have signed my name to this specification in the presence of two subscribing witnesses.

ALBERT H. CLOSSON.

Witnesses:
James H. Bain,
Harry L. Mickle

Chapter 3

Earl Richardson and Silver Creek

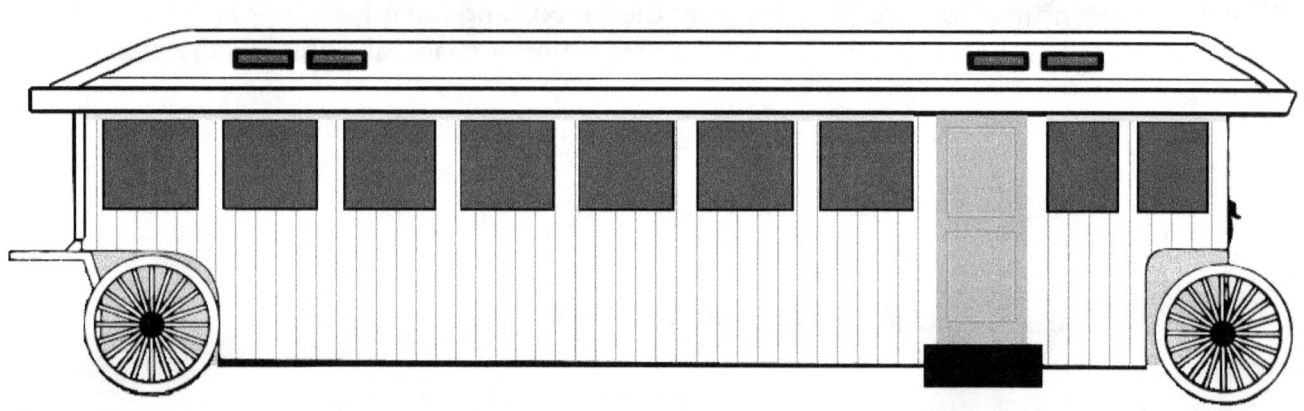

The Old Lunch Wagon.

I saw, standing upright in a vacant lot,

An old lunch wagon:

Battered, weatherbeaten, forlorn;

Its days of service long outlived.

On its windows, such as still remained,

Were pictures rude of statesmen—

Washington, Jefferson, Jackson, Lincoln.

Its steps, worn by many footfalls,

Were partly buried in the mud.

And I thought: If this old wagon

Could only talk, what memories

Might not it share with us—of nights

Long past, and men and women

(For most part of a common mold).

Who talked the argot of their fleeting day;

And youths, who, while the eggs they ordered sizzled,

Upon the little gas stove in the front,

Told tales of stirring combats and escapes from

Policemen huge, who cursed in baffled rage:

And others who, with gusto great, related.

Between large bites of apple pie or sinkers,

Their stories of affairs with women.

Proud creatures of amazing grace and beauty,

Who looked but once, then weakly yielded,

Enslaved by some compelling charm;

And"'drunks, -who, heavy-footed, clumsy.

Entered in early morning watches.

Stumbling, reeking and filling the air

With foolish mouthings;

And women, a few—silly girls a-titter.

And older ones with bold and painted faces,

Who talked in accents hard and cold.

What tales the old lunch wagon might unfold

Could it but voice its memories.

"Probably the fact that the country as a whole has taken to wheels is responsible for the rejuvenation of the old dog wagon into a modern dining car."[1] This May 19, 1926 quote from the Dunkirk Evening Observer is an important background for the next three chapters. Of just as much importance was the fact that Americans were becoming used to "the growing habit of a sandwich and a cup of coffee between meals whenever the spirit moves." A combination of the popularity of the automobile and the movement of the country away from an agrarian society into more of the city lifestyle. The evolution of the lunch wagon was a third facet to the rejuvenation. These portable restaurants now deserved new names such as lunch car, dining car or the newly coined term of diner.

The 1920s brought new life to the lunch wagon business. During the 1910s and World War I, lunch wagons started to fade in novelty as they were moved off the streets and into permanent locations. As the 1920s roared in, the lunch wagon evolved. Builders were making their wagons longer and wider. Some were a good thirty feet long, and the vast majority were fully intended to be placed permanently, except if the vehicle needed to be moved to a new location.

The terms the lunch wagon builders used for their vehicles also changed. Some builders went with "lunch car" and others "dining car." Both of these terms were intended to be directly related to the luxurious accommodations of real railroad dining car eating. In the Great Lakes and Midwest, more so than in the East, the terms "lunch car" and "dining car" were synonymous with railroad eating. These choices of terms were intentional. They were meant as a positive reference, intended to bring more customers to the lunch car.

The interiors also progressed. In the lunch wagon, the cooking and storage was tucked away in the small end of the wagon, and maybe a few stools were available for customers. An early Closson lunch wagon has eleven stools, but many wagons had far fewer available. Many customers would eat standing up. As the lunch car evolved, the counter was stretched out lengthwise with

Above:

The vast majority of Richardson lunch cars stayed close to Lake Erie. Sheldon Neebuhr, a resident of Silver Creek ran this car in Conneaut, Ohio from 1923-1935. Note how similar to a Closson lunch wagon the Richardson model appeared.

customers on one side, and the kitchen and storage on the other along the entire length of the car.

In the East, most lunch cars came with tile floors and often tile on the walls, and sometimes behind the cooking area. Very little metal was found inside except for the coffee urn and maybe the area behind the grill. In the Richardson lunch cars, wood was the main element. The walls were all covered in wood panels or wainscotting. The floors were linoleum, a cheaper alternative to the more expensive and time-consuming task of laying down tile. While companies like the Jerry O'Mahony Dining Car Company of New Jersey started to add metal siding to the exterior of their diners in the late 1910s, companies in the Lake Erie region would not follow suit until the mid to late 1920s.

In the early 1920s, the term "diner" was first coined, quite possibly by the Jerry O'Mahony Dining Car Company, but the terms of "lunch car" and "dining car" would prove to be more popular in the Great Lakes during this period. Diners in the Great Lakes would need more of the railroad association than they would in the Northeast. The area around Erie, Pennsylvania and Jamestown, New York coined the

Above:
Hamburg, New York

In the 1920s, lunch cars typically were placed in a commercial district. A 1925 Silver Creek article stated that Hamburg was the location of the first Richardson built wagon.

Above and Next Page:
Two views of the inside of a Richardson lunch car. Booths had not yet made their way into lunch cars. Four stools on one end looked outside the end windows for extra counter space. There was very little metal used inside of a lunch car at this time. Even the refrigerator was clad in wainscotting. For obvious fire reasons, the grill hood was made out of metal.
(Marilyn Gollnitz)

terms "dynor" and "dinor" in the mid 1920s. The term "dynor" didn't make it beyond one or two diners in Jamestown, but the term "dinor" did become very popular in and around Erie and vicinity before World War II.

Not only did the diner change its name and appearance, but society was changing too. The 1920s brought with it the prosperity of a victorious United States after World War I. Americans were becoming more urban, and at the same time many gained more leisure time and freedom with the automobile. The first automobile travelers showed everyone else that travel in a car could be done. The 1920s brought a major push to pave more highways, connecting a greater part of the country together. Goods also began to be delivered by motorized truck at a higher rate. Even some diners began to be moved real distances by motorized trucks during the 1920s. Railroads and horses were no longer the only choices.

The automobile was as new to many families as the lunch wagon was some thirty years ago. Still in its infancy, car travel was slow, bumpy, and dusty. After traveling in an automobile, many tourists did not feel they were accepted in a nice hotel or respectable restaurant. The lunch car of the day was intended to have higher class than the lunch wagon it replaced, but it was still intended to feed anyone who would come through the door.

Around 1900, Westfield, New York received their first lunch wagon. That was about ten years before Dr. Welch would move the Closson Lunch Wagon Company to Westfield. A few years before then, a different Westfield resident already had his own wagon set up in Silver Creek for a few years. The story goes that Earl Richardson came to Silver Creek for Old Home Week in 1909 and never left. His lunch wagon did so well, he kept the business going. The residents of Silver Creek, and those first automobile travelers who were dusty and weary, came to rely upon Earl Richardson and his lunch wagon for dependable meals. The main mode of travel in 1909 was trolley cars and railroad service. It would be another ten to fifteen years before the tide would turn in favor of the automobile. Richardson kept his ties to Westfield, with his family staying there, but Silver Creek welcomed him with open hearts and empty stomachs.

By 1921, Earl somehow got the idea of building lunch cars and selling them, often to residents of Silver Creek. Perhaps it was the prosperity of the 1920s that helped him on his decision. Or, was it with Silver Creek being located on Route 20, a major east-west road from the Midwest to New England? At the time, there were only three known places to buy a lunch wagon: Jerry O'Mahony in Bayonne, New Jersey; P. J. Tierney and Sons in New Rochelle, New York; and the Worcester Lunch Car Company in Worcester, Massachusetts. Jerry O'Mahony started building lunch wagons in 1913 and quickly became one of the premiere builders. Tierney was easily the largest builder of lunch wagons at the time, having started in 1917, a few years later than O'Mahony. The Worcester Lunch Car Company had a stranglehold on New England, but rarely sold lunch cars outside of that region. Anyone could still buy an old horse-drawn trolley car and fix it up, but Richardson knew there was a business for a nicely accommodated and well built lunch car.

The 1910s was the beginning of the motor travelers who ventured out across America. This was not similar to traveling today. The only accommodations were in city hotels, which were meant for the railroading public, not the "dirty" traveler. Traveling on dirt roads in open carriages in vehicles that were prone to break down or get flat tires made traveling more difficult. Many of the first travelers were called tin can tourists, as they carried their food with them, and cooked it in tin cans on the engine of their cars. But soon, more Americans started traveling the open road, and many ate food at any place they could find along the road. With most travelers only being able to drive 10-15 miles per hour, these travelers did not make much headway each day. One could imagine that Richardson's Lunch Wagon was a welcoming sight to weary travelers. People who were hot, sweaty, and dirty from the road did not mind as much about their appearance when it came to eating in a diner. Trolleys were still in business in the 1920s, and railroad travel was still in service. People stopping in

(Hanover History Center)

An Old Timer at Ravenna, Ohio

Below: **Howard Clute took this Richardson built diner to Ravenna, Ohio. Years later, while working for Ward & Dickinson as a traveling salesman, he took this photo of his former diner. Less than ten years old, he still called it an "old timer."**

Silver Creek had the option to stop at Richardson's place.

There is no doubt that Closson's lunch wagon company had some influence on Mr. Richardson's decision, especially with the design of the body. Just like the Closson wagon, Richardson's car had the same large wheels, recessed into the body. At the beginning, it seems that the building of dining cars was a small business, similar to when Albert Closson first started out back in 1903. If he did not sell to more than a few local residents, the business might not have received any coverage in the local newspaper at all.

One of the first blurbs in the Silver Creek Times mentioned that Earl bought back the lunch cars he originally sold to Cook and Yonk, both Silver Creek residents, in July of 1922.[2] In the next few years, he sold many of the wagons he built to numerous Silver Creek residents. One of those residents, Neil Paul, was reported to be, "traveling through Ohio looking for a good location to place a diner."[3] He chose Bellevue, population about 8,000, located on Route 20 between Toledo and Cleveland. This would be of double importance, especially to the Richardson dining car concern. Ohio was a mostly untapped region for the lunch car. There were some lunch wagons around the state, but their saturation was minimal at best, especially when compared to New England and upstate New York.

With the prosperity of the 1920s and the relative success coming to Earl Richardson, others began to follow his lead. Peter Schneider built a wagon in 1922 in Gowanda, New York for his daughter and son-in-law, Arthur Nelson.[4] It seems that this would be the only lunch car he would build. But in 1923, Dr. L.D. Fitzpatrick formed a company to be known as the "Silver Creek Dining Car Company" with Ernest Fox and G.E. Fowler as Vice Presidents and R.P. Galloway as Secretary-Treasurer.[5] Already, Dr. Fitzpatrick had hired the Fox Bros. of Forestville to build one wagon for him. He must have seen the success and decided to make a go of it as a sideline income to doctoring.

Left:
Earl Richardson was able to place a number of his diners in Ohio locations. This one owned by Silver Creek resident Clement Yonk went to Bryan, Ohio. After a few years of running the diner, Clem sold to a local concern, first buying a diner in Silver Creek before going on the road for Ward & Dickinson.

(Photographic Archives of the Williams County (Ohio) Public Library)

Below:

One of the first diners built by either Dr. Sharpe or Dr. Fitzpatrick's concern went to East Aurora, New York. While the style is similar to a Richardson built lunch wagon, the exterior has a bit more of a cruder look to it. The interior photo that accompanies shows what a typical lunch car of the time looked like.

(American Diner Heritage)

Shortly afterwards, Dr. J.J. Sharpe, a Silver Creek dentist, joined the company. By the time Dr. Sharpe had his sixth lunch wagon built in 1925, Dr. Fitzpatrick had left the concern. The article dated July 9, 1925 in the Silver Creek Times mentioning his sixth wagon explained some of the unique qualities this wagon boasted:

> Doctor Sharp is shipping this week to Woodlawn [we assume south of Buffalo] one of the lunch wagons which he has now been building for some time past. This wagon has a number of new features. The griddle and hot plates are of double capacity and there are two coffee percolators. A most ingenious arrangement is made for taking care of ice cream and ice water. A container for ice cream can is built into the wagon. The ice cream, of course, is packed by the ice cream manufacturer, with salt and ice. The melting of the ice in contact with salt makes a very low temperature, which usually goes promptly to waste. In the Sharp lunch wagon this waste is carried off through a coil of pipe in such a way as to give plenty of ice water without additional expense and it also cools a large compartment used for storage of bottled soft drinks. The water is drawn through a spigot which is turned on by a push of the glass to be filled.
> The finish is exceptionally good, being mostly in veneered mahogany panels. By an ingenious arrangement, the transoms for ventilation swing in the middle, giving maximum ventilation and easy operation. the sash move up and down as in house sash. There is a large storage capacity and a closed compartment for cigars and

> cigarettes where the main stock is kept. Only a few at a time, for immediate sale, are exposed to view.
>
> There is a good sized refrigerator, a steam table and all the usual equipment for dishwashing, etc. Altogether, the Doctor has now shipped six wagons, adding considerably to the local circulation of funds and helping local business.[6]

Other Sharpe built diners were sent to Randolph, East Aurora, New York and Medina, Ohio, while one diner stayed in Silver Creek, initially run by Miss Florence Clute. Sharp's lunch wagons varied the most in appearance of any of the local builders. The lunch wagon that operated in East Aurora starting in November 1923 was long and narrow with large wheels, but the wheels were entirely metal. The transom window configuration had three on the front half of the diner and two on the back half. He later built a car that easily resembled a Richardson or early Ward & Dickinson that went to Medina, Ohio. This diner was transported to Medina in May 1925, so it was built probably just before the Woodlawn diner. The Medina diner also had mahogany veneer on the interior of the diner and close examination of the pictures reveals a veneer bubbling up on this newly built diner. Sharpe would end up building barrel-roof diners, a change from the design that would dominate Chautauqua County builders.

By November of 1923, Earl Richardson decided to move into a factory building, in order to build his lunch cars on a larger scale. The Silver Creek Times reported at this time, "Richardson is an asset to the community, and his many friends will wish him continued and even greater success in his chosen field."[7] Unfortunately for Earl, a windstorm and a fire, on separate occasions, hindered his progress. In late January of 1924, a fire destroyed the old plant of the Columbia Postal Supply Company at 4 Porter Avenue that Mr. Richardson was renting.[8] Fortunately, he had just delivered a lunch car to nearby Falconer for Howard Chapman & Charles Hoeffner, so he only lost equipment in the blaze. The windstorm happened in late June of 1924 and collapsed a building in the process of being built, so little was lost in the mishap other than time in

getting a new factory built.[9]

A new factory building did get built on Hawkins Street. Before Richardson's untimely death from appendicitis on June 7, 1925, the Grape Belt & Chautauqua Farmer announced that he had built "twenty-six cars this past year".[10] This showed that as 1925 rolled around, Richardson's pace of building had picked up to around two cars a month. Cars of solid oak construction were beginning to find their place in the dining car industry.

More than any other lunch car builder in the region, Earl Richardson sold a fair number of his diners to Silver Creek residents. Besides the aforementioned Neil Paul, other Silver Creek residents introduced Richardson-built dining cars to Ohio. Paul helped to finance Ed Root with his lunch car in Galion. Sheldon and Fred Neebuhr brought a car to Conneaut, Ohio, Clement Yonk went to Bryan, and Howard Clute placed one in Ravenna. Yonk and Clute both built up healthy businesses before selling their establishments to local concerns. No less than thirteen other residents took a Richardson lunch car to out of town destinations in western New York and Pennsylvania.

Ward & Dickinson, the company that would truly put Silver Creek on the map, seemed to have great luck in starting their business out. In 1921, Charles Ward, a successful hotel operator, came from Clyde, Ohio to run the Powers Hotel in Silver Creek. It was said that he left signs along the highway from Clyde so his friends could find his new concern. Lee Dickinson was a land speculator, businessman, and prominent resident of Silver Creek.. He also became Mayor in the 1920s, just before starting the dining car company.

Somehow, they came together and had a lunch car built for Wilbur Blanding in 1924 which was placed in Lockport. They were smart enough to hire local contractor Berthel Kofoed to lead the construction. Three more wagons were built behind Peter Kofoed's

Above:

This Sharpe lunch car was located in Medina, Ohio and was initially operated by Lawrence Bader, a former Silver Creek resident. Dr. Sharpe imitated a couple of designs during the time he built diners.

(American Diner Heritage)

Left:

By 1925, Dr. Sharpe had refined the stylings of his lunch cars. Note that unlike the Richardson models that had seven windows to the left of the door and two to the right, the Sharpe model had six on the left and three on the right. With the interior photo, you will notice there is not wainscotting on the ceiling. Sharpe put veneer in an attempt to upgrade the look of his diners.

Case Goods Factory, each bringing more popularity and possibilities to the concern.[12] They quickly realized the great demand for their dining car and decided to start out 1925 in a factory building, right in view of what would become the intercontinental US Route 20.

This chapter deserves more, but there is much lost information concerning Earl Richardson and his importance to the entire dining car industry. Perhaps without him, more than any other person, the Great Lakes diner scene might have been a much smaller blip on the screen of history.

1 Dunkirk Observer, Dunkirk, New York May 19, 1926
2 Silver Creek Gazette, Silver Creek, New York July 14, 1922
3 Silver Creek Times, Silver Creek, New York June 17, 1924
4 Silver Creek Gazette, Silver Creek, New York July 28, 1922
5 Silver Creek Gazette, Silver Creek, New York June 1, 1923
6 Silver Creek Times, Silver Creek, New York July 9, 1925
7 Silver Creek Times, Silver Creek, New York November 8, 1923
8 Silver Creek Times, Silver Creek, New York January 31, 1924
9 Grape Belt & Chautauqua Farmer, Dunkirk, New York June 24, 1924
10 Grape Belt & Chautauqua Farmer, Dunkirk, New York June 9, 1925
11 Silver Creek Times, Silver Creek, New York November 12, 1925

Below:

The Bailey Diner in Buffalo, New York was also built by Dr. Sharpe. Sidney Schweikert first owned this diner and would continue to go back to Dr. Sharpe for two more diners. Both diners were placed in the suburb of Woodlawn, one run by himself and the other by his wife.

(David Ries)

Above:

The lunch car in Warsaw, New York had a prominent spot in the village, right next to the movie theater. (Warsaw Historical Society)

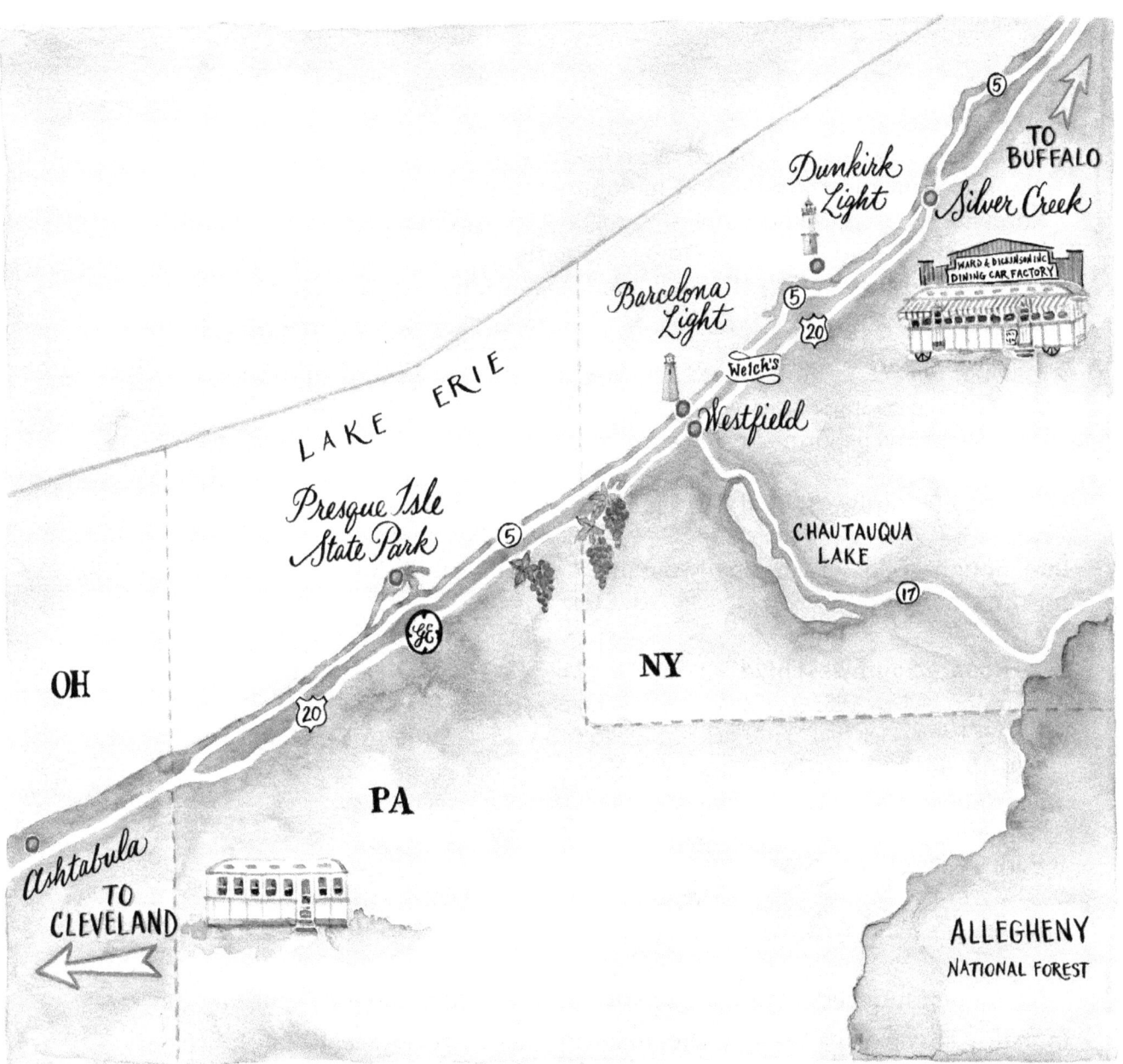

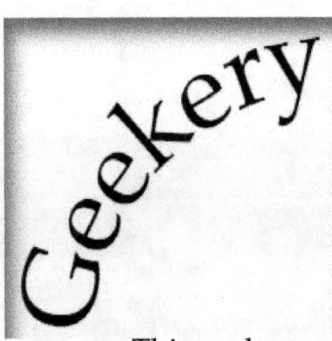

This geekery section is based upon the map above. With so many of the diner manufacturers located in Chautauqua County and U.S. Route 20 and Route 5 such important east-west highways for travelers, the area had more than its share of lunch cars. Below is a simple directory of diners and owners from Irving, New York on the east and Geneva, Ohio on the west.

This list is not a complete list. Some of the unverifiable diners on this list may not be factory built diners. There will also be missing diners. There were even a couple of changes made as late as the layout of this book. If you can add to this list or make any corrections, please get in touch with me.

Lake Road & Southwest Blvd – Irving, New York (**Ward & Dickinson**)
Veva Lewis (1932-1935)
Info: Bought used, was originally the first Kendall Diner. Moved somewhere in 1935, unsure where.

Lake Road & Southwest Blvd – Irving, New York (**Ward & Dickinson**)
Arthur Booth (Nov 1935-) ; Estella & Marie Ebling (Nov 1936 - July 1938+) ; Ralph Denny (1939) ; Thomas Letta (Oct 1940-) ; Angelo Millitello & Angelo Peternostro (Dec 1945-) ; John Fox (1950s-1960s)
Info: Replaced Veva Lewis' diner. Russell Minardi was owner.

@ Park – Silver Creek, New York
Mrs. Myrtle O'Connors (1925) ; Clarence Hagen & Frank Sharron (July 1926-July 1927)
Info: Diner seems to have been in Silver Creek from 1925 to 1927.

Info: Walter Plum had a **Ward & Dickinson** diner at the Zoo for a year.
Info: Roy Payne had a **Ward & Dickinson** at the Kraeft Garage. Kraeft & Schwerk bought and ran it until 1927 when Walter Wasmund took the diner to Cleveland, Ohio.

Central Ave – Silver Creek, New York (**Richardson**)
Earl Richardson (1921-1925) ; Clement Yonk (May 1926-Mar 1927) ; Harrington Bros.(April 1927-)
Ernest Centner (1931-July 1948) ; Vincent & Gerald Sorge (July 1948 -Oct 1951)
Info: The 1921 diner may have been replaced with a more current diner in 1924 or 1925.

265 Central Ave (Foot of Hill) – Silver Creek, New York (**Sharpe**)

Florence Clute (-Aug 1933) ; Ernest Blanding (Aug 1933-July 1946) ; Bernard Symonds (July 1946-Feb 1948) ; Sam Villafranco & Danny Conny (Feb 1948-Mar 1952) ; Carmen Contino & Frank Chappione (Mar 1952-Feb 1959)

349 Central – Silver Creek, New York (**Ward & Dickinson**)
J. P. Lown (Oct 1938-Jan 1944) ; Alex Dickson (Jan 1944-) ; Mrs. Gladys Blakley (-Jan 1947) ; Russell & Philip Dolce (Jan 1947 - 1962+) ; Village of Silver Creek (-Today)
Info: Placed in front of factory. Became Steve's Diner later and currently sitting next to Fire Department.

Route 20 West – Silver Creek, New York (**Ward & Dickinson, Ward & Dickinson**)
Ray Dimon (1927-1948)
Info: Ray did not run the diner. Diner replaced in 1932, with old diner going to Irving, New York.

Info: In Sheridan at a Bungalow camp, there was a lunch car run by Mrs. Nina & daughter Margorie Orr in 1932.

404 Main – Dunkirk, New York (**Mulholland**)
Mr. & Mrs. Alfred Smith (Aug 1925-) ; Mrs. Eva G. Helwig (1930) ; Katherine & Harold Sheehan (1935 - 1940) Anthony J Polito (-June 1948) ; Fred Odel & Richard Scholtys(June 1948-Oct 1949) Ray E. Bogardus & Richard N. Smith(Nov 1949-)
Info: Main Diner then Dunkirk Diner

2 Lake Shore Drive – Dunkirk, New York (**Mulholland**)
Mrs. Gertrude Giebner (1935- 1945)
Info: Harbor Diner. Announced new Harbor Diner in 1945. Kenneth Powell opened a diner here in April 1934.

405 Central – Dunkirk, New York (**Mulholland**)
William W. Cease (1925-1944)
Info: Part of a small chain of restaurants in Dunkirk. replaced by onsite restr by 1944.

Info: Gard's Diner was on the edge of town and was a Ward & Dickinson diner. It was there in the 1960s.

41-43 W Main – Fredonia, New York (**Richardson ;** May 1927 **Ward & Dickinson**)
Harry Hotchkiss (April 1924 – August 1927) ; Barry Lint & Mr. Pitt (August 1927-) ; Mrs. Bertha Hall (1930) ; Kenneth S Powell (1935) ; Steward L Burlage (Sept 1936-1940) ; Alex Dickson (Aug 1942–Dec 1944) ; Herbert Baye (Dec 1944–Feb 1948) ; Mr & Mrs Ray Arnold (Feb 1948 – Feb 1952)
Info: Fire 1929, Fire 1948. Moved to Kimball Stand, to be run by Mike Palermo.

16 Water Street – Fredonia, New York
Walter's Lunch Car (1933) ; Water Street Diner (1935) ; Walter Tucholski (1938) ; Eric Gullburg (1942–1946) ; Frank B Gustafson (1946) ; Burns B Morris & William S Tant (July 1946-) ; Robert Fales (July 1947-)

24 W Main Street – Fredonia, New York (**Trolley Pittsburgh Bessimer & Lake Erie 1882 model**)
W.J. Hall (1920) ; George Kopp (1923–?, April 1933-) ; John C. Donnelly (1927–1930) ;Mrs Florence P Crimens (1933-1940) ;
Lilas & Harry Stanton (June 1940-1956+)

Rt 60 @ US Rt 20 – Fredonia, New York (**Ward & Dickinson ;** 1949 remodeled **Sorge**)
Harris Mead & Gardner Freling (June 11, 1949-) ; Joseph Militello (-Nov 1954) ; Mr. & Mrs. Samuel Militello (Nov 1954-Sept 1962) ; "Irish Billy" Collins (Sept 1962-)
Info: Was the second diner at the Kendall Station just outside of Silver Creek.

Main St – Brocton, New York (**Richardson**)
George Dickinson (June 1923 – December 1924) ; Clyde, Elliot & Howard Manning (Dec 1924 – Dec 1925) ; Mrs. Fred Guenther (Dec 1925–) ; Blanche & Daniel Keegan (-1929 – 1930s)

41 West Main – Brocton, New York (**Mulholland**)
Leland & S.M. Powell (1931 – 1947) ; Milton Nickols (1955) ; Lucille Palmer

Main @ Union – Westfield, New York (**Ward & Dickinson**)
Gerald Mead (Oct 1934-)
Info: Diner moved to Corry, Pennsylvania for a few years then to Sherman, New York.

East Main – Westfield, New York (**Ward & Dickinson**)
Bert Maggio (June 1938-1951+) ; Vinnie Calarco (late 1940s) ; Joe Villafranco (1955-1960) ; Georgia Smith (1963)
Info: Diner came from Dunkirk, New York where it was operated by a Leo Vidal for two years. Probably opened in 1934, though could go back to 1931. Also owned by Thomas Vidal and Julian Billeke.

East Main – Westfield, New York (**Richardson**)
Bruce Merry & Clark Guest (-Feb 1926) ; Bruce Merry (Feb 1926-Apri 1926) ; Wallace Stafford (May 1926-1936)

Main @ Elm – Westfield, New York (**Ward & Dickinson**)
Harold Washburn & Walter Moore (Jan 1929-Aug 1934)
Info: Diner moved to Bethlehem, Pennsylvania by William Bourne and Walter Moore.

Main @ Elm – Westfield, New York (**Ward & Dickinson**)
Manuel Triantefellow (Sept 1934-1946 owner, not operator) F.J. Wright (Oct 1934-Mar 1935) ; S.N. Betts (Apr 1935-Jan 1936) ; Mr. & Mrs. Leon "Steeg" Hanks (Feb 1936-Aug 1936) ; Pat Park (Aug 1936-1946) ; Pat Park (1946-July 1968 owner) ; Louise Taylor (1968-) ; Charles & Susan Bingham ; Grace Beck Perry (-1993) ; John Ellison (-1995) ; Sandy Lewis, Dennis Lutes, and Kelly & Robert Atkins (1995-)
Info: Was previously in Erie, Pennsylvania

West Main – Westfield, New York (**Ward & Dickinson**)
Getrude Briggs & Thelma Joiner
Info: Beacon Bradley Diner. Have photo from 1960s. No idea when it arrived at location.

Main St – Sherman, New York (**Ward & Dickinson**)
Bud Fields and Ray Chylinski (1946-Sept 1946) ; Lee and Betty Buesink and Verna Cox (Sept 1946-Sept 1947) ; Nelson Williams and Lloyd Smith (Sept 1947-Aug 1948) ; Harry Barnes (Aug 1948-Aug 1952) ; Dan and Hazel Hemmink (Aug 1952-Oct 1955) ; Felix and Agnes Pulinski (Oct 1955-Sept 1962)
Info: This is the diner that was originally in Westfield, New York and was moved to Corry, Pennsylvania.

c. Erie @ Chautauqua Sts. – Mayville, New York (**Mulholland,** 1949 **Sorge**)
Harley Barber (Nov 1928-Apr 1929) ; [Clarence] Meade Bros.(Apr 1929-) ; Mr. & Mrs. Clyde Ford ; Mr. & Mrs. Rexford Little ; Grant Hawkins ; Otto & Jerrold Webber (-May 1952) ; Mr. & Mrs. Thomas E. Cardwell (1975) ; Tim & Gail Gatto (Feb 1986-)
Info: Diner was moved to Sinclairville around 1949 when it was replaced with a Sorge built diner.

Entrance to Chautauqua Institution – Chautauqua, New York (**Ward & Dickinson**)
Grant and Madelene Hawkins (1945-1948) ; Chuck Wheeler (1948-1975) ; Jim Jackson (May 1976+)
Info: I have a feeling this diner came from Lancaster, New York.

Main Street –Northeast, Pennsylvania
Arthur Wasmund (-June 1925) ; Marion Manning (June 1925-)

Main Street –Northeast, Pennsylvania(**Guy Russell**)
John Tefft(1930) ; Bruce McFadden (July 1944-)
Info: Guy Russell built one diner in his front yard in Ripley, New York.

4019 Main – Lawrence Park, Pennsylvania (**Silk City**)
Harold E Curtis (1948-1959) ; Wm E. & Jeanne Hammill (1960) ; Kenneth C. Flaugh (1961) ; Mrs. Thelma E. Parker (1962-1968)
Info: On National Register of Historic Places.

3655(became 3341) Buffalo Road –Wesleyville, Pennsylvania (**Richardson**)
Mr. & Mrs. Arthur Carr and Mr. & Mrs. Roy Payne (1924) ; Walter H & Sibyl Wasmund (1926-1927) ; Earl E. Vender (1928) ; Michael Frank + Thomas O'Donnell (1933-1939) ; Paul F. Sperry (1941-1942) ; William D. Parker (1943-1944)

3402(became 2902) Buffalo Road – Wesleyville, Pennsylvania (**Mulholland**)
Chas N. & Merle B. Wells (1929-1939) ; Martin J Atkins (1940) ; John C. Shockow (1942) ; Basil F. Henderson (1944-1946) ; Wendell & Joseph E Russ (1947+)
Info: Russ removed diner and replaced with stick built building that is there today.

3604(became 3212) Buffalo Road – Wesleyville, Pennsylvania
George R. Heath (1939-1944) ; Norval & Myrna Allsopp (1946-1951) ; Blanche Markle (1952-1955) ; Mrs. Helen H. Goodrich (1956)

3335 Buffalo Road – Wesleyville, Pennsylvania
Mrs. Grace Hetrick (1948) ; Mrs. Elsa K. Lane (1949-1952) ; Basil F Henderson (1953-1954) ; Mrs. Mildred Burke (1957) ; Walter Iliff (1958-1961) ; Mrs. Eloise J. Birkner (1962)

407 East 18th – Erie, Pennsylvania (**Unknown**)
Joseph Evans & Gilbert Tong (1930) ; Andrew C. Pietrasanta & Gilbert Tong (1931) ; Mary Ganczkowski (1932) ; Joseph Shelly (1933-1934) ; Raymond Bargelski (1935)

25 West 8th – Erie, Pennsylvania (**Ward and Dickinson**)
Ernest Reynolds + John L. Kreider (1930-1931) ; Mark Hopkins (1932)
Info: Newspaper says diner moved to Westfield, New York Sept 1933. because of 4 years of back taxes owed. Timeline has not matched up to a diner yet. I have a feeling the diner went to Schenectady, New York.

2506 Parade – Erie, Pennsylvania (**Unknown**)
Edward Schnee (1929-1930) ; Paul F Sperry (1931)
Info: Sperry moved to Ann Arbor, Michigan. The diner he owned seems to have been a Ward & Dickinson or similar make. It seems to lead he took this diner with him to Michigan.

2519 Parade – Erie, Pennsylvania
Paul F Sperry (1927-1931) ; Monroe L Saterlee (1932) ; David Rummel (1933) ; Arthur Harriett (1934) ; Mrs Kath Shultz & Helen Fuller (1935) ; Arthur E & Katherine Shultz (1936-1965)

16 West 9th – Erie, Pennsylvania
Harry D Newberry & Clair J Spath 1934

1150 East Lake – Erie, Pennsylvania (**Ward & Dickinson**)
John H Stead (1931-1933)
Info: This was Ward & Dickinson diner #36. Diner came from Delray, Florida. This is now the Main Diner in Westfield, NY.

1315 State – Erie, Pennsylvania
Carl & Lawrence Cunningham (1932-1934) ; Andrew Barnes (1935-1947) ; Richard Jenks (1948) ; Robert L. Whitford (1949) ; Marguerite Boudau (1951) ; Mrs Dorothy Hamilton (1952) ; Stelios Psillas (1953-1959) ; Sarah T Vosler (1960) ; Robert C. & Wilma L. Bahm (1961-1962) ; Jason & Sally David (1963) ; Mrs. Elsie M MacAloney (1964)

13 West 10th – Erie, Pennsylvania
Philip L Cary (1931) ; Leigh Dailey (1936-1942)
Info: Cary owned other diners with verified Ward & Dickinson diners.

3624 Peach – Erie, Pennsylvania
Robert Ross (1954) ; Carl O. & Rachel Fallier (1957-1967)
Info: Postcard shows a 1950s style diner.

2607 Parade – Erie, Pennsylvania
George F & Leo C Reinhardt (1931-1944) ; George Opalenik (1946) ; Valentine J. Woznicki (1947) ; Robert Osborne & Eliz Marshall (1948-1957)

1403 Peach – Erie, Pennsylvania (**Tierney**)
George F & Leo C Reinhardt (1929-1935) ; Carl Rummel (1936-1963)

432 State – Erie, Pennsylvania
George F & Leo C Reinhardt (1928-1929) ; Lawrence C. Cunningham (1931-1933) ; George F & George L Reinhardt (1933-1951) ; Frank J. Merve (1952-1958) ; Ona L. & Lemuel E. Hollen (1959-1960) ; Betty A Ross (1961) ; Nancy Borkoski (1962) ; Donald E. Wragg (1963) ; Nancy Pellican (1964) ; Mrs. Joan Knapp (1966-1968)

1105 Parade – Erie, Pennsylvania (**Closson**)
John H Stead (1924-1929) ; Norman A Detzel (1930-1940) ; William G Kern (1941-1944) ; William G Kern (1946-1960) @ **1102 Parade**

712 Peach – Erie, Pennsylvania (**Richardson, Ward & Dickinson, Silk City**)
Chas Tiedeman + Clayton Haggerty (1925) ; Jessie & John J. Schoos (1926-1930) ; Robert MacKendrick (1931-1960)

5 East 18th – Erie, Pennsylvania (**Ward & Dickinson #55**)
August M. Liebau (1927-1930) ; Barbara Loper (1931-1942) ; Gerald J. Seelinger (1943-1968)

156 West 13th – Erie, Pennsylvania (**Ward & Dickinson**)
Ernest Reynolds (1930-1931) ; Barbara Loper (1932-1937) ; David J. Rummel (1939-1941) ; Betty Snider (1942) ; Benjamin & Eleanor Kays (1943) ; Walter R. & Mildred Smith (1944) ; Mrs. Margaret Gerard (1946-1957) ; Robert Buss (1958) ; Arthur J. Balthes (1960-1961)

1720 Parade – Erie, Pennsylvania
William F. Treuwart (1927-1943) ; Joseph Micelli (1944) ; Walter Kruszewaki (1946-1955) ; Mary A Niedzielski (1956-1962)

110 East 11th – Erie, Pennsylvania
Mrs. Bertha Klingensmith (1936-1944) ; Fred I. & H. Ruth Miles (1946) ; Jason Manos (1947) ; Jason Vencenyo (1948-1954) ; Mrs. Frances & Albert C Leissner (1956-1961) ; Thomas Lynch (1962)

1621 West 26th – Erie, Pennsylvania
E. Arthur Cunningham (1948-1959) ; Albert C. Leissner (1960) ; Gloria C Emerick (1961)

1109 Peach – Erie, Pennsylvania (**Ward & Dickinson**)
Leigh L. Dailey (1927-1928) ; Philip L. Cary (1929-1930) ; Paul Howard (1931-1939) (& Ralph Geness 1931) ; Calvin N. Lambert (1940-1944) ; John J. Straub (1946-1951) ; Millie Cook (1952-1956) ; Sally Erickson (1958-1959)

26 East 26th – Erie, Pennsylvania
Carl & Alfonse Striegel (1928-1939) (& Teresa Alexander 1936-1939) ; Russell Bevaloqua + Russell P Moscato (1946) ; Blaine A. & Barbara Loper (1947) ; Robert E Althof (1948) ; William T Jones (1949) ; Ralph Shearer (1952-1953) ; Leonard J. Petrucelli (1954-1959)

2516 State – Erie, Pennsylvania
John L. Steiner (1933-1937) ; Jason Osborne (1939-1940) ; Stelios Psillas (1947-1948) ; William Vicos (1949-1960)

3723 Peach – Erie, Pennsylvania
Jason Osborne (1941-1942)

1303 West 26th – Erie, Pennsylvania
Leon E. Herpich (1935-1937) ; Howard Flint (1939-1944) ; Buddy Russell (1946) ; Alf J. Pettinato (1947) ; John Bongivino (1948) ; Nick & Angelo & Katherine Panos (1949-1953) ; Alberto Verno (1954-1958) (moved to 1314 W 26th) ; Michael & Josephine Picardo (1959-1968)

2002 State – Erie, Pennsylvania
Joseph & Anna Weis (1927-1933) ; Margaret Weis (1934-1935) ; Lester Goetz & Margaret Weis (1936-1940) (1142 West 12th) ;
Mrs. Margaret Heinlein (1941) ; Walter W. Pattison (1942) ; Clarence J. Denmark (1943-1944) ; George P. & Paul M. Hewitt (1946-1955)

309 State – Erie, Pennsylvania
John Felbinger (1937-1944) ; Carl Alessi (1946-1947) ; William A. Snow (1948-1956) ; Mrs. Thelda Manendo (1957) ; Mrs. Mary Geisecke (1958-1964) : Carl L. Foulk (1965-1968)

222 Main Street West – Girard, Pennsylvania (**1913**)
Peggy & Dick Crosby (1989-Dec 2013) ; Dean Martin (Jan 2014-)
Info: Unknown make, but dates back to 1913.

244 State Street - Conneaut, Ohio (**Richardson**)
Sheldon Neebuhr (1922-1935)

226 Broad Street – Conneaut, Ohio
Autie N Shadix (1935-1941) ; Maurice E. & Wayne Jones (1947-1959) (moved to 255 State) ; William H. Bailey (1963- 1974)

217 State Street – Conneaut, Ohio
Eugene D. Johnson (1935, 1941) ; Charlie Hutchenson (1939) ; C.D. Coon (1947) ; N.M. & Mrs. Addie Kraus (1950) ; Mr. & Mrs. Earl Braden (1954)

202 Main Street East – [Lakeville] Conneaut, Ohio (**Trolley**)
Mrs. Edith Cutshall (1941) ; F.L. Auger (1947) ; Alex K. Michalos (1950-1968) (& Virgil M. Frisbee thru 1954)

277 Main Street – Ashtabula, Ohio (**Richardson**)
Mrs. Louise A & Charles F. Phillips (1926-1934)

4754 Main Street – Ashtabula, Ohio (2nd was **Sorge**)
Wilbur S. Hopkins (1931) ; Philip L. Cary (1934-1943) ; Mrs. Clara Whelpley (1944-1971)

321 Center – Ashtabula, Ohio (**Ward & Dickinson**)
Lloyd W Haws (1934-1943) ; Doris I. & Clinton G. Mallory (1944-1960)
Info: Philip Cary owned the diner.

457 North Ridge Road West – Ashtabula, Ohio
Olive E. Evans (1937) ; Mrs. Louise Lee (1939) ; Mrs. Francis O. Hautala (1941) ; Mildred Mimick (1943) ; Robert Truesdell (1944) ; Wade T. Westlake (1946) ; Raymond R. Maurer (1948)

1907 East Prospect – Ashtabula, Ohio
Joseph Zalokar (1939-1946) ; Jay Christos (1948-1962)

4231 Lake Avenue – Ashtabula, Ohio
Lawrence A. Voorhees (1941-1944) ; John P. O'Neil (1946-1948)

381 North Ridge – Ashtabula, Ohio
Paul A & Mildred Minick (1944-1951) ; Carmel Bennett, Dora Tamburro & Marie Niemi (1953) ; Harry & Rose Dykes (1954) ; Paul A & Mildred Minick (1955) (became 2229 Prospect West.) ; Catherine D. Zullo (1957) ; Donald F. & Marian N. Wood (1958-1960) ; Virginia Ohl (1961)

250 Center – Ashtabula, Ohio
Leo D. Joseph (1948) ; Wesley Zorn (1951-1954) ; Mrs. Catherine D. Zullo (1955) ; Mrs. Dorothy W. & Earl T. Young (1957) ; Lee Gardner (1958) : Harry O. Barnard (1962) ; Mrs. Emma M. Kaydo

(1964-1965) : Mrs. Pauline Williams (1967)

1138 Prospect – Ashtabula, Ohio
Harrison Urch (1950) ; Donald L. Radik (1951)

1010 Prospect – Ashtabula, Ohio (**Valentine**)
Janet L. & Raymond R., + Ralph Wright (1950-1976)

33.5 East Main – Geneva, Ohio (**Cleveland Painesville Ashtabula Trolley #97**)
G. Constant Carafas (1929-1931) ; Eugene G. Johnson (1934-1941) (70 E Main) ; Mrs. Estelle Brown (1963) (62 E Main)

35 North Broadway – Geneva, Ohio
Harold Taylor (1926-1931)

52 North Broadway – Geneva, Ohio
Forrest Hopes & Mrs. Addie George (1934) ; John M. Knapp (1937-1939) ; V. Leslie Stiffler (1941) ; Clara B. Karver (1963)

103 West Main – Geneva, Ohio
Forrest Hopes & Mrs. Addie George (1937) ; Earl Miller (1939-1941)

Chapter 4

Ward and Dickinson Dining Car Company

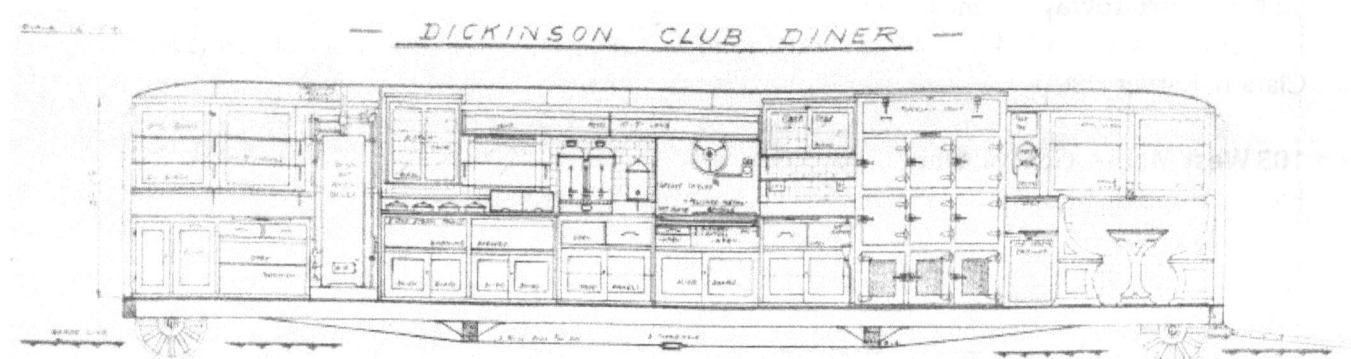

Ward & Dickinson diner

She brings me money every day.

She treats me in a mighty nice way.

And even when I go away

She's working for me just the same.

She brings me motor cars

Two bit cigars (I smoke 'em all the while)

Diamond rings and other things.

To keep me dressed in style.

I love my Dinah, Dinah

Lordy, how I love my Ward and

Dickinson Dinah.

This Page:
Gerald Blanding's diner in Lockport, New York. This was the first diner built by Berthel Kofoed for Ward and Dickinson. Compare this interior to the interior of a Richardson lunch car in the previous chapter and you will notice only some subtle changes.
(American Diner Heritage)

Below:

The McCraig family outside their diner in Toledo, Ohio. This was the fourth Ward and Dickinson diner built and the first in the new factory. The Ward dining car was already taking shape.

(American Diner Heritage)

The Ward & Dickinson Dining Car Company came the closest of any company to matching the output of O'Mahony and Tierney, who quite possibly were building a diner a day at this time. For roughly ten years, the company dominated the diner trade in the eastern Great Lakes.

As Lyle Myers stated in a 1972 interview for the Buffalo Courier, "Tourists passing through the community [Silver Creek] would stop at the rambling plant and look over the cars in the yard, awaiting shipment. Pretty soon they'd sign up for a diner."[1] The Ward and Dickinson plant was called the "Pride of Silver Creek" in the local newspaper during the 1920s. A company that at its prime had about 100 employees. For about 10 years, this company from the little known village of Silver Creek became a major player in the diner business and had the majority of the diner business in the Great Lakes area and their fair share of central New York and Pennsylvania.

Lee Dickinson lived in Silver Creek and made his money on land speculations, especially in Florida and Texas, and oil well drilling. He was definitely the financial backbone of the company. Charles A. Ward previously came from Clyde, Ohio to run the Powers Hotel in 1921. Although, before that, he was in Colorado and West Virginia. Lee Dickinson was called a "modern Croesus" by the Buffalo Times due to some of his actions while in Florida in 1925. Dickinson, "finding a hotel in St. Petersburg full up, promptly bought the hotel and helped himself to the best accommodations."[2] He also bought a barber shop with a long line because he was in a hurry to get a shave. The Silver Creek Times retorted back that Dickinson was a shrewd businessman. "What he buys he hold unless he sells it at a profit or makes a good trade, and as we all know he would rather trade than sell any day."[3] When Charles Ward came to Silver Creek, he was said to have put up signs along the highways pointing his old friends to Silver Creek.

In the summer of 1924, Charles Ward and Lee Dickinson hired local contractor Berthel Kofoed and set out to build a lunch car under a tree behind Kofoed's Garage.[4] Although the

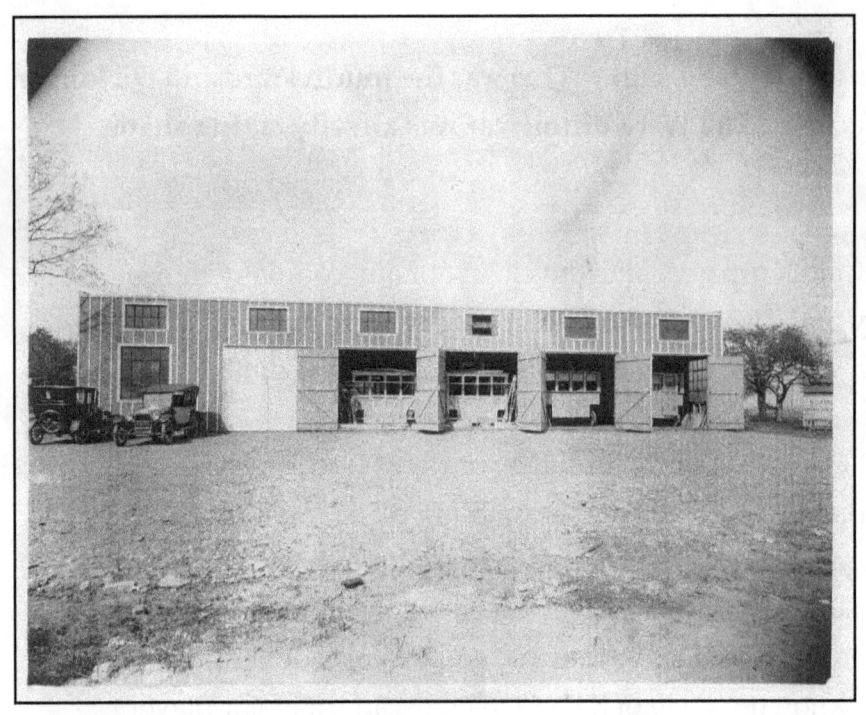

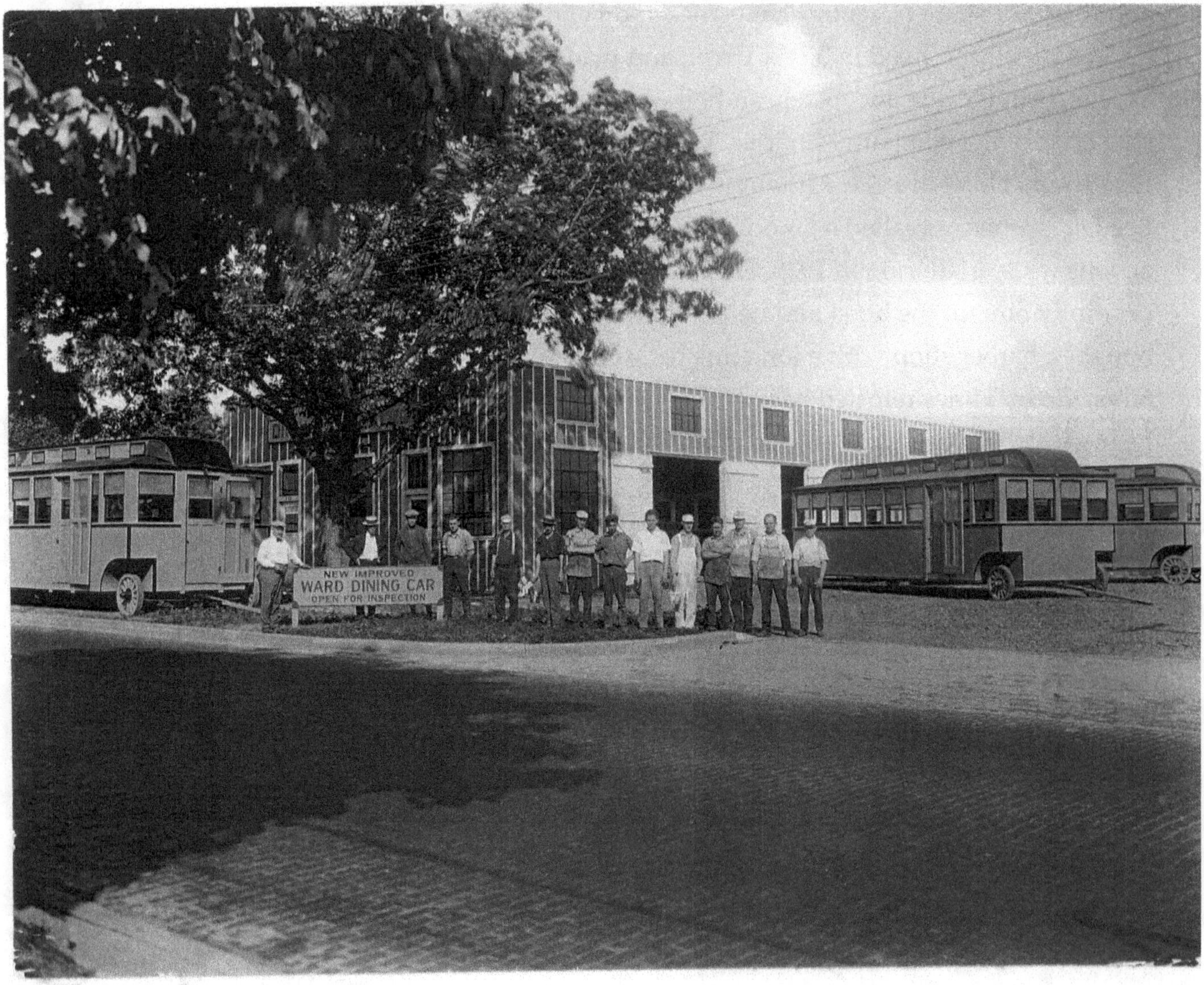
NEW IMPROVED
WARD DINING CAR
OPEN FOR INSPECTION

The Ward and Dickinson factory in the summer of 1925. This is what a traveler on soon to be US Route 20 would see when they entered Silver Creek. The factory was an improvement to the dining car business and also a fantastic advertisement.

(Hanover History Center)

Below:
The first of the Dean's diner chain, located in Indiana, Pennsylvania. Deans had at least three Ward and Dickinson diners over time with one of the other diners in Blairsville, Pennsylvania.

local newspaper claimed that the first lunch car was run by LeRoy Payne besides Kraeft's Garage, this first car actually went to Lockport, to be run by Wilbur E. Blanding. The Blanding surname would become well known to the line of Ward and Dickinson dining cars. The team would have a total of four lunch cars built outdoors, each one bringing more acclaim and success to the possible venture.[5]

By the start of 1925, Berthel was put to the task of erecting a factory building. The business was expected to be a short affair, so a building with six bays and an expected life of maybe 10-15 years was put in place on Central Avenue on top of Oak Hill, where they quickly began to build more and more lunch cars. And as quickly as they could build the diners, orders continued to come in from all over. At first, many of the orders were centralized around the southern shores of Lake Erie, but soon, the orders expanded to farther reaching places.

The first car built inside the new factory was intended to go to Florida, to be operated by Elmer Birdsey and Howard Dickinson.[6] For some unknown reason, the lunch car, at ten feet wide, was found to be too wide to be shipped to Florida[7], and instead was sold to Robert McCraig and shipped to Toledo, where it was called the Betsy Ross Diner. Fortunately, as many Ward and Dickinson dining cars were shipped by rail, the unknown problem was solved, and future diners did make their way to Florida.

The dimensions of these first lunch cars built by Ward and Dickinson were 30 feet by 10 feet. The cars started out being clad in wood wainscoting, and painted typically in white. Unlike Richardson's lunch cars, the Ward and Dickinson models almost exclusively had small radius wheels. The company explicitly stated that their "dining cars are semi-steel vehicles (not a building)." The wheels being used to move the lunch car to its final destination from the train and

if the car ever needed to be moved again. There are also rumblings that the wheels had a second advantage. By being built on wheels, the dining cars did not classify as a building and thusly were not taxed by New York state as a new building.

As pointed out in the personal memoirs written by Donald Kofoed, son of Berthel, in 1991, there was another reason most of the diners looked the same. "Father built wooden wagon wheels once, enough for all the diners they built. Likewise the axles." Donald, who worked at Ward and Dickinson for a number of years, credits his father with the creation of the Ward and Dickinson dining car. Kofoed also made a deal with Pittsburgh Paints and had a special shade of green made for the company.[8]

Only one Ward and Dickinson lunch car is known to have bucked this trend of the smaller wagon wheels. That was one diner that stayed in Silver Creek and sold to Walter Plum. Plum ran Silver Creek's Zoo in 1925. If it was not for two independent sources that verify this car to be built by Ward and Dickinson, one could easily mistake it for a Richardson built diner.[9] The Zoo whose main attraction was alligator and ostrich, was started in 1924 as a way to gain publicity for the village. The publicity for the village and the budding lunch car building businesses was reiterated on March 12, 1925 by an editorial in the Silver Creek Times.

"There will be times when all four lunch wagons in Silver Creek will be rushed to the limit and perhaps turning customers away. It stands to reason that the tourist trade will be heavier than ever before this year, and there will be times when all facilities will fall short of caring properly for it. With four lunch wagons on the job catering to tourists we have a constant advertisement not only for the town itself but for the lunch wagon manufacturers, and we venture to say that many good inquiries will be received and sales made as a result of the unusual spectacle of lunch wagons in pairs, practically adjoining each other, in the same small town. Let us pull together and make the place

Above

Diner number 8 was an odd looking Ward & Dickinson diner. The diner stayed in Silver Creek for two years before being presumably being sold to an unknown party. Plum ended up in Erie, Pennsylvania.

itors this year."[10]

It also took a few lunch wagons for the classic swirled green upper sash to make its appearance. Unfortunately, it is not known which was the first car to sport these famous Ward and Dickinson trademarks. Like most windows, Ward and Dickinson's windows were double sashed. This allowed the windows to be opened. Some diners even came with an attached screen that would recess into the diner when the window was closed. The upper sash was smaller on Ward and Dickinson's cars. Charles Ward decided to put in some swirled glass into the upper sash, probably to block the sun. In matching the color of most of their diners, the glass was swirled with a mix of green and white pigments.

Diners that the company built in 1925 did not have booths. Only specially built diners on the east coast had tables for either two or four, the vast majority having a counter lengthwise, and others having a second counter along the windows. Ward and Dickinson's diners had a regular counter, but they also had separate counters at the ends of the diners over the wheels recesses. Sometime in late 1925, two booths were placed in one end of their diners. They would use this fact to promote the concept of ladies having an acceptable place to eat at in a diner.

Sometime by the late summer of 1925, the company began to clad their diners with automobile quality steel. First and foremost, this made the diner "fireproof" in the eyes of fire departments. Perhaps this was in response to the Elwood City, Pennsylvania fire chief denying the request of Ernest W. Blanding. Blanding wanted to place diner number eight in February 1925 in Elwood City's business district.[11] Lunch cars built by the east coast companies like Worcester, O'Mahony and Tierney were already clad in steel.

Charles Ward patented this metal clad "Ward Dining Car" in January, 1927 as a design patent number 73,246. This protected the design, but just like any good idea, didn't stop its progression. Ward's initial design patent was quite simple. It started with 20 gauge auto body steel panels, painted white. Except on part of the back side, a

Above:

This early Ward and Dickinson ended up in the Valley section of Syracuse, New York. Quickly, the company recognized the need for canopies over the windows to block direct sunlight from the customers and employees eyes if necessary.

(Hanover History Center)

double sashed window would be above each steel panel. The top sash containing swirled green and white glass. The windows were trimmed in green. This would be the general look that Ward and Dickinson would stay with until the end.

The design patent showed the 30 foot model with seven windows to the left of the front door and two to the right, but the size of the diners was one thing that would quickly change. The next step in this progression of the Ward Dining Car was just slightly different on the outside. The new Ward Diner had overhangs, unlike the earlier models. This gave a perception of a larger diner. One of the company's advertising cards shows this diner in front of a baseball stadium, possibly in nearby Buffalo. Next came the Deluxe model. the new deluxe model was 40 feet in length. This extra ten feet was mostly used for a separate partitioned room at the end of the diner where a stove and dishwasher would be placed, out of view of the customers. In later brochures, Ward and Dickinson would claim that they introduced the idea of a separate kitchen.

Compared to what diner owners originally had, this was a great advancement for people who could not afford to build an addition on the back of their diner. The placement of the oven and dishwasher in the end room of a Ward and Dickinson Deluxe dining car, away from sight of customers, greatly allowed for better flow of employees, especially during busy times of day.

By the time Ward and Dickinson covered their diners with steel and fancy green and

Right:

Slight improvements were made by Charles Ward which was officially named "The Ward Diner." Charles even patented the exterior design. The exterior was now covered with automobile quality metal and the roof was extended beyond the ends of the diner itself.

(Hanover History Center)

Below Left:

Estelle and Clive Howard, Silver Creek residents bought this diner in Le Roy, New York. The diner moved to Perry and then the junction of US Rt 20 and Rt 36 where the diner is shown.

(Sharon Roesch)

In 1926, the company tried building diners with two tables for three people separate from the main counter. They also tried chair back stools.

(Vincent P. Martonis)

white swirled glass they made quite the statement.

When the first Ward and Dickinsons came into many towns, they made quite the splash on the culinary scene.

Cortland Standard, August 24, 1926

> The diner was built by the Ward & Dickinson company of Silver Creek and is of a type which is replacing the old style lunch wagon. The vehicle, which is an innovation in this city, will be operated independently by its proprietor. The Silver Creek concern which puts out these diners builds the restaurant vehicles in such a way that they are clean and up to date. The interior is finished with a two-color combination of apple green and white tile sidewalls. Ample lighting facilities are afforded by the group of windows built into the wagon, while seats are available for eighteen persons. Tables in the west section of the diner will be reserved for the ladies. The diner is equipped with modern culinary facilities, the Ward & Dickinson company providing a portion of the furnishings. In addition to the regular facilities, the diner has a counter, an ice machine, steam tables, two ovens, burners and plates, an electrical fan and ventilator to carry off all fumes and smoke over the burners.[12]

Ballston Spa Daily Journal July 5, 1927

> The "dining car," this is no lunch wagon, is one of the finest of its kind

and with a capacity for seating eighteen people at one time. It is trimmed in white and light green. The counter service will seat twelve and chairs at table for six others. The stoves and apparatus for keeping the food hot or cold are of the very latest equipment.[13]

During Armistice Day of 1925, the employees of this booming company in Silver Creek feted their employers. The employees were so grateful for their excellent treatment and working conditions. The Silver Creek Times reported, "The proprietors, C.A. Ward and L. F. Dickinson were very pronounced in their efforts to provide a factory, working conditions and wages that their employees might support themselves and families and live as American people should live."[14] Lee Dickinson continued this concern for Silver Creek and its residents by announcing in February of 1926 that all employees at the factory must be citizens of Silver Creek. Dickinson, being the mayor of Silver Creek at this time, saw it as an important facet of business to improve the lives of the residents of Silver Creek.[15] Ward and Dickinson sponsored a band and a baseball team known as the Diners. The band even serenaded the customers of the newly opened Park Restaurant, a place the Silver Creek Times called, "a restaurant that is an inducement for tourists to remain and spend some time in our town and also to return again."[16]

By the end of 1926, the company had 100 diners built with 96 in use. Studying the company, researchers are fortunate for two reasons. Being located in a village of 5,000 people, much of the news coming from the company was reported early on. Also, a ledger documenting the first 100 diners built by the company was located by Vince Martonis, Town of Hanover Historian. He discovered that a relative of the family had this ledger in her possession up in Buffalo, and she donated the ledger to the Hanover History Center. As a side note, a salesman for the company also took

Above:

Author is shown working on a Ward and Dickinson diner. Many of the Ward and Dickinson diners had little sliding doors on the far ends of the ceilings where various items could be stored.

Advertising copy of the DeLuxe model.
(American Diner Heritage)

pictures of various Ward and Dickinson diners around 1932-33 which was also in the possession of this relative.

The ledger shows some unique trends. Two companies, the Ohio Dining Car Company of Cleveland and the Toledo Dining Car Company respectively bought ten and nine diners for their companies. Both attempts at similar looking "chains" were short lived and were out of business by mid 1927. Demand for Ward and Dickinson dining cars was so great that each of these 19 diners were quickly sold to new owners, often for close to the original selling price. Interestingly enough, the majority of these 19 diners ended up in Eastern States. Even the eight car Fisher System in Buffalo was a short lived venture where all the diners were successfully resold by Ward and Dickinson.

If we were to look at the first owners of these 100 diners, only 34 % lasted more than five years in the diner business, and 43 % stayed with that particular diner for more than two years. The companies in the east talked about trading in older diners for newer diners. But for Ward and Dickinson only 10 of the first 100 diners were documented as being traded in for newer diners. As viable as the diner business could be, it seemed it was tougher to make a good enough business to allow for upgrading in the Great Lakes region.

In central and western New York especially, many owners did not consider upgrading to newer diners. If an owner got to a point where they thought their diner was too old, or they needed more room, they would add on to the diner with another building, or like in Wellsville and Naples, they would take down the outer walls of the diner and completely enlarge the place. Both of these diners show no resemblance to a Ward and Dickinson diner today, except that they both have framed pictures of the

A company salesman in the early 1930s took various photos of diners across the country. Above is Cincinnati, Ohio and below is Bellefontaine, Ohio.

(Hanover History Center)

original diners. Others, though would just do a quick remodel, or a repainting, and then open back up. For example, in LeRoy, New York, the proprietor for thirty years, Winnie Hamister, would give the inside of the diner a fresh coat of paint and new curtains every year.[17]

The high turnover of owners did not stop the increased business of Ward and Dickinson. In the first three years of business, they increased the size of their factory twice and went from just ten employees to at least 100.[18] The company made sure their their employees, especially their most visible, were very knowledgeable in their field. Howard Clute was one of their traveling salesmen. He previously ran his own diner in Ravenna, Ohio for just over a year, before selling it to a local concern. Howard was joined by Robert McKendrick, who first worked for the Dunkirk Dining Car Company as one of their traveling salesmen. The plant foreman, Berthel Kofoed, was a well known contractor in Silver Creek before joining Ward and Dickinson, and stayed on with the company almost to the end.

Clement Yonk also went to work for Ward and Dickinson after running his own diner. In November of 1924, he moved to Bryan, Ohio and ran a "very prosperous" Richardson built diner, before selling it to locals. He then bought the Richardson Demonstration car in Silver Creek.[19] The next year, 1927, he went on the road for Ward and Dickinson setting up diners for new customers, going as far as Oakland, California.[20]

In November of 1927, Charles Ward left the company. A newspaper article from the time stated Lee Dickinson bought out C. A. Ward's shares in the company and placed Mr. Ward's ill health as the deciding factor.[21]

Another possible factor could be gleamed from the local paper and conjecture.

More photographs from the company salesman. Above is Hammond, Indiana and below is Rochester, New York. Pratt's Diner below was actually called the Wayside Diner and would be replaced by a Rochester Grills diner just five years later.

(Hanover History Center)

Below Left:
Wall's Dining Car in Hamilton, Ohio was the second Ward in Hamilton. The first moved to Maine after a few years in town.

Below Right:
Wall's under new ownership of Mildred and Howard Brossman.
(Marybelle Beigh)

Charles Ward announced that he went out of town in early 1926 on business. He stated that plans had begun in hopes to shortly announce a new factory and interest for Ward and Dickinson, something that was not yet made in the United States. The story made front page news and stated that the new factory would soon give employment to every resident in Silver Creek.[22] The new factory never materialized, and perhaps there was some behind the scenes issues that caused Mr. Ward to leave Ward and Dickinson. An interesting sidebar was that only four months after leaving Ward & Dickinson, Charles Ward popped up in Clarence, New York the head of his own dining car company.

In August of 1928, Lee Dickinson had Ward and Dickinson incorporated. In the article, the net income was listed (see table). The article noted a, "recent business depression which now appears to be over." The balance sheet as of July 31, 1928 showed $505,413.75 in assets and $48,809.57 in liabilities, an incredible rating of 10 to 1. All this meant that the company could survive the shock of the great depression.[23]

Business was booming. Even the used diners sold in 1928 were going for higher prices than they were originally priced for. The Fisher System diners were initially bought for $4,950 each in

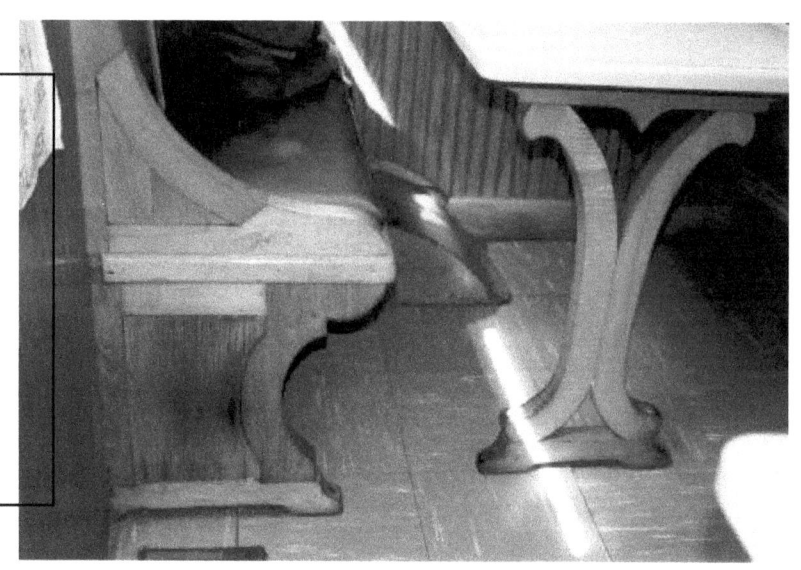

Ward & Dickinson Net Income

Year ended Dec, 31. 1925 -- $60,258.84
Year ended Dec, 31. 1926 -- $99,792.53
Year ended Dec, 31. 1927 -- $78,832.89
7 mo. ended July, 31. 1928 -- $68,791.63

Above Left:

The Club diner was a variation on the DeLuxe diner. Introduced around 1929 the diner did not have a separate room for the kitchen, but did have more room behind the counter and a few more stools at an extended counter.

(Frances (Dibble, Blackburn) Anderson)

Above Right:

Booths found their way into Ward diners by 1927. Cushions were added many years later as the diner originally had simple oak made booths.

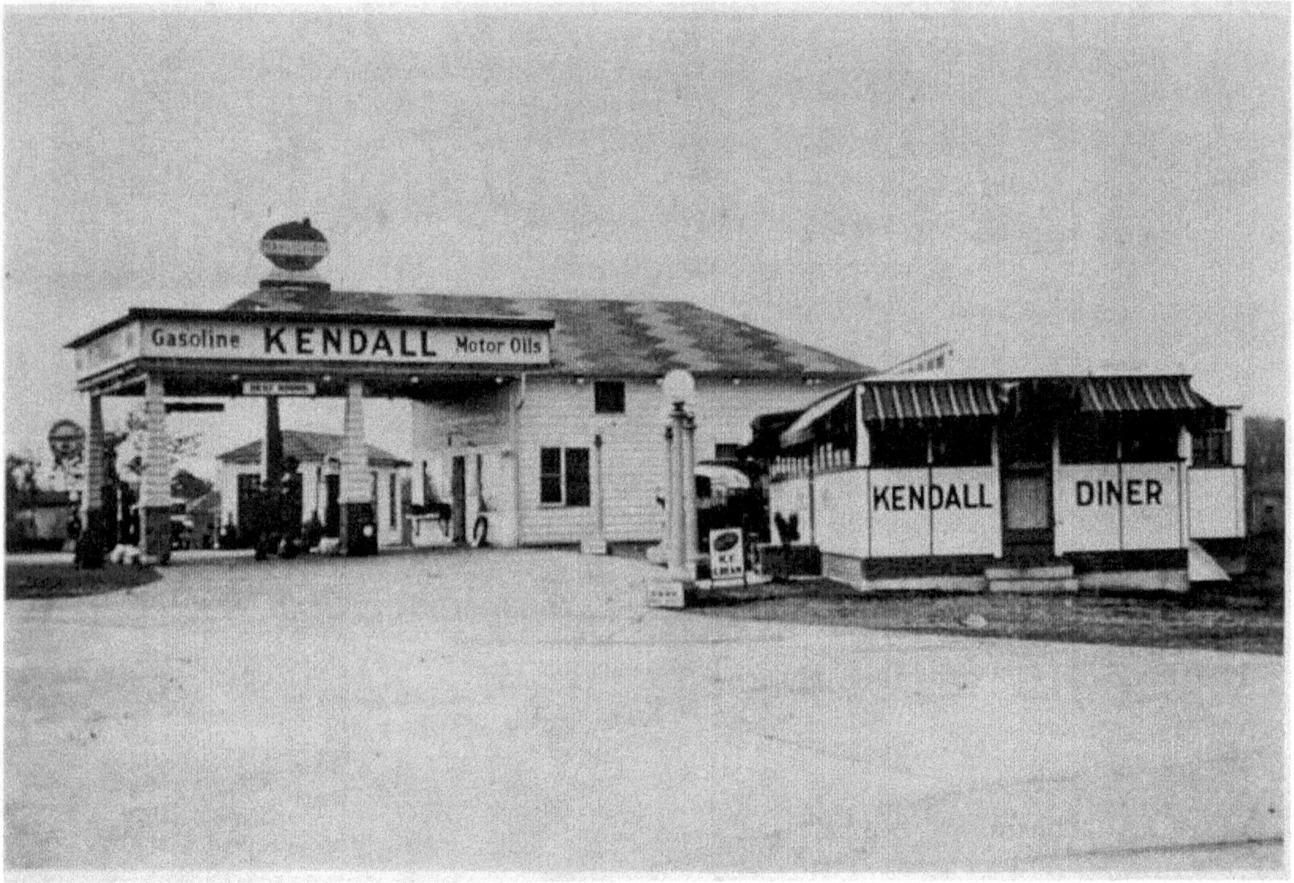
Gasoline KENDALL Motor Oils
KENDALL DINER

KENDALL TOURIST CAMP.
U. S. MOTOR ROUTE NO. 20.
KENDALL

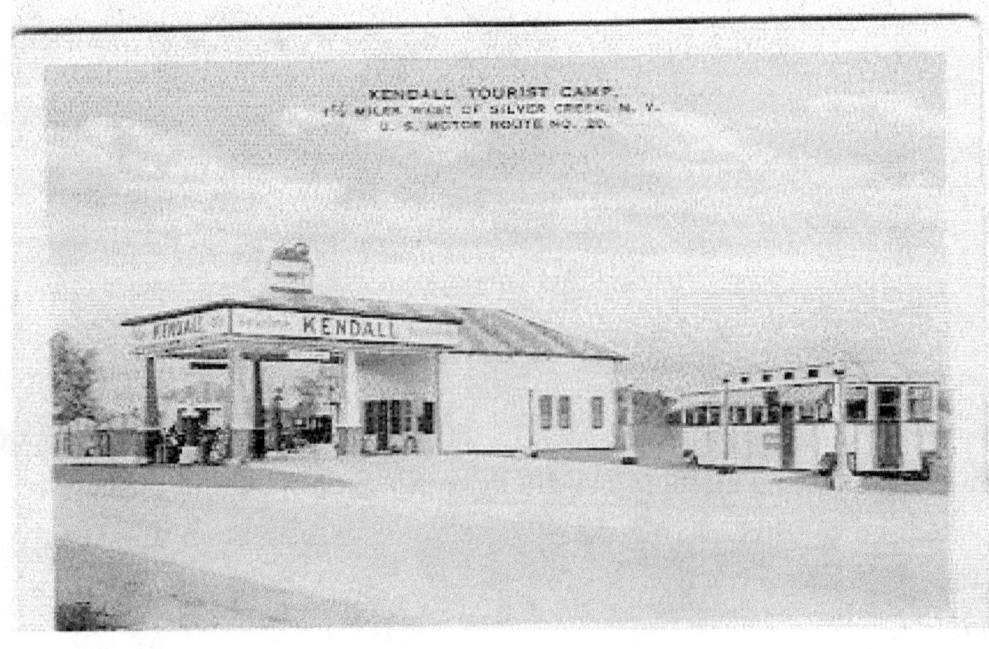

January 1926 and two of them were resold for $6,250 in January 1928. Another diner sold for $5,000 in June 1927 and was resold for $6,250 just six months later.

Around 1928-1929 would come the next improvement in the Ward and Dickinson line. A "Club Diner" was designed with minor tweaks learned over the last couple of years from conversations with proprietors. Booths probably already found their way into Ward and Dickinson dining cars by the time the Club diner was designed, but other small tweaks to the interior was probably the focus. Each tweak to the interior made operating a diner with busy crowds just a little easier.

With Route 20 being a major east west road which went through Silver Creek, and automobile travel growing by leaps and bounds, more people discovered Ward and Dickinson's factory and stopped to take a look, as Lyle Myers recounted in 1972. This wasn't the only way automobile travel helped to sell these diners. Nearly every decent sized village between Syracuse and Toledo, Ohio on Route 20 had at least one diner, and a majority were Ward dining cars. The diners were not only located downtown, but also on the outskirts, often near a gas station or tourist court.[24][25]

The largest Ward and Dickinson diner built had a width of five windows instead of four, so it would have been roughly 13 feet wide, a width that could not be moved by train. One of these wider diners went to Auburn, New York. It would be the third Ward

Above:
The thirteen foot wide Kendall Diner leaving the factory.
(Hanover History Center)

Preceding Page:
The Kendall Diner was a diner, service station and forty-eight tourist cabins just west of Silver Creek. The inset shows the original diner. First an extension was built on the right side of the diner for more seating, then the new diner seen above was brought in around 1932.
Ward and Dickinson built at least two of these wider diners with the other known wide diner going to Auburn, New York.

and Dickinson Diner at the location. Another went to the Kendall Station and Tourist Camp just outside of Silver Creek on what was then Route 20. The diner replaced a 30 foot model that already had one on-site addition attached on the end with the booths. This busy diner thrived up until this part of Route 20 was bypassed by a newer and wider road in the late 1940s. On the other side of Silver Creek, a mile or so east of the village was Irving, mostly a junction of Routes 5 and 20. Here, there were two diners that set up shop. There was also the Sunset Bay Diner, only a stones throw from Irving, set up next to a gas station. While the building itself was brought to Sunset Bay from Silver Creek, where it was a coffee shop, it is unsure if it was an actual diner, or just a building.[26] Later, Ward and Dickinson would have a different answer to making a wider diner.

Ward and Dickinson put out a brochure aimed at focusing on America's love affair with the automobile. They noted a study which found that 75% of those registering at hotels were now coming in by automobile. In reminding prospective diner operators about the automobile, they stated that edge of town locations would be perfect for a Ward and Dickinson dining car. They stated that Ward and Dickinson had a department whose sole goal was to make surveys and to secure lease and rental information in the best locations. They extolled the idea that if you had a downtown

Above:
The Standard Oil Company of Indiana bought a Ward and Dickinson diner that they placed at one of their gas stations in the Chicago area. A concept that was ahead of its time did not seem to lead to the sale of more diners.

(Vincent P. Martonis)

Below:

Nine diners in all were sent to Toronto, Ontario, Canada. The venture was named the Electric Diners. The hope was to set up a chain of diners all across Ontario. The plan never developed and the company went bankrupt in 1930. The diners were auctioned off. Two ended up in Grimsby, Ontario and one in Hamilton, Ontario with at least one staying in Toronto.

(Toronto Harbour Commission Archives/Mike Filey Collection)

restaurant that your diner out on the outskirts of town could advertise your restaurant or hotel, or vice versa.[27]

Ward and Dickinson also advertised in Restaurant Management Magazine in anticipation for the Restaurant World's Fair in Cleveland, Ohio in October 1930. The advertisement stated, "let us explain the advantages of operating Dining Cars in conjunction with your restaurant."[28] On September 12, 1929, the Buffalo Courier-Express announced that the company signed a sales contract with Dining Car Sales Corporation of New York City for the distribution of Ward and Dickinson dining cars in the region that served Tierney and O'Mahony so well.

> A contract has been entered into with the Dining Car Sales Company of New York City to handle a new type car for the Atlantic Seaboard area, which it is estimated will at least double production of the present plant in Silver Creek, which has been materially increased in size and equipment to take care of this added volume of business.[29]

Around the same time, the B-G Sandwich Shops, a long time chain which had about a dozen locations in Chicago came up with an experimental idea for Ward and Dickinson. B-G wanted to place a dining car on location at a Standard Oil Company of Indiana gas station in Chicago. The concept received national press. A. H. Buck, founder and president of B-G was reported to have worked as a waiter on opening day and planned to spend much time at the diner during the first summer. "While the business side of the gasoline-food combination is being watched, attention is also given to the mechanical

side, that is providing restaurant facilities through the use of dining cars. The advantage of dining cars for gasoline stations are that they keep the food department separated from the gasoline and lubrication departments..." The article even noted that by-pass roads around downtowns were already being built, and with the portability of a dining car, they could easily be moved to directly meet the traveling public.[30]

The restaurant business was said to be depression proof, people still had to eat. And fortunately for many diner owners, people still traveled. What the depression did do to the business was to slow down sales of new diners. Ward and Dickinson let go of Bob McKendrick from his salesman job around 1930-31 and probably kept Howard Clute until the mid 1930s. McKendrick would go on to own a Ward and Dickinson Deluxe model on Peach Street in Erie, Pennsylvania, a city well represented by diners.

Lee Dickinson announced he was leaving Ward and Dickinson in April of 1930.[31] But he did not entirely let go of all business concerns. Rumor has it that he still went into silent ownership with some new diner proprietors, helping to get them off the ground. Also in September of 1930, Dickinson installed a "Tom Thumb" [miniature] golf course on Central Avenue in Silver Creek. Foster Parmelee of Buffalo was chosen as the new President of Ward and Dickinson.

In the history of Ward and Dickinson, most of their diners obviously stayed in the Great Lakes states. Most of the Ward and Dickinson diners went to the western two-thirds of Pennsylvania or stayed in upstate New York. A few, though, went quite far. A couple diners went to Florida, with one being run by William Dickinson a relative of owner Lee F. Dickinson. William tried setting up a

Above:

Some additions really fit in well with the original diners. Bob's Diner in Providence, Rhode Island was one of these diners where either the addition was built by Ward and Dickinson, or someone who went through the extra effort to match the addition up to the diner.

(Hanover History Center)

syndicate of five diners in Florida that never materialized. Diners would seem to fail in Florida until Air Conditioning was commercially available. By 1930, William was the sales manager for the company. A few went deep into Worcester Lunch Car territory, near Boston like Amesbury and Haverhill. A few diners even went to Canada, a country whose history of diners is still deeply hidden. A businessman from Toronto, Ontario set up a chain of nine Ward and Dickinson diners known as the Electric Diners.[32] These diners received special attention from Lee Dickinson who brought factory foreman Berthel L. Kofoed and Percy Johnson up to Toronto to set up these diners in March of 1928.[33] The venture in Toronto failed and the nine diners were put up for auction.[34]

In 1930, Ward & Dickinson representative Harold Kurtz wrote the committee in charge of preparing for the 1933-1934 Century of Progress World's Fair to be held in Chicago. Ward & Dickinson was excited to provide their dining cars to service food for the fair. They stated that they had buyers in line for the dining cars after the event

Above:

This three piece diner was part of the Moore Diner chain in Reading, Pennsylvania. The main section had the monitor roof with a parellel section right behind that. Then a third section was grafted on the right end, perpendicular to the other two pieces. The diner shown was being moved from its original location to a new location also in Reading.

(Photo courtesy of Ron Romanski and Geo. M. Meiser, IX: The Passing Scene, Vol. 10)

Right:
Although not the name when this photograph was taken, the diner in Valparaiso, Indiana was best known as the Pullman Diner. The name does evoke a comparison with a railroad car. Although there were two street car diners in Valparaiso, this one was a Ward and Dickinson diner. (Rich Halstead)

was over in 1934.[35] Unfortunately the World's Fair declined the offer, which would have been a great boon for Ward and Dickinson. In one of the brochures they supplied the Century of Progress, it stated that the Pace Restaurant Corp had bought four dining cars, run to supplement their chain of restaurants in Chicago.

Diners were often attached to on-site buildings to give more room for customers and kitchen space. Diners in Canandaigua, New York and Providence, Rhode Island had on-site buildings attached to their diners that matched the diners dimensions and window patterns. Ward and Dickinson knew that if they could build their own factory built "additions", they could add to their profits.

Paramount Diners patented the "split diner" in July, 1941. But Ward and Dickinson were using this concept many years before this date. In fact, this idea for

Preceding Page:
The Quarrier Diner in Charleston, West Virginia opened up in 1932 and so was popular that the owners needed to expand just two years later. They decided to buy a separate diner, set it up right next to the original diner and change the name to the Twin Diner.
(Jerry Waters)

Ward and Dickinson dated back to 1931. They stated that their new dining car could seat sixty people and both sections were separated by glass partitions.[36] The company would build two diner shells and place them together lengthwise. The building facing the back would not have a monitor roof. The second building allowed room for extra dining space, bathrooms and kitchen and storage space. Two of these diners still exists today in Meadville and Bradford, Pennsylvania, although the buildings are now used for other purposes.

The Moore's Diner chain of Reading, Pennsylvania bought a few of these double unit diners. The Moore Diners were straight from the factory to be operated as a single diner. At least one of the Moore diners had a third section appended on the end of the two units, perpendicular to the other two.

The Moore Diner chain was started with Lee Dickinson became a silent partner with Chautauqua County resident Walter Moore. Moore started with a diner first in Bethlehem and then Williamsport, Pennsylvania. Walter Moore came from a family who ran various diners in western New York. The diner from Bethlehem, Pennsylvania was moved from Westfield, New York where it did business for roughly five years.

Below:

A true rarity for Ward and Dickinson. This photograph was in the same collection of salesman photographs mentioned a number of pages earlier. So many things make this diner unique. The roof was way ahead of its time, mimicking the mansard look of the 1960s and the short size and lack of a front door are also quite unique. One can only imagine what the ceiling and roof lines looked like from the inside of the diner. The only Fairmount Diner anyone can find is a western suburb of Syracuse, New York.

(Hanover History Center)

Moore sold the Bethlehem diner, moved to Williamsport for a year or so before settling in Reading, Pennsylvania.

The Quarrier Diner in Charleston, West Virginia was different than one of these "double wide" diners. The Quarrier was nicknamed the Twin Diners due to two diners being placed side by side. The Quarrier differed from the others in another way because there was a single Ward & Dickinson diner placed on location in 1932, and a second diner was grafted a few years later due to demand. One of the Moore diner chain may have used a similar concept as two monitor roof lines are visible from a photograph.

The end for Ward and Dickinson came when there was just no more interest in their style of diner. Lee Dickinson knew the company was not going to last more than ten to fifteen years when he had the factory built in 1925. Diner styles changed quite a bit for the diner manufacturers in the metropolitan New York area, but Ward dining cars barely changed with respect to the visual appearance of both the interior and the exterior. Its been passed down that the last diner built by the company was the current Steve's Diner, diner #316. Built for Jack Lown who ran a Ward in Ithaca previously. The diner stayed in town and was later moved to the outskirts of the village. The diner was saved by retired Police Chief Louis Peletter and is now used as a community center/museum. Recent information, though, places the possibility of the last diner built going to State College, Pennsylvania, and being a double unit diner operated by long time diner proprietors Gertrude Richardson and Anna Haigh. Or the last diner may have been sent to Elizabethtown, Pennsylvania at roughly the same time.

A November 30, 1937 article stated, "B. L. Kofoed has taken over management of the Ward and Dickinson dining car factory and will remodel cars besides furnishing

supplies for lunch cars. Mr. Kofoed is an authority on lunch car manufacture and has been superintendent of the Ward and Dickinson factory for many years."[37]

Donald Kofoed noted that some time during 1938, business had dried up so much that Mr. Dickinson offered his father, Berthel, a cut in pay to half of his salary. Berthel refused and resigned. At this time business was mostly paper work. The actual resignation was reported in the December 2nd, 1937 edition of the Silver Creek News-Times:

> Mr. B. L. Kofoed, who for the past 13 years has been occupied building and managing the Dining Car Factory for Ward and Dickinson, will again take up his former occupation as a general contractor and distributor of new, modernized, dining car equipment.[38]

Although Berthel left the employment of Ward and Dickinson, they still did build a few more diners at the factory after this time. Diner #310 was delivered in October 1938 and diner #318 was built in December 1939. We do not know of a diner built after #318.

Harry Richardson was hired by Ward & Dickinson when he was not working on building houses. Harry was even hired by Lee Dickinson to build houses for him in Florida. He was an expert carpenter and also went out to Dayton to help Raymond Richardson (distant relatives, if at all) get his business off the ground. Harry was related to Elmer & Aletta Richardson who ran a Ward and Dickinson in Warren and Youngsville, Pennsylvania, along US Route 6. Harry's grandson Eric Richardson, relates stories of Eric's father Franklin Richardson traveling with Harry (Franklin's father) for Ward and Dickinson to help install diners. Eric's uncle Dave who was younger than his brother Franklin remembers traveling with his mother to visit his father and brother in places like Elmira, New York and Cincinnati, Ohio.[39] After Ward and Dickinson closed shop, Harry and Franklin even went to Geneva, New York in May, 1940 to build a diner/restaurant for G. W. Bush, who had a ten year old Ward and Dickinson.[40]

Glenn Bush was also owner of the former Carroll Diner in Auburn, New York around 1937 when a forty foot Ward & Dickinson was replaced by the rare wide width Ward similar to the one that became the Kendall Diner outside of Silver Creek.

1 Buffalo Courier-Express, Buffalo, New York November 3, 1972

2 Buffalo Times in Silver Creek Times, Silver Creek, New York November 12, 1925

3 Silver Creek Times, Silver Creek, New York November 12, 1925

4 Grape Belt and Chautauqua Farmer, Dunkirk, New York November 13, 1925

5 Silver Creek Times, Silver Creek, New York November 12, 1925

6 Grape Belt and Chautauqua Farmer, Dunkirk, New York January 16, 1925

7 Grape Belt and Chautauqua Farmer, Dunkirk, New York January 23, 1925

8 "Those Were The Days: A Collection of Memories", Written 1991-1992 Donald William Kofoed

9 Silver Creek Times, Silver Creek, New York April 1, 1925

10 Silver Creek Times, Silver Creek, New York March 12, 1925

11 New Castle News, New Castle, Pennsylvania March 24, 1925

12 Cortland Standard, Cortland, New York August 24, 1926

13 Ballston Spa Daily Journal, Ballston Spa, New York July 5, 1927

14 Silver Creek Times, Silver Creek, New York November 12, 1925

15 Silver Creek Times, Silver Creek, New York February 4, 1926

16 Silver Creek Times, Silver Creek, New York July 22, 1926

17 The Demise of the Diner by Weegie Pratt April 15, 2002

18 Grape Belt and Chautauqua Farmer, Dunkirk, New York November 2, 1925 and March 30, 1926

19 Grape Belt and Chautauqua Farmer, Dunkirk, New York April 27, 1926

20 Silver Creek Times, Silver Creek, New York November 17, 1927

21 Silver Creek Times, Silver Creek, New York November 12, 1927

22 Silver Creek Times, Silver Creek, New York March 11, 1926

23 Silver Creek Times, Silver Creek, New York August 30, 1928

24 Watkins Express, Watkins Glen, New York December 7, 1938

25 Genesee Country Express and Advertiser, Dansville, New York July 30, 1936

26 Silver Creek Times, Silver Creek, New York May 10, 1928

27 "Feeding the Traveling Public", published by Ward and Dickinson Dining Car Company, located at UIC Library, Chicago, Illinois

Right:

This Ward and Dickinson diner in Cleveland, Ohio was part of the American Diner chain. The chain did not buy exclusively one brand of diner and would also own Brill and O'Mahony diners. This particular diner did not last long at this spot as there was a market here by the end of the 1930s.

(Cleveland Public Library/Official City of Cleveland Photograph)

28 Restaurant Management, October 1930

29 Buffalo Courier-Express, Buffalo, New York September 12, 1929

30 "Gasoline-Food Combination Watched As New One-Stop Service." National Petroleum News, September 2, 1931

31 Silver Creek Times, Silver Creek, New York March 28, 1930

32 Toronto Star, Toronto, Canada February 9, 1928

33 Silver Creek News, Silver Creek, New York March 22, 1928

34 Toronto News, Toronto, Canada January 11, 1930

35 Correspondence between Century of Progress and Ward and Dickinson located at UIC Library, Chicago, Illinois

36 Gowanda Enterprise, Gowanda, New York May 28, 1931

37 Dunkirk Observer, Dunkirk, New York, November 30, 1937

38 Silver Creek News-Times, Silver Creek, New York December 2, 1937

39 correspondence with Eric Richardson

40 Geneva Daily Times, Geneva, New York July 26, 1940

Kuppy's Diner

Kuppy's Diner in Middletown, Pennsylvania would still be in iconic diner and story even if it was not Ward & Dickinson diner. There are two stories that need to be told; one about the family that runs the diner and one about the diners themselves. First the story about the Ward and Dickinson diners.

In 1933, Percy Kupp bought a Ward and Dickinson DeLuxe diner with attached kitchen for his middletown, Pennsylvania location. He ran it successfully for five years before trading it in for a model that had six booths on the right end, and a kitchen was built on the back side of the diner. The old diner was rumored to have gone to Elizabethtown, Pennsylvania where it was rented out. This story sounded good, because a diner was rented out to the Baker family and ran for a number of years. There was only one problem with the story. The photograph of the original Kuppy's did not match the photograph of the supposed same diner in Elizabethtown, caught in a flood that moved the diner off of its foundation.

Enter some information from a Conditional Sales Docket found in the end of Chapter 9. This record shows a new Ward and Dickinson diner being sold by Percy Kupp to the Baker family in late 1939. The diner was not sold by the Ward and Dickinson company or Lee Dickinson. Piecing this information together, it would seem that the old Kuppy's diner spent a year in Elizabethtown before being replaced with a newer diner. So the next mystery is the final destination of the original Kuppy's Diner. Another mystery awaiting an answer.

The story of the Kupp family is a rare story. Four generations of the same family running the diner, with a fifth generation working at the diner. Percy Kupp said, "If you serve good food at reasonable prices, people will be satisfied." Each generation has kept true to this mantra and added something special to the diner. Nearly every diner has daily specials, but the food at Kuppy's puts the "special" in Daily Special, many of the recipes handed down from generation to generation.

Former customer Charles Selcher had been coming to the diner since it opened August 5, 1933 and was still coming on his 100th birthday in 2013. The number of regulars and their stories could fill multiple chapters in any book. So if you're in the area, go find out why so many regular keep coming back to Kuppy's for years upon years.

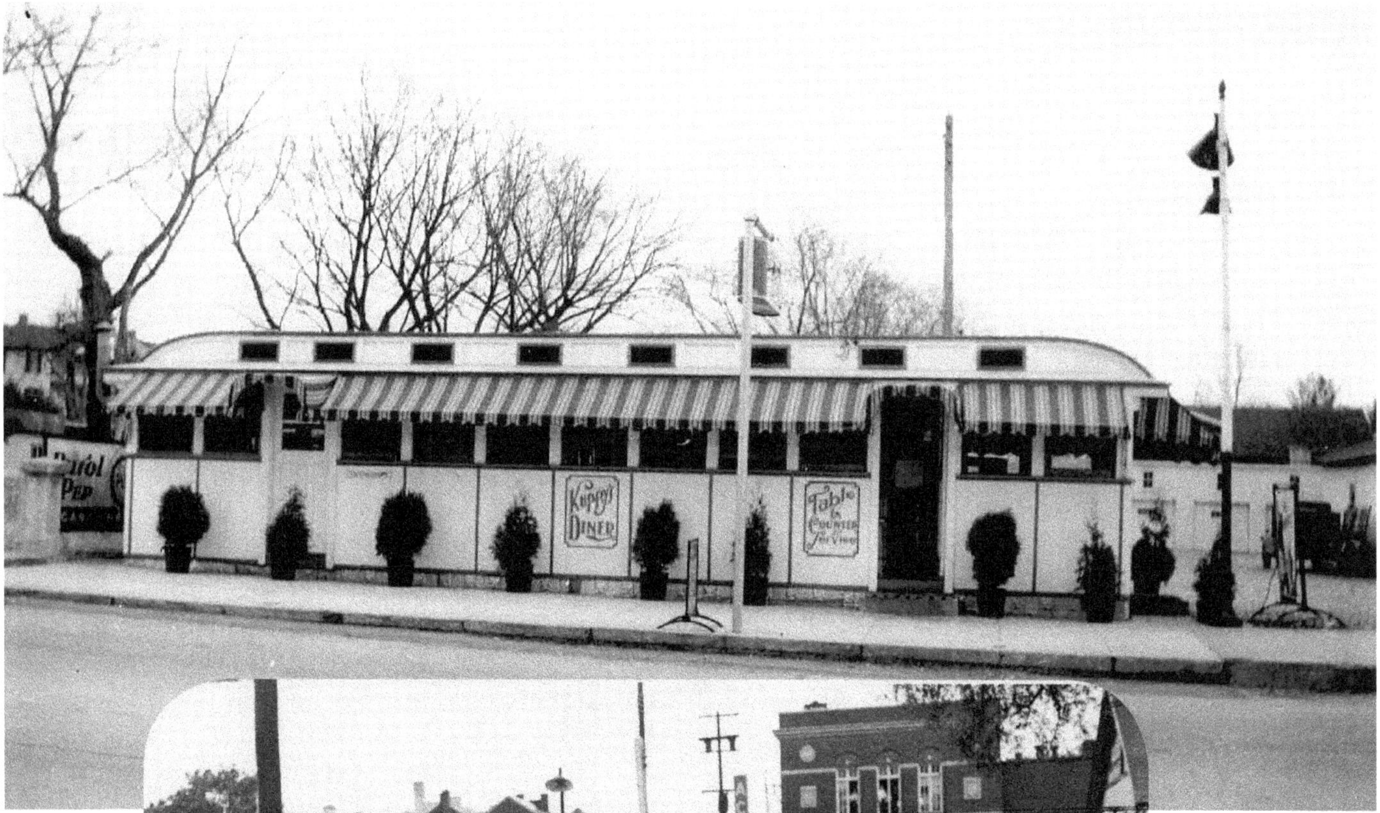
Kuppy's
DINER
Table
&
Counter

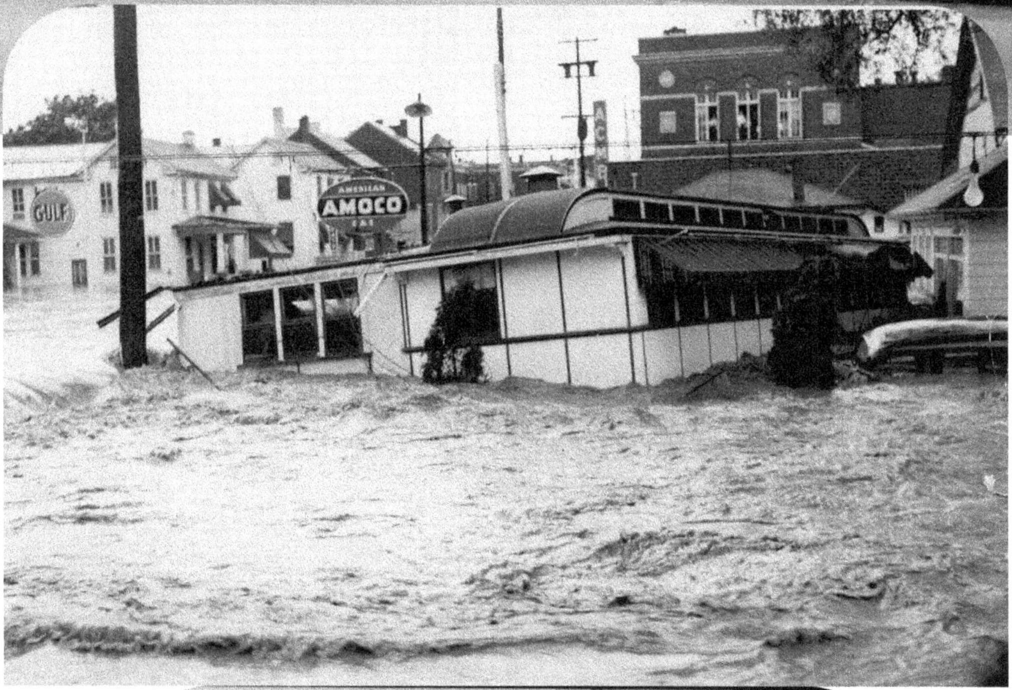
GULF
AMOCO

DINER

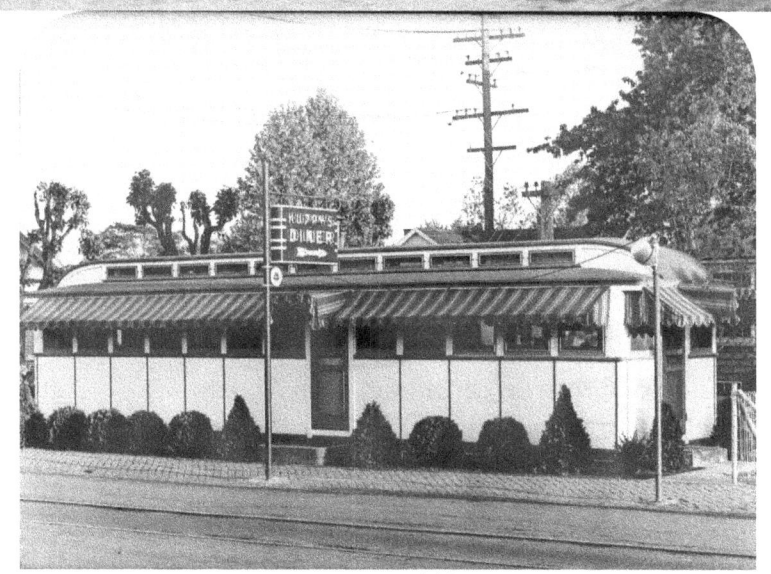

Introduction: This is my list of known Ward & Dickinson diners. We think the company built 320 diners. This is not a perfect list. Some diners disappeared, were moved by the owner without news coverage, replaced by a new diner, which may or may not have been a Ward & Dickinson diner. Did that old diner move to a different location? Was it demolished? Is the local lore correct? In many cases, we just don't know.

The company numbered the diners, starting at number one. The serial number was stamped on to a piece of metal under the bread counter. The first 100 diners on this list were provided by Vince Martonis of the Hanover History Museum. He came across this list while interviewing a lady in Buffalo, New York. It turned out she had some materials from the Ward & Dickinson offices, including the ledger for the first one hundred diners built. So for numbers 1 through 100, these numbers represent the actual numbers of the diners. Starting with 101, the numbers are just incremental and represent number more than a reference. If I know the actual number of that diner, it will be placed in (#).

1 August 1924 – 1940   44 Pine St. Lockport, New York.   Fire in January 1940
2 November 1924 --   Williamsville, New York   Herman Swartzman. No info.
3 November 1924   220 Washington, Jamestown, New York. Was replaced with larger Ward & Dickinson. Spent time in Mt. Jewett, Penn
        June 1930 –   Niantic, Connecticut   George Gergulis. No Info.
4 November 1924 –Sept 1927   Kraeft Garage, Silver Creek, New York
        October 1927 –   891 E. 152nd, Cleveland, Ohio. No Info.
5 January 1925   Toledo, Ohio. Robert McCraig (McCaig?) Possibly Perrysburg
6 February 1925   New Brighton, Penn. See #13. One was moved to Indiana, Penn and run as Dean's Diner
7 March 1925 – 1940+   Main @ Water, Gowanda, New York   C.N. Ubel
8 March 1925   Beaver Falls, Pennsylvania   No Info.
9 February 1925   Silver Creek, New York   Ran one year at Zoo, then disappeared.
10 February 1925   Grove City, Pennsylvania
        Edinboro, Penn   Ledger said diner was now in Edinboro
11 April 1925 –   Angola, New York
12 April 1925 --   8 Chestnut, Bradford, Pennsylvania. Moved to Congress Street?
13 April 1925   Abridge, Pennsylvania.   See #6
14 June 1925 – 1957   236 Grant, Buffalo, New York
15 May 1925 – October 1927   Batavia, New York.   Robert Augram replaced with new diner.
        3030 Bailey, Buffalo, New York for three years then March 1930 -- Waterford, Penn
16 July 1925 – January 1926   Cattaraugus, New York

March 1926 Williamsville, New York Herman Swartzman. No Info.
17 August 1925 – 1941 360 Niagara, Buffalo, New York
18 July 1925 –April 1929 Kane, Pennsylvania. Kane got new diner. Short time in Johnsonburg, Penn and Hammond, Indiana
July 1932 – c.a. 1964 Redfern Terrace, Batavia, New York
19 July 1925 – 1940 172 Allen, Buffalo, New York
20 September 1925 Tonawanda, New York Louis Gingras died. 1927 article mentioned wife had diner on leased land
21 August 1925 –1956 1435 Main St., Niagara Falls, New York
22 September 1925 – July 1928 18 Genesee, Auburn, New York Diner replaced by larger Ward and Dickinson
August 1928 – 33 West Main, Waterloo, New York
23 September 1925 – 82 S. Division, Buffalo, New York. Diner disappeared from directories
24 September 1925 – July 1928 Akron, Ohio
October 1928 664 Green, Waynesburg, Pennsylvania. Fred & Kathryn Norris
25 September 1925 – February 1929 Buffalo, New York
February 1929 – 11 Union, Hamburg, New York
26 October 1925 -- 79 North, Owego, New York Diner enlarged over years. Restaurant still at location.
27 November 1925 – October 1928 Seneca Falls, New York
October 1928 – 1931 51 Triangle, Buffalo, New York
May 1931 – October 1938 661 Fairfield, Bridgeport, Connecticut
June 1939 – Columbia, Pennsylvania Howard Hovey
28 January 1926 – November 1929 Buffalo, New York
November 1939 – 1960 Main St., Franklinville, New York
29 December 1925 – November 1926 Miami, Florida
November 1926 – February 1932 476 Abbott, Buffalo, New York. Diner dismantled by company.
30 November 1925 – July 1954 164 W. Chippewa, Buffalo, New York. Diner demolished and replaced with stick built restaurant.
31 December 1925 – June 1928 Syracuse, New York
June 1928 – February 1932 Schenectady, New York. Diner dismantled by company, but restaurant still listed in city directory.
32 November 1925 – May 1934 612 Genesee, Buffalo, New York
October 1935 – 104 Lincoln, Uniontown, Pennsylvania
33 December 1925 – 1532 E 55th, Cleveland, Ohio. George Hamilton. No Info.
34 December 1925 – 1932 Hamilton, Ohio
July 1932 -- Gardiner, Maine. Margaret Lawson. No Info.
35 January 1926 – 1930 Sharon, Pennsylvania. Sold to Albert Hauge. Diner disappeared

from city directory
36 February 1926   Delray, Florida then Erie, Pennsylvania
     October 1934 – Today   40 E Main, Westfield, New York
37 January 1926 – 1982   129 S. Elmwood, Buffalo, New York   Shultz family
38 January 1926 – 1931   Buffalo, New York
     July 1931 –   107 State, Clarks Summit, Pennsylvania.   Stanley Cooper. Restaurant on location today.
39 February 1926 – 1930s   Ludlow, Penn   A.W. Steiner ran at gas station on U.S. Route 6
40 February 1926 – 1951   6 W. Michigan, Indianapolis, Indiana.   Grover Rainey
41 February 1926 – 1946   Avon, New York   Just outside of village green
     August 1946 – July 1957   25 Borden, Perry, New York
42 February 1926 –   Bailey @ Kensington, Buffalo, New York   Last mention 1930
43 March 1926 – 1955   168 Chestnut, Meadville, Pennsylvania
44 February 1926 –   St Petersburg, Florida. William Dickinson tried setting up a syndicate of five diners. Seemed to fail.
45 March 1926 –   Camden, New Jersey   No Info.
46 March 1926 –   Camden, New Jersey then Collingswood, New Jersey until January 1933
     February 1933 –   Tupper Lake, New York. Diner moved in town in 1943.
47 March 1926 – 1935   Kalamazoo, Michigan
     1936 –   Main St., Lawton, Michigan
48 March 1926   Cleveland, Ohio.   First of ten sent to Cleveland for very short lived chain.
     June 1927 – 1969   74 Milton, Ballston Spa, New York
49 March 1926   Cleveland, Ohio
     Sept 1929 – 1962   9 N. Mercer, Greenville, Pennsylvania
50 March 1926   Cleveland, Ohio
     June 1927 – June 1930   10 Port Road, Marcus Hook, Pennsylvania
     1930 –   608 Chester Pike, Norwood, Pennsylvania
51 March 1926   Cleveland, Ohio
     August 1927 – 1990   242 State, Watertown, New York
52 March 1926   Cleveland, Ohio.   Short time in Rome, New York
     December 1927 – 1949   1111 S Salina, Syracuse, New York
53 March 1926   Cleveland, Ohio
     June 1927 –   Erie, Penn.   Louis Del Porto.   No Info.
54 May 1926 – December 1932   Lake St., Le Roy, New York
     December 1932 – 1940   Perry, New York
     1940 –   US Route 20 @ New York Route 36, York, New York
55 June 1926 – 1968   5 East 18th, Erie, Pennsylvania
56 April 1926   Cleveland, Ohio
     June 1927 – May 1935   Remy Plant, Anderson, Indiana

January 1936 –   Clarion, Pennsylvania
57 April 1927   Cleveland, Ohio
June 1927 – 1932   Kendall Gas Station, Silver Creek, New York
May 1932 –   Irving, New York
58 April 1926   Cleveland, Ohio
June 1927 – 1966   234 S Cayuga, Ithaca, New York
59 April 1926   Cleveland, Ohio   Short time in Oil City, Penn
1929 – 1951   78 Broad, Waterford, New York
60 May 1926 --   Steubenville, Ohio   F.M. Hunter said he was trying to sell.
61 July 1926 – 1967   353 Oliver, North Tonawanda, New York
62 July 1926 – 1932?   Buffalo, New York   First at 2514 Main then 1083 Kensington before disappearing from city directories.
63 August 1926 – 1930   19 Clinton, Cortland, New York.   Replaced by new Ward & Dickinson.
Jan 1930 – 1940   Littleton, New Hampshire.   Replaced by Sterling diner.
64 December 1926 – 1930   Wilkes Barre, Pennsylvania   five months in 1932 in Lock Haven, Penn
Dec 1932 –   Raymond Blvd, Newark, New Jersey
65 June 1926 – 1956   10 E 7th, Chester, Pennsylvania.   Louis Flynn.
66 July 1926 – June 1927   Camden, New Jersey
June 1927 –   Chester, Penn. Louis Flynn.   May have been at site of Post Office until 1934 when P.O. was built.
67 October 1926 – 1964   457 E Delevan, Buffalo, New York
68 September 1926 – 1929   Buffalo, New York   Short stints in Youngstown and South Akron, Ohio
December 1934 –   Dover, Ohio
69 July 1926 – May 1929   Watertown, New York
May 1929 – 1957+   337 Crescent, Ogdensburg, New York
70 August 1926 – June 1933   Willoughby, Ohio
June 1933 --   4726 S Salina, Syracuse, New York   diner remodeled beyond recognition today.
71 July 1926 – June 1927   Racine, Wisconsin for three months then Toledo, Ohio
June 1927 – 1957   19 Port Watson, Cortland, New York
72 July 1926 – June 1933   Syracuse, New York
June 1933 -- 1954   Pulaski, New York.   Fire in 1954, said extensive remodeling afterwards.
73 September 1926 –   Pontiac, Michigan   Also see #79. Addresses in ledger either didn't match city directory very well.
74 August 1926 –   Glassboro, New Jersey. Replaced by small Kullman diner.
75 August 1926 – 1929/1930 Albion, New York. Replaced by larger Ward and Dickinson. Some possible confusion on date.

Jan 1931 --					793 Bromley, Scranton, Penn	Diner may have gone to Eldred, Penn in the 1940s
76 August 1926 – Dec 1926	Salamanca, New York
	December 1926 – 1932	11 W 11th, Anderson, Indiana	Location had diner with same footprint in 1940s
	1932 –				Lake Placid, New York
77 October 1926 –			Toledo, Ohio. Part of a short lived chain of diners in Toledo, Ohio
	March 1927 – 1940	219 W Pennsylvania, Warren, Pennsylvania
78 Sept 1926 –			Toledo, Ohio Followed by stints in East Bradford, Turtle Creek, Erie, Penn and Ashtabula, Ohio
	May 1932 –			Amesbury, Massachusetts
79 September 1926 –		Pontiac, Michigan. See #73
80 August 1926			Minneapolis, Minnesota	Display diner at Minnesota State Fair
	1926 – 1974			110 S Cedar, Auburn, Indiana
81 September 1926 –		Toledo, Ohio	Brief stints in Weirton, WV, Manchester, NH, Branford, Conn and Kennebunk, Maine
	August 1934 – 1937	Springfield, Massachusetts. Then disappeared from city directory.
82 September 1926		Toledo, Ohio. Stayed in Toledo. Mrs. Agnes McGrath
83 September 1926		Toledo, Ohio
	1927 – 1940s			7 Park St., Glens Falls, New York		Replaced a Closson lunch wagon.
84 September 1926		Toledo, Ohio In DuBois, Pennsylvania until 1930
	June 1930 – 1956		33 S Main, Wellsville, New York
85 September 1926 – May 1930	Toledo, Ohio. Then Salisbury, Mass
	May 1931 --			Newburyport, Massachusetts
86 September 1926 – 1930	Lockport, New York. Traded in for new diner.
	March 1931 – 1934	Potsdam, New York. Winter gas explosion practically ruined diner.
87 October 1926 –			N 3rd nr Read, Clearfield, Penn		J.P. & Catherine Lown, who moved to Silver Creek in 1938 to run diner.
88 October 1926 – 1942		116 E Wayne, Butler, Pennsylvania
89 October 1926 – June 1927	Kenosha, Wisconsin
	June 1927 – 1940s		44 Mohawk, Scotia, New York	Either renovated or moved to Ballston Spa, New York
90 November 1926 – January 1928	Akron, New York
	Jan 1928 – 1937		307 N Franklin, Syracuse, New York	Called the Akron Diner while in Syracuse.
91 October 1926 –			Pittsburg, Penn.		Ledger states: Car moved to either 5603 Penn or Carapolis, Penn
92 December 1926 –		612 Penn, Wilkinsburg, Penn	Feiler. May have gone to Reading, Penn in mid 1940s
93 September 1926		Toledo, Ohio
	June 1927 – 1950		216 W Erie, Lorain, Ohio

94 September 1926 –   Toledo, Ohio   Short stints in Glens Falls, NY, Torrington, Terryville and Newington, Conn
       June 1932 –   Philadelphia, Pennsylvania
95 October 1926 –   Detroit, Michigan.   R.T. Hurst asked city to move diner to 1208 W. Vernor Hwy around 1931.
96 December 1926 –   Pittsburg, Pennsylvania
     September 1927 – 1934   Schenectady, New York
     1934 –   283 Main St., Johnson City, New York
97 November 1926 – 1939+   2211 Industrial, Flint, Michigan
98 November 1926 – May 1927   Waverly, New York
     May 1927 – 1950   212 Water, Binghamton, New York
99 December 1926 – 1985   117 E Center, Medina, New York
100 December 1926 – Today 75 N Broad, Hillsdale, Michigan
101(117) July 1927 –   Amsterdam, New York.   Appeared in 1927 city directory, then disappeared.
102 May 1930 – 1961+   Albion, New York
103(244) May 1932 – 1949   Kendall Station, Silver Creek, New York.   Replaced older diner.
     1949 – 1962+   Near Jct 60 & US Route 20, Fredonia, New York   Remodeled by Sorge.
104 1930s – 1963   505 E Water, Elmira, New York
105 ?? – Today   Willimantic, Connecticut.   Possibly a used diner.
106 1937 – 2012   178 E 9th, Oswego, New York Possibly a used diner, was brought into town at night.
107 November 1927 – 1960   Batavia, New York   Augram's replacement diner. Moved to East Main St.
108(210) – Today   412 E Main, Bradford, Penn   With attached back room.
109 1933 – Today   802 Erie Blvd W, Syracuse, New York Totally remodeled.
110(310) 1938 – Today   Brown @ Poplar, Middletown, Penn   Replaced older Ward and Dickinson.
111 ?? – Today   121 E Manlius St., East Syracuse, New York
112(309) Sept 1938 – Today   Central Ave., Silver Creek, New York   Moved a couple of times in and around Silver Creek
113(215) 1931/1935 – Today   Phelps St., Oneida, New York
114(187) 1929 – 1933   Glens Falls, New York   Used to service factory workers
     September 1933 – Today   Church St., Port Henry, New York
115 1931 – 1939   476 Broadway, Kingston, New York.   Replaced by Sterling diner, "moved to Rochester"
116 February 1932 --   1022 Quarrier St, Charleston, West Virginia
117 1932 – 1956   628 State, Schenectady, New York   May have been in Erie, Penn first.
118 March 1927 – 1944+   Main St., Palmyra, New York   Sent to garden store.

119 1936 – 1968 44 W Main, Ilion, New York
120 ?? – 1938 Reading, Pennsylvania. Fegeley's. Replaced by O'Mahony
121 ?? LaPorte, Indiana Based on company matchbook. Never could find in city directories.
122 1930 – 1951 299 W Main, Waterbury, Connecticut
123 1929 – 1940 893 Broadway, Albany, New York. Replaced by Silk City diner. Said placed to rot behind diner.
124 1929 – 1962 128 Hudson, Albany, New York
125 (151) c.a.1938 – 1963 Kittanning, Pennsylvania. At gas station outside town. Used diner from unknown location.
126 1928 – 1946+ 58 Railroad Place, Saratoga, New York
127 1933 – 1962 104 Oriskany Blvd, Utica, New York
128 1934 – 1940s 272 South St., Utica, New York Replaced by Silk City diner.
    1940s – 1967 1101 Oriskany Blvd, Utica, New York
129 1933 – 1940 23 Genesee, New Hartford, New YorkReplaced or remodeled? New on-site diner.
130 1933 – 1964 407 Erie Blvd E., Syracuse, New York
131 ?? Temple Diner, five miles north of Reading, Pennsylvania
132 1928 – 1968 42 Jackson, Batavia, New York
133 Dec 1931 –   Brockport, New York Over years, got remodeled beyond recognition.
134 1931 – 1961 30 W Main, Malone, New York
135 1928 – 1940s 141 N Main, Gloversville, New York. Remodeled beyond recognition by 1940s, restr survived later.
136 0000-00-00 Pittsburg, Penn Three diner chain of Ward & Dickinson diners mentioned in brochure.
137 0000-00-00 c. Strawberry & Montour Sts, Pittsburg, Pennsylvania. Scotty's Diner.
138 0000-00-00 Pittsburg, Penn holding the spot, waiting for more information.
139 1935 – 1939 109 W 3rd, Williamsport, Pennsylvania. Disappeared.

140 1928 – 1930 Toronto, Ontario There were nine diners in Toronto. No clue which specifically went where.
    1932 – 1965 Grimsby, Ontario Two went to Grimsby
141 1928 – 1930 Toronto, Ontario
    1932 – 1965 Grimsby, Ontario
142 1928 – 1930 Toronto, Ontario
    1933 – 1971 600 Hughson South, Hamilton, Ontario
143 1928 – 1963 Yonge by Waterfront, Toronto, Ontario
144 0000-00-00 Placeholder. There were nine in Toronto, we know where

four went.
145 (156) July 1931 – Mansfield, Penn. We have not found location for this diner before it moved to Canton.
?? – ?? Canton, Penn. It was rumored that the diner in Canton came from Mansfield.
146 1932 Cabot St., Gloucester Crossing, Massachusetts Replaced by Sterling diner. called Hesparus
147 1932 – 1951 5 E. Pennsylvania, Warren, Pennsylvania
148 1943 – 1980 628 River Road, East Liverpool, Ohio. Probably used.
149 ?? Salem, Ohio
– 1961 48 Main St., Mount Alliance, Ohio Shaffer's Diner
150 1932 – 1951+ Youngville, Pennsylvania Could be diner from Sharon for all we know.
151 Nov 1929 – May 1948 710 Peach St., Erie, Pennsylvania Replaced Richardson, replaced by Silk City.
152 August 1933 – 1938 Brown @ Poplar, Middletown, Pennsylvania Original Kuppy's Diner
1939 Elizabethtown, Pennsylvania May have spent a year in Elizabethtown before ???
153 February 1934 – 1950 1201 13th Ave., Altoona, Pennsylvania Replaced by on-site restaurant.
154 1939 – 1970 421 Penn, Reading, Pennsylvania One of three of Moore's Diner, two added dining rooms.
155 1937 – 1976 Main St., Homer, New York Could be 2nd used Clinton St. diner.
156 1938 – 1960?? 411 Penn, West Reading, Pennsylvania Looks like two diners placed together.
157 1938 – 1958 33 S 6th, Reading, Pennsylvania Moore's Diner, two added dining rooms. Moved in town 1958.
158 1935+ 900 Shore, Pittsburgh, Pennsylvania
159 1950 – 1964 Buttonwood Diner, Reading, Pennsylvania Either Scotty's or Feiler's from Pittsburgh. Used.
160 (181) August 1930 – 1932 State College, Pennsylvania Moved few doors down in 1932. Replaced with Ward & Dickinson
1932 -- ?? State College, Pennsylvania
161 July 1932 – Today State College, Pennsylvania $27k diner. 100% remodeled today.
162 1927 – 1949 Milford, Pennsylvania Replaced by Mountain View diner. Was a 40'x10' model
163 ?? Gettysburg, Pennsylvania
?? York Springs, Pennsylvania Twin Keys. Postcard
164 0000-00-00 15 S 10th St., Allentown, Pennsylvania
165 1933 – 1940 5th Avenue, Lansingburgh, New York Replaced by Silk City

diner.
166 1929 – 1934   Dalton, Massachusetts
1935 – 2000   West Housatonic, Pittsfield, Massachusetts
167 1931 –1933   711 S Main, Tulsa, Oklahoma Part of failed chain of two diners. Disappeared
168(126) January 1928 – Sept 1932   Carlisle, Pennsylvania   On-site restaurant put at address
1932 – 1949   Hagerstown, Maryland   May have moved to new site in Hagerstown.
169 1930 – 1949   166 W First, Oswego, New York
170 February 1932 – June 1937   415 Ridge, Rochester, New York   Replaced by Rochester Grills
171 1931 – 1954   709 Portage, Niagara Falls, New York
172(249) 1932 – 19??   20 Groton, Cortland, New York
    19?? – 1958   Main Street, Cortland, New York
173 ??   Fairmount, New York
174 0000-00-00   Canton, Ohio
175 0000-00-00   Canton, Ohio
176 0000-00-00   Akron, Ohio
177 1933 – 1970   183 E Taunton, Providence, Rhode Island   Remodeled by 1950s
178 1933 – 1966   1025 Barnum, Stratford, Conn
179 0000-00-00   Birmingham, MI
180 1932 – 1950   13820 Michigan, Dearborn, MI
181 0000-00-00   Ferndale, MI
182 1929 – 1963   63 Park Ave., Mansfield, Ohio
183 0000-00-00   Yorkshire, New York   Called Green and White Diner in 1940
184 1932 – 1935   Haverhill, MA   Al's Ward 7 Diner.   Replaced old lunch car. Moved shortly afterwards.
185 June 1930 – Today   415 Ford, Ogdensburg, New York   Fire and remodeling over the years.
186 1933 – 1966   233 Court, Watertown, New York
187 February 1930 – Today   28 E Main, Johnstown, New York   Remodeled greatly around 1950
188 1941 – 1962   York, Pennsylvania   Two diners placed together. Probably used.
189 October 1930 – Sept 1935   25 Clinton, Cortland, New York   Replaced by O'Mahony. Possibly became #155 in Homer
190 August 1928 -- 1938   18 Genesee, Auburn, New York   Second Carrollet Diner. Replaced by large Ward and Dickinson
191 August 1930 – 1965   23 High, Hamilton, Ohio
192 1928 – 1942+   S First @ Oneida, Fulton, New York
193 1929 – 1957   14 E Main, Falconer, New York
194 1932 – 1950   157 E Main, Kent, Ohio

195 1934 – 1960 321 Center, Ashtabula, Ohio
196 May 1927 – 1948 41 N Main, Fredonia, New York
       1948 – ?? Kimball Stand, New York
197 August 1931 – 1953 8 W Erie, Corning, New York
198 0000-00-00 144 Norwich Ave, Norwich, Connecticut
199 March 1927 – 1935+ Canandaigua, New York Moved to West St. in 1935
200 1931 Tulsa, Oklahoma Here for 1 year then disappeared
201 1935 – 1942 Hazleton, Pennsylvania
       1945 – 1972 Bellmawr, New Jersey Club Diner Replaced
       1973 – 2000? Paulsboro, New Jersey Rumored that it moved to Florida
202 0000-00-00 Chicago, Illinois Pace's
203 0000-00-00 Blairsville, Pennsylvania
204 (306) 1945 – Today Chautauqua, New York Unknown where it came from. Lancaster?
205 January 1929 – July 1934 Westfield, New York Walter Moore ran then moved diner.
       August 1934 – 1953 306 Broadway, Bethlehem, Pennsylvania Replaced by Silk City diner
206 0000-00-00 Warren, Ohio
207 1934 – 1947 North Utica, New York Jack & Andy's chain. Replaced by Fodero diner.
208 0000-00-00 Dunkirk, New York At Gasoline City outside of town.
209 ?? Westfield, New York Beacon Bradley Diner, west of village.
210 0000-00-00 Chicago, Illinois B&G Sandwich Shop
211 Feb 1931 – 1935 Le Roy, New York
       1935 – Today 7 3 N Main, Wellsville, New York Remodeled 1950s
212 1937 -- Today 863 Park, Meadville, Pennsylvania Attached dining room.
213 February 1931 – September 1963 Meriden, Connecticut Replaced by used Paramount diner from Hartford, Conn
214 1932 – 1934 Bellefontaine, Ohio Disappeared
215 May 1929 – Jan 1938 Clearfield, Pennsylvania
       1939+ Indiana, Pennsylvania
216 0000-00-00 St. Marys, Pennsylvania
217 1940 – 1976 Charleston, West Virginia Empire Diner. Two diners placed together.
218 ?? – 1947 Coudersport, Pennsylvania Probably used.
219 December 1929 – April 1940 Geneva, New York Replaced by on-site built by Harry & Franklyn Richardson
220 1932 – 1942 632 N LaBrea Ave, Los Angeles, California
221 0000-00-00 Sacramento, California No Info

222 1928 – 1940   1218 Franklin St., Oakland, California
223 0000-00-00   Oakland, California   No Info
224 0000-00-00   Hammond, Indiana
225 0000-00-00   Cincinnati, Ohio
226 1932 – 1949   154 S. 3rd, Easton, Pennsylvania
227 Sept 1932 – 1950   933 S 5th, Allentown, Pennsylvania
228 1934 – 1962+   229 Franklin, Johnstown, Pennsylvania
229 Empty
230 0000-00-00   Lewiston, Maine
231 June 1929 – 1951   Merchants Row, Middlebury, Vermont
232 1932 – 1950   831 W. Genesee, Syracuse, New York Replaced by Mountain View diner
233 February 1930 – 1957   1048 Charles, Rockford, Illinois
234 September 1929 – 1961   156 W 13th, Erie, Pennsylvania
235 0000-00-00   Lincolnway @ Washington, Valparaiso, Indiana
236 Nov 1929 – January 1939   Wellsboro, Pennsylvania   Replaced by Sterling diner
237 1931 – 1939   Defiance, Ohio
        1939 – 1960s   Sandusky, Ohio
        1960s –   Marblehead?, Ohio
238 0000-00-00   188 Water St., Bath, Maine
239 January 1934 – 1951   251 W Union Blvd, Bethlehem, Pennsylvania
240 May 1935 – ??   21 N. Main, Niles, Ohio   Replaced older diner that had a sliding front door.
241 1938   Corning, New York   Assuming Vernon Harvey took the diner with him.
        1940 – 1971   381 W Main, Amsterdam, New York
242 September 1934 – ??   Westfield, New York   Mead's Diner
        ?? – 1946   Corry, Pennsylvania
        1946 – 1962   Sherman, New York
243 1927 – 1948   80 Bassett, Albany, New York First spent some time at Broadway @ S. Ferry
        May 1949 –   Glenmont, New York Either replaced or remodeled and then fire in 1961.
244 October 1927 – 1940   134 9th Ave N, Nashville, Tennessee
245 May 1935 – 2000   18 Lake St., Le Roy, New York
246 1936 – 1961   1306 E Main, Endicott, New York   This diner is an odd case. In the one year anniversary photo, a Ward & Dickinson is shown in front of a barrel roof diner. The ad mentions one diner is new, but does not specify which, clearly.
247 1932 – 1951   321 W 4th, Williamsport, Pennsylvania

This list does not include a number of diners that we are unsure just where they belong on this list. There are a couple of diners that popped up in new locations. Two diners come to mind. Both, we are very confident are one of the first 100 diners, but we are not sure which one of those. For example, the Lincoln Diner in Olean, New York. A photograph shows a diner that looks to be built in 1925-1926 based upon its style.

For a list of these diners, please go online to http://www.nydiners.com/wdpp.html and check out the mysteries page. You can also get more information on the above diners at the same page.

One of the interesting, to me, mysteries is the Lincoln Diner in Olean, New York. From the one photo of this diner that I have seen, I am positive it was one of the first one-hundred diners, due to the lack of overhang on the end of the roof. The question now becomes which one of those diners does it match up with? The Lincoln Diner came to Olean as the Lincoln around 1934. If I had to make a guess, I would lean towards the missing Sharon, Pennsylvania diner. The big problem with that diner is that there are roughly four years in between. In any event, this is what makes diner sleuthing so fascinating; you never know when you're gonig to find that missing link and everything comes together.

Above:
Scotty's Diner in downtown Pittsburgh, Pennsylvania.
(Ed Engel)

Chapter 5

Others Followed in Building Diners

When the novelist Theodore Dreiser made a car trip across upstate New York in the summer of 1915, he repeatedly admired the rural scenery, but complained about the lack of good places to eat and sleep along what were then bumpy and commercially undeveloped roads. Riding through the little town of Avoca in Steuben County, Dreiser searched intently for a restaurant that would serve him "a decent meal" but had to settle for a disappointing sandwich. Not long afterward, his hunt for a reliable eating place became so frustrating that he ended up buying eight bananas, and, as he recorded for posterity, "I believe I ate them all."

Dreiser's problem was that he'd embarked on his excursion a few years too soon. By the 1920s, millions of people would be traveling by car, and New York State's highways would undergo the beginning of a transformation.

Suddenly the shortage of services for travelers disappeared. Tourist cabins, tea rooms, filling stations, diners, a vast number of new buildings began competing for motorists' attention.

- Philip Langdon
Legacy of roadside buildings being sorted out

With Ward and Dickinson an unmitigated success right out of the gate, the rest of the 1920s became relatively good times for other diner builders in western New York. For historians, the unfortunate fact is that most of the newspaper coverage always seemed to surround Ward and Dickinson and rarely any other builder. But this didn't mean that Ward & Dickinson was the only company to take advantage of the dining car craze. Earl Richardson had fought through many setbacks, including a factory fire and separate factory collapses during construction. In 1925, he was building at least two diners a month.

But in the middle of 1925 something happened that no one could foresee. Earl had appendicitis and died on the operating table.[1] This may have forced his son Raymond, who had just graduated from the University of Michigan and married to take over the family business. While Earl personally knew most of the customers he sold lunch cars to, Raymond was in school and Westfield during that time and did not have any of the connections his father had.

The obituary in The Grape Belt & Chautauqua Farmer stated: "Mr. Richardson has helped many young men in a business way and assisted in giving an education to several of the young people. He was very popular with the business men and a member of the Moose, Odd Fellows and Masonic Lodges."

Raymond Richardson soon reorganized the company and named it the Rich Dining Car Company with Merle Richardson as vice president.[2] The company spent a year in Silver Creek, and then in mid 1926, Raymond decided to move the company to Dayton, Ohio. His newly married wife and new business partner and father-in-law L.A. Wilson were both from Dayton, but in the newspaper he stated that the market for diners in the eastern states was saturated.[3] A move to Dayton also put the company in uncharted waters, which meant there were possibilities, but also a different audience to win over.

While in Dayton, the company received an initial newspaper article and not much else. The Rich Dining Car Company did put out a little advertising, focusing on the

portability of their diners.[4] Otherwise, not much else is known of the company's time in Ohio. The Rich Dining Car Company was out of business by 1928 and Raymond was working as a manager at a grocery store in 1929. The family stated that a mini recession in 1926 and 1927 hurt the business venture. Raymond would later separate from his wife, go back to college, and work for the Navy. While many Richardson diners built in Silver Creek have been documented, no diner built in Dayton has ever been tracked down. [Save this next sentence for a photo.] The only extant example of a Richardson is the Penn Yan Diner in Penn Yan, New York. For some unknown reason, the local newspaper on April 10, 1925 called this diner a "Galion dining car," which has long been a mystery to diner historians.

The Mulholland Company started out fast in 1925 with their move to building dining cars. They previously built automobile bodies, focusing on ambulances and trucks. In 1925, Mulholland started dedicating part of their work force to building diners. Quite possibly, with their work with automobile bodies, they could have introduced metal clad diners to western New York. While the other companies, like Ward and Dickinson were using wooden frames, Mulholland was using metal frames. Even though different materials were used for their frames, the diner did look quite similar to a Ward and Dickinson. History has not told us who copied who, but in every business, there is some level of copying going on.

Above left:
A Richardson built diner in Buffalo, New York run by Henry Clees.
(Nancy Garner Clees)

Above right:
The Penn Yan Diner, another Richardson, was remodeled a little in the 1930s. Particle board was added to the ceiling and walls. New stools with a little cushion were added and the small counter at the far end was taken out.
(Dean Smith)

A May 1926 article in The Dunkirk Evening Observer said they were building a diner a week and had already built thirty, with two doing business in Dunkirk.[5] Mulholland was starting to hit their stride in the dining car building business.

Mulholland had a little help along the way. A company was formed by local residents to distribute Mulholland dining cars. The Chautauqua Farmer & Grape Belt on September of 1925 noted the founders:

> A $30,000 corporation has just been organized to handle the sale of the dining cars which are being manufactured by the Mulholland Company at its plant in Washington Ave. Dunkirk. The new corporation has for its directors: Robert J. Gross [banker] of Dunkirk, Roscoe B. Martin [banker, historian], Mathew P. Wilson, William H. Marvin [sheriff], C. Warren Knapp [bank employee, director], and Walter Record [attorney] of Forestville. The corporation is to be known as the Dunkirk Dining Car Corporation and will begin operations at once.[6]

The Dunkirk Dining Car Company was quite aggressive in attempting to sell Mulholland's diners. At one time they had six salesmen[7] out on the road looking for new locations to place the diners, or they would manage company-owned diners until a local concern could be found to buy the diner. Wallace Gillson, E.A. Cees, C.G. Hammond, Robert McKendrick and Ray Schwartz were five of these salesmen. Wallace Gillson sold a diner to his parents, which they ran in Olean, New York. When he was let go from selling diners he went to work operating theirs until roughly World War II. When that diner was demolished, a February 1972 article mentioned that he amassed twenty-six sales for the Dunkirk Dining Car Company.[8] Robert McKendrick would go on to work for Ward and Dickinson before running his own diner in Erie, Pennsylvania. McKendrick and Schwartz were also managers for company-owned diners in Mansfield

Above:

A 1930 Dunkirk, New York city directory advertisement and a colored enhanced photo from a Mulholland brochure. The diner is Cease's Diner in Dunkirk.

(American Diner Heritage)

and Marion, Ohio before both diners were sold to local concerns. These managers would stay on board to help the new owner become comfortable with the operation of the diner. The Dunkirk company would even bring in chefs to aide the new owners, as they did with a diner sold to a Mayville, New York concern.[9]

As has been stated, Mulholland was building diners that were mostly similar to a Ward Dining Car. There were some minor differences with the roof line, and the standard Mulholland dining car always had nine transom windows. But the most important difference was the frame. Like many eastern builders, Mulholland's frames were of an all-steel construction, something invisible to the naked eye.

In 1928, Mulholland sent one of their diners to the Chautauqua County Fair. There was no mention of the Dunkirk Dining Car Company having anything to do with the placement. The article gushed on how women were extolling the placement of all the cookery in the dining car: "There is hardly a housewife that can not obtain valuable ideas from visiting the Mulholland display." It also stated that the company studied each diner now in business and any improvement found in the field was incorporated into the arrangement of the next dining car.[10]

Around 1931, Mulholland came out with a different looking diner, whose base price was $3,500 for a 24-foot car. Constructed in a different way, larger diners could be ordered in multiples of three-foot increments. The main visual difference in the construction was an oval roof with a "graceful curve" extending about a foot over each end. To fix the sweating problem, apparently an ongoing concern, the diner was insulated on both sides of the pillars, which the company said greatly reduced the possibility of sweating. A unique difference in the interior was that linoleum was not used just for the floor, but also on the ceiling and interior walls, "cemented under heavy pressure to insulating board."[11]

These Dunkirk concerns were not without their issues. The company was sued by Alexander Cameron in Herkimer County Court for selling what he called a defective diner. Cameron claimed that it did not have adequate ventilation, and moisture

This Spread:
The same Cease's Diner in Dunkirk, New York is shown in various stages.
(American Diner Heritage)

Various interior photos of two different Mulholland diners. One shows lineoleum under the counter. Other slight variations in the two different diners are stools verses chair back stools.
(American Diner Heritage)

produced while cooking was not being carried out, causing multiple moisture problems. He also accused Mulholland of using inferior wood.[12] The Dunkirk Dining Car Company was not able to sustain their business model. After the company was discontinued, William A. Draves was hired to settle Dunkirk's affairs. The Dunkirk Evening Observer reported on the disappearance of Mr. Draves on August 1932 as front page news. "Mr. Draves said that working alone in his office had affected his nerves and that he suddenly decided to take a couple of days vacation." He drove to Buffalo, intending to also stop in Kenmore where the Dunkirk concern had interest in a diner. He did not contact his wife to let her know about his plans, and when he did not come home that night, she contacted his friends and the police. His friends and associates had, at one time during the day, thought that Mr. Draves was kidnapped, and organized their own search party. Mr. Draves was found by police in his hotel room in Buffalo, resting.[13]

Today, there is essentially only one Mulholland diner anyone can visit. The Green Arch Restaurant in Brocton, New York started as the Empire State Diner in 1931 and is one of the rare Mulhollands with an oval roof. Though remodeled, it still retains the shell of the original diner. Besides the severely remodeled diner in Union City, Pennsylvania, another Mulholland made it into the 1990s. The former Elite Diner of East Liverpool, Ohio is a diner still talked about fondly in this part of Ohio.

The Dunkirk Dining Car Company was not the only company related to Dunkirk, New York that had questionable endings. Jim Pickup tells the story behind his father's diner in Olean, Pickup's Diner:

> Dad had invested in the "Modern Dining Car Company" back in the 1920's when he was operating a grocery store in East Olean. The company would build the diners and put them on location and sell them. It ended up that he had 2 partners in the business and his partners were tapping the till until the company went broke. The diners were built in Dunkirk, NY and when the company went belly

Next Page:

The Empire State Diner in Brocton, New York was Mulholland's last gasp at creating a new lower priced diner in the beginning years of the Depression. The diner had two booths on the right side of the diner and a counter on the left. the ceiling had more of a graceful shallow curve than your typical barrel roof diner.

(American Diner Heritage)

up, he was left with 3 Diners on location. One each in Batavia, East Aurora and Brooklyn. In 1929, selling the Batavia and East Aurora diners was no problem. Selling the diner in Brooklyn was another story. One which has several tellings but the "family tale" was the most interesting.

With the "Mob" ruling the Brooklyn area, telling you with whom you would do business, no one wanted to buy that diner. No company would move the Diner until he found one company that went in at night, (talk about a "Midnight Requisition") jacked it up, transported it to the freight yard and loaded it on a flat car to ship it to Olean. And as the records show, the diner was first put on location at 322 West State Street and was known as the State Grill.[14]

Very little is known about the Liberty Dining Car Company. It seems that Charles Ward really wanted to start his own dining car company when he left Ward & Dickinson in 1927. In early 1928, Ward and John L. Heider, a lawyer with offices in Buffalo, leased the former Buffalo Truck and Tractor building in Clarence for three years and placed the company's offices in Buffalo, twenty miles away.[15] They also placed a demonstration model in Buffalo that they ran to show prospective owners how the diner should be run. When the newspapers mentioned the start of this company, they connected Charles Ward with his former Silver Creek business, Ward and Dickinson. Albert and Howard Meyer were vice-president and treasurer, respectively. Howard G. Britting was the secretary and was the president of the Bank of Williamsville, which was probably useful for financial transactions with customers. At least three Liberty dining cars were in operation in Buffalo with the majority of documented Liberty dining cars being in operation in western New York. One dining car was sent to East Rochester, New York in August of 1928:

Above:

The Liberty Dining Car Company's factory in Clarence, New York. A number of diners are shown which were seemingly ready to ship to buyers. Many Liberty diners stayed in Western New York, but a number made it to New Hampshire and one replaced a Richardson diner in Bellevue, Ohio to former Silver Creek resident Neil Paul. Paul's diner was numbered #58.

(Clarence Historical Society)

Above:

Photographs from a Liberty brochure. Liberty quickly added room for six booths to their diners. They even had room for storage of necessities in cabinets next to the booths. Like other companies, they gave the buyer the option to purchase chairback stools.

(American Diner Heritage)

Above:

Sharpe/National started building diners with monitor roofs but switched to barrel roofs. Shown below is Clute's Diner which stayed in Silver Creek.

(left - Hanover History Center)(right - Vincent P. Martonis)

Above:

A Goodell diner in Zelienople, Pennsylvania. (Everett Bleakney)

Above:

Gordon Tindall waves from the Goodell diner he restored and ran for a number of years in Lanesboro, Minnesota. The diner started out in Wellington, Ohio from 1927 to 2002.

Right:

Advertisement for Goodell. Goodell was primarily a Hardware store and used building diners as a side income.

You Can Buy
AT AN ATTRACTIVE PRICE

A Quality Dining Car

Manufactured by us at our factory here in Silver Creek, N. Y.

Exterior trim of the Best Grade of Cypress: Interior trim of Solid Philippine Mahogany. Decorated with the proper combination of Cast Hardware. Photos furnished on request.   Your inspection solicited.

Goodell Hardware Co.
Office 30 Main St.   Phone 321

> The Liberty Diner, a beautiful $8,000 dining car was opened on North Main street at East Rochester last week by Leon F Balling. The dining car will be open every day and night, every day of the year.
>
> The Liberty dining is the latest creation in dining cars. It is manufactured at Clarence, N. Y. It seats twenty people and there are accomodations (sic) for breakfast booths for women patrons. Comfortable cane stools are found in the car at the counter.
>
> The car is equipped with a sanitary dish washer and an electric refrigerating system and an automatic electric roaster.[16]

Their diners, obviously, were very similar in appearance to the Ward Dining Car. Small differences, such as the lack of swirled green glass in the upper sash, and minor ceiling and roof differences, make discerning the two different makes in black and white pictures a tough job. In 1929, Charles Ward designed a "new and improved" diner. Ward wanted to keep the diner movable by rail, so he didn't change the width or the exterior look. But he also knew that the addition of booths was becoming a desirable selling point to many new diner owners. To address his concern, he added a total of six booths to one end of the dining car. In front of the first pair of booths, facing the counter and cooking, area was a cabinet designed to keep any dining room necessities.

The Liberty Dining Car Company did not last into 1932. The Depression must have been a major factor. Perhaps enough customers could not afford the initial payments anymore. Perhaps they didn't market their diners as well as Ward and Dickinson was able to market their diners. But Charles Ward did design a layout of diners that would be used by companies like O'Mahony, Kullman or Mountain View for any of their diners that they would send long distances by rail from their New Jersey factories. In 1929, O'Mahony shipped a 40' x 10½' diner on a flat car to Columbia, Missouri. Known as Gaebler's Club Diner, it only had nineteen stools.[17] But by the time Null's Diner was shipped to Medina, Ohio sometime in the 1930s, six booths were placed at one end of

Null's Diner.

Today, only one Liberty dining car remains, though it has been greatly remodeled. The Red Arrow Diner in Milford, New Hampshire is still a popular restaurant, though only the shell of the diner is original. Liberty seemingly did a fair business in the state of New Hampshire but most of their dining cars stayed in western or central New York. In Clarence, New York, the hometown for Liberty, the local historical society did save pieces of another Liberty dining car that made it into the 21st Century. This diner had been incorporated into a larger building and last did business as Mazio's Pizza.

There were still a few more concerns in Chautauqua County that would build a small number of diners. As mentioned, Dr. J. J. Sharpe built lunch wagons under the Silver Creek Dining Car Company name. Sometime around 1926, he would change the company name to the National Dining Car Company and start building diners with a barrel roof instead of monitor roofs. By the end of the year, he decided to expand the business:

> The National Dining Car Co., of Silver Creek, of which Dr. J. J. Sharp is the head, is enlarging their plant on Main Street to double its present size. The sale of cars is steadily increasing and the company found it necessary to enlarge their plant to meet the demand.
>
> The company had made no special effort in the sales end of the business, being satisfied to supply the demand as it came to them, but orders have increased so materially that more commodious quarters were found to be a necessity.[18]

In April 1927 The Silver Creek Times reported that a National car was being constructed for Henry Smith of North Tonawanda, New York. Smith, who married a Blanding, was currently operating a Richardson dining car since May 1923, and had built up a "very lucrative business". The car was 36 feet long with an interior finish of solid mahogany and white enamel. The article reported that National's standard dining

Above:

The Miss Batavia Diner in Batavia, New York. The curve in the lower roof of this forty foot Liberty dining car really stands out in this angle.

(Miss Batavia Diner)

car was 32 feet long. The interior of Sharpe's diners were solid mahogany.[19] As noted in Chapter Three, Sharpe previously had issues with bubbling veneer. So he switched from veneer to solid woods. At the time, mahogany was not as cost prohibitive as it is today for a diner.

In 1928, his factory suffered a fire that completely ruined his building. It was stated that there was a diner in the process of being built in the factory at the time of the devastating fire. This was the last time a Silver Creek newspaper reported on the happenings of Dr. Sharpe's business.

Sometime in 1926, the Goodell Hardware store decided to build diners. A relative of Goodell stated to Vince Martonis, Town of Hanover Historian, that they built four cars a year into the 1930s. It would seem safe to say that they built roughly twenty diners in all. Their diners started out wood-framed and clad with wood wainscoting, the only metal being the iron truss rods in the cupola and below the body. By late 1927 the diners were clad in steel, similar to the other manufacturers. Only three Goodell diners have been noted. There was a Goodell diner in Zelienople, Pennsylvania. The Court House Diner in Bath, New York was destroyed by fire in the 1970s, and the former Cecil's Trackside Diner in Wellington, Ohio was moved to New York by Michael Engle with critical assistance from Toni Deller and Daniel Zilka in 2002. This diner was restored by Gordon Tindall starting in 2007 and moved to Lanesboro, Minnesota in 2010. Gordon's reconstruction notes that the construction of Goodell diners was a very straightforward build. While Ward and Dickinson dining car bodies were made to fit together nicely with tongue-and-groove, Goodell's builders favored nails and screws to hold many parts of the frame together.

In North Tonawanda, New York, the Spillman Engineering Company got into the portable restaurant business. They designed and built a building they called the "Dinette Diner." Spillman is best known for building Merry-Go-Rounds, but by 1930 decided to grab a piece of the dining car trade with a building that better resembled a cottage than a typical dining car built anywhere else.

An April 1930 article discussed at length the first Dinette Diner built, and placed at Main and Goundry in North Tonawanda. This diner was purchased by C. V. Starkweather, secretary of the Spillman Engineering Corporation, and served as a model for the company.[20]

Not much is known concerning how many diners they were able to sell. It is believed they sold a diner to a Mr. Campau on Delaware Street in the Town of Tonawanda. A later newspaper article also stated they were placing a Dinette Diner on 42nd Street in New York City to serve as a sales model. A Mr. C. A. Dann was even mentioned as being the lead Sales Manager in New York City for selling Dinette Diners.[21] A Dinette did make it out to Sandusky, Ohio, a city that also had a Ward and Dickinson, Brill/Dina-Car, O'Mahony, Mountain View and a trolley-built diner.

Spencer Stewart of *www.dinerhunter.com* commented on the company:
> The Dinette Diner Company was a subsidiary of Spillman Manufacturing, a North Tonawanda, New York firm which made carousels. They launched their line of "Dinette Diners" in 1930, opening their prototype at 107 Main St., North Tonawanda.
> Shortly after, they opened a second diner on 42nd St., New York City. A separate Dinette Diner corporation was organized nearby with offices in the Bowery Bank Building, 110 East 42nd, New York. They hired on Mr. C.A. Dann, "a man who has probably sold more dining cars than any one individual in the country" as the sales manager for the company.
> The styling of their diners was very unusual for the time period, and their construction methods and materials were somewhat unconventional. What may jump out at you immediately is the exterior- it doesn't look like a diner. Where's the enamel? Where's the stainless? Where's the barrel or monitor roof? No, instead of streamline moderne, "the structure is of the English cottage type

Top Picture:

May's Diner in Sandusky, Ohio in 1939. Spillman Manufacturing built portable restaurants that looked more like cottages than diners.

(Sandusky Library Follett House Museum Archives)

Bottom Pictures :

Interior view of the Dinette Diner in Sandusky, Ohio known as May's Diner. The interior was much more diner like than the exterior. Booths were upholstered instead of being solely made of wood like most other Great Lake manufacturers of the time.

(Sandusky Library Follett House Museum Archives)

with a roof of variegated autumn shades with heavy rolled eaves. The exterior walls are of grey stained shingles. The windows, beautiful indeed, are of the cottage casement type, opening out, and with diamond ground design."

The interior had much more of a standard diner look about it, but with what was, for the time, a huge width. Like Bixler and Rochester Grills, Dinette Diners built their diners in four foot "slices", which were shipped in a box car or truck to the site. As such, they could be wide enough for booths, and the length of the diner was not limited by transportation. This idea had been done before, by the Fremont Metal Body Company, a precursor to Bixler, as early 1925. But it still represented a huge technical advantage over what was coming out the big factories of the day.

The interior walls and floors were covered in linoleum, with a barrel vault ceiling, with beams at each of the section seams. Interior woodwork was gumwood with a walnut stain. "The Dinette has seating capacity for 30 persons, 14 at the counter and 16 at the end and side tables. The tables are of walnut with two tone "Lino" tops having brown centers and jasper green borders. The chairs have hat racks, green leather upholstered seats and are of the low back design.

The counter is of table height with a wide overhang on the front edge so that one sits close to the eating top without having to bend over to his food. The counter is raised off the floor by porcelain legs, providing plenty of toe room underneath. One sits at the counter exactly as is customary at one's own table. No balancing on foot rests or hunched up limbs. In addition this type of counter is the last word in sanitation, permitting free circulation of air and eliminating the

Right:

Hilton's Diner in Brookville, Pennsylvania was one of two diners of this unknown diner style. Around the late 1930s, an unknown diner builder built at least four diners in this style for towns in Pennsylvania like Clearfield, Linesville and Brookville. The Hiltons came from Westfield, New york where they worked in a Ward and Dickinson diner for a couple of years.

(Archie Hilton)

RAY'S DINER
Located Corner of Plank Road and Union Avenue on Route 36
—A CONVENIENT PLACE TO STOP AND ENJOY GOOD FOOD—

Featuring
FULL COURSE DINNERS—LUNCHES AND SANDWICHES
OPEN DAILY-24 HOUR SERVICE
ARTHUR KRAMER
GENERAL CONTRACTOR
SPECIALIZING IN BUILDING — REPAIRING AND REMODELING
2424 5th AVE.   **PHONE 2-8173**

usual dirt and vermin traps. The counter stools have apple green porcelain bases with green leather upholstered tops. The front of the counter is finished in "Formica" panels of ivory with contrasting pillars and trim in modernistic color and design.

Between the ceiling and the roof is a 30 inch air space, ventilators opening into it from the ceiling and a heavy duty exhaust fan at one end which ensures freedom from steam or odors- the air in the Dinette, by means of the above system is completely changed every three minutes."

Dinette Diner was playing the environmental game of the '60s/'70s thirty or more years before it came back into vogue. They were trying to outclass "dining car" builders by making their product more elegant, and at the same time more technologically advanced. Bigger, better, cleaner and more cozy.

Think of a 1960s diner in the same regard. More sections, wider, longer, better kitchen equipment. In so many ways more modern, but covered in stone, mansard roofs, and lit by wagon wheel chandeliers. Just like Diner Dinette, trying to revolutionize the diner industry while distancing themselves from the diner image.[22]

Besides the Dunkirk Dining Car Company, there were other dealers in new and used diners. George Gregory, who owned three Ward & Dickinson diners in Buffalo, New York around 1927, had numerous want ads announcing that he was selling diners all over Buffalo. The Bradford Sales Company of Buffalo announced that they were agents for new dining cars in 1926. In 1934, the company made the news in Plymouth, Pennsylvania when they placed a diner in that village.[23]

Other entrapeneurs either worked with dining car manufacturers or on their own to

Above:

Ray's Diner in Altoona, Pennsylvania opened up at least ten years after the other diners of a similar style. In the grand opening advertisement a contractor of Arthur Kramer is mentioned. This is our only possible clue to the builder of these diners.

Below:

This building in Portville, New York was built on-site in the late 1930s but was originally called a diner. Other on-site buildings that were intended to be used as diners were even wider and had higher roofs.

get diners started in various locations. Leslie and Mernie Cross worked for a short time with Ward & Dickinson establishing diners in a town for a year or two before selling to a local concern. They would show people that running a diner could be a profitable business before moving on to a new diner in a new location. Philip L. Carey also ran diners in at least Meadville, Pennsylvania and Ashtabula, Ohio before selling to local concerns.

Lastly is the smallest known concern. Guy Russell was listed as a "dining car builder" in the 1930 census. Russell built no more than one or two diners in his home town of Ripley, New York. One of the diners was placed in his front yard on US Route 20 and was sold to John Tefft in November 1930. Teft moved the diner to North East, Pennsylvania, the next village west on Route 20.[24]

In 1931, a Dining Car Organization was formed in Buffalo by two local dining car operators, Paul Sterling and Jesse Crawford. Nothing is known about the organization other than a list of members gleaned from a newsletter they published, which was sparse with historical facts.[25]

There are also a number of mysteries when it comes to the builder of particular diners. A handful of diners located in north and west Pennsylvania have remained a mystery to diner sleuths. All of the diners exhibit an overly round barrel roof with a thin monitor roof. Diners of this style have been noted in Pennsylvania locales of Linesville, Clarion, Brookville(2) and Altoona.

And in many upstate New York, Ohio and Pennsylvania towns there existed home built diners that exhibited diner like qualities in appearance. Many of these diners were not restricted by the actual need to ship the finished diner to its final destination, so they were often wider than your typical diner. And even though they were stick built buildings, they still exhibited diner like qualities like a barrel roof. One diner in Smethport, Pennsylvania, built in 1938, even

exhibited a monitor roof to really capture the appearance of a diner.

1 Grape Belt and Chautauqua Farmer, Dunkirk, New York June 9, 1925
2 Silver Creek Times, Silver Creek, New York May 27, 1926
3 Dayton Journal, Dayton, Ohio July 31, 1926
4 Silver Creek Times, Dayton, Ohio October 25, 28 and November 14, 1926
5 Dunkirk Evening Observer, Dunkirk, New York May 19, 1926
6 Grape Belt and Chautauqua Farmer, Dunkirk, New York September 25, 1925
7 Silver Creek Times, Dunkirk, New York May 19, 1926
8 Olean Olean, New York February 8, 1972
9 Mayville Sentinal, Mayville, New York November 2, 1928
10 Grape Belt and Chautauqua Farmer, Dunkirk, New York September 25, 1925
11 Mulholland brochure ca. 1931
12 Utica Daily Press, Utica, New York March 17, 1928
13 Silver Creek Times, Dunkirk, New York August 17, 1932
14 Email correspondence with Jim Pickup
15 Buffalo Evening News, Buffalo, New York February 21, 1928
16 Wyoming County Times, Warsaw, New York August 2, 1928
17 Columbia, Missouri newspaper, April 25, 1929
18 Silver Creek News, Silver Creek, New York November 25, 1926
19 Silver Creek Times, Silver Creek, New York April 27, 1927
20 The Evening News, North Tonawanda, New York April 9, 1930
21 The Evening News, North Tonawanda, New York January 10, 1931
22 Correspondence with Spencer Stewart
23 Wilkes Barre Sunday Independent, Wilkes Barre, Pennsylvania July 8, 1934
24 Silver Creek Times, Dunkirk, New York November 14, 1930
25 Diner News & Guide, Dan Sullivan, editor. Published by Diner's News Company, Buffalo, New York

Included are three chattel and or sales posted in newspapers concerning diners mentioned in this book. The listing of what came included with a diner are fascinating and help a person to understand how a diner was laid out and what came with each diner. The completeness of the Rochester Grill diner in Cortland, New York is quite fascinating.

Some copies were difficult to read, so there are mistakes in translation. Much of the translation was done via OCR. A few items which were completely illegible were omitted.

JUNE 3, 1938 – CORTLAND STANDARD

Notice of Sale

Notice is hereby given, that the undersigned will, on the 8th day of June, 1938, on the front step of the Club Grille. 16-18 Main Street, Cortland, New York, at 10 o'clock. In the forenoon of that day, sell to the highest bidder, a certain Sectional Restaurant building and equipment size APX 14' x 44', Serial No. 101. as per specifications annexed hereto and made a part hereof. Such Sectional Restaurant and equipment have been repossessed by the undersigned under and by virtue of a certain conditional sales contract between Nellie D. Perline, purchaser and Barnard & Simonds Company Inc. seller, and subsequently assigned through conveyances to the undersigned. Specifications and equipment to be sold are as follows:

Plumbing — Toilet fixtures, sink faucets and connections to floor furnished

Electric — Fans, electric lighting (exclusive of bulbs) fixtures are supplied. Rochester Grills furnish wiring and plumbing plans only for estimating. All work must be done in accordance to local code.

1. Exterior Finish: White and apple green combination.
2 Interior Finish: Ivory, white and light green with mahogany trim.
3 Flooring; Maple and fir Joists 2" x 8" yellow pine. Sills: 8" steel channels.
4 Posts—Steel: Side and end post 1 3/4" x 1 3/4" x 3-16". Corner posts 3" x 3" x 5-16" Side and corner posts have steel supporting brackets welded on.
8. Side and End Panels: Frames made of birch, sheathed with 10 gauge steel outside and Masonite Inside. Space between walls is packed
with rock wool.
6. Planchers: Made of No. 1 yellow pine with ventilating opening covered with copper wire cloth.
7 Rafters: 3" x 3" x 5-16" cold rolled steel.
8 Roof Panels; Mads of poplar Outside sheathed with white pine ship-lapped inside with Masonite.

9 Roofing: Composition slate surface.
10 Windows: Special steel casement type. Can be opened and closed without removing screen.
11. Flor Frames: Frame of birch concealed steel reinforcement.

12 Doors: Combination type. Removable glass sash and removable copper screen sash made of pine.
13. Hardware: All visible hardware is chrome plated.
14. Ventilation: Side wall weatherproof automatic ventilating system.
15. Floor Covering: In front of counter only. Kind: Armstrong linotile.
16. Paneling: Imitation mahogany panels 38" from floor not included in kitchen or toilet.
17. Hood: Porcelain hood covering coffee urns, steam table and griddle, with three 8-inch vents through celling. (Green outside, white underneath)
18. Hood Plate: Of porcelain under hood (white).
19. Electric Light Fixtures: Ceiling fixtures four, table lamps five, kitchen celling fixtures two, toilet celling fixtures two, corridor ceiling
fixtures one, awning lanterns five.
20. Exhaust Fans: Under hood in diner one, under range in kitchen one, in corridor one.
21. Celling Fans: Two.
22. Open Booths: Table and benches made of birch, mahogany finish. Tables equipped with standard polished plate glass five.
23 Back Bars: Built of whitewood and equipped with drawers and shelves. Tops are covered with Monel Metal and chrome plated copper.
24. Lunch Counter: Counter is built of white wood, trim of birch with mahogany finish with green steel porcelain panels. Top has glass
display 8" high the full length of counter.
25 Stools Equipped with brass pipe foot rail fourteen.
28. Coffee Urns: A three-piece battery of urns. Copper, nickel plated. Capacity, 3 gallon coffee and 6 gallon water, 3 gallon coffee. Interior lining is Pyrex glass.
27. Griddle: 6 burners griddle, 4 open burners in a group.
28. Steam Table: Rochester Grills standard 8 crock with two meat platters with overhead warming oven.
29. Gas Range- 3 burner South Bend. Oven 23" wide, 20" deep. Canopy for range.
30. Work Table: Equipped with cutting block and shelves.
31. Work Table: For kitchen equipped with cutting block.
32. Toaster: Toastmaster 4 slice
33. Sink: Under counter rinsing Sink. In kitchen: Double compartment with drain boards galvanized
34. Refrigerator: 32 cu. ft. capacity.
35. Hot Water Heater: 30 gallon automatic.
36. Coat Hooks: Quantity as needed.

37. Salad Tray: With 3 pans each and equipped with 50 ft coil pipe and push back faucet.
38. Menu Boards: Four letters 1,500.
39. Mirror Ladies' toilet.
40. Toilet fixtures in color ladies toilet white gents. Lavatory equipped with two faucets, chain and rubber stopper with S trap. Toilet
with fittings.
41. Cashier's Booth: One.
42. Shelves in Kitchen: Three.
43. Pie rack combination with silverware tray one, silverware tray one.
44. Spice Rack.
45. Dishes and Kitchen Equipment: 6 doz. stack up cups, 8 doz. R.E. saucers, 4 doz. 10 ¾" grille plates,
6 doz. 6 1/4" plates, 4 doz. 4 7/8" fruits, 4 doz. 7 3/8" coupe soup, 1/2 doz. 4-oz. unhid, mustards, 1 doz. 11 3/8" R.E. platters,
2 doz. 9" plates, 6 doz. No. 376 barrel glasses 5 oz, 1 doz. No 37 No-Nik tumblers 4 oz, 6 doz. 1-oz bottle creams, 1 doz. prs. salt and pepper chrome, 1 doz. china sugars, 6 only No. 306 tip top syrup jugs N-P tops, 6 only 5-oz, oil crusts, ½ doz, No. 10 G. tea pots (Halls), 6 doz. Berkshire teaspoons overlay, 6 doz. Berkshire forks, 6 doz. stainless steel knives Berkshire, 6 doz. Berkshire dessert spoons, 9 only chrome plated Havanap holders. 1 only 17" potato masher. 1 only No. 70 cap strainer, 1 only No. 2 Edlund can opener, 1 only heavy 14-qt. galv. pail, 1 only 1-oz. retinned cream dipper, 1 only No 18 30-qt. L & G stock pot, 1 only No. 238 8-qt L & G sauce pan, 2 only No. 224 6-qt L & G sauce pans, 2 only No. 15 8" steel frying pans 2 only No. 30 11 ¾ steel frying pans. 1 only No. 26 14 ¼" steel frying pan. 1 only No. 1062 10" French fryer, 1 only No. 2702 2-qt white enamel pitcher, 1 only No 109 retinned skimmer, 3 only No. 77 12" retinned ladles. 2 only No. 314 14' basting spoons, 1 only 15" French wire ship, 2 only 15 x 30 strapped roast pans, 3 only 1-gal enameled urn measure, 1 only No 51 griddle scraper, 1 only No. 50 square grater, 1 only chrome pancake turner, 1 only Dexter 10" spatula, 1 only stainless steel paring knife, 1 only 13" bread knife 1 only 10" butcher knife, 1 only 12" carving knife, 1 only Dexter 12" cook's knife, 2 only Dexter 12" steel, 1 only Dexter cook's fork. 1 only round hamburg mould, 1 only oblong hamburg mould.

JULY 5, 1932 - BELLEVUE GAZETTE

Liberty Dining Car Corporation
vs
Neil F Paul and Mabel L Paul, Defendants

In pursuance of an Order of Sale issued from the clerk's office of the Court of Common Pleas of Huron county, Ohio, on the 27th day of June 1932, and to me directed in the case above named, I will expose to Sale at Public Auction, on the premises of Neil F Paul and Mabel L Paul in Bellevue, Lyme township, Huron county, Ohio on Friday, the 8th day of July 1932, at 2:00 O'clock in the afternoon of said day, the following goods and chattels, to-wit:

"One Liberty semi steel dining car Serial No 58 together with equipment to-wit: One counter, 12 stools, 2 booths and tables, floor covering, 1 clock, 1 electric refrigerator, 1 electric dish washer, 1 electric exhaust fan, 1 range, 1 heating tank, 1 steam table, 1 twin coffee urn, 1 cream dispenser, pie cases, cigar case, electric lights and globes, set of silverware, 1 set of dishes, 1 set of glassware, 1 awning, cutting boards, range hood, 21' glass counter tops, 2 glass table tops, 1 gas heater and other miscellaneous items, standard equipment."

JANUARY 9, 1939 – KINGSTON DAILY FREEMAN

1 Ward & Dickson Diner, located at 476 Broadway, in the City of Kingston N.Y. together with all the furniture, equipment and fixtures contained therein, as follows:
1 Counter
2 Booths, complete
12 Stools,
1 Set of Twin Coffee Urns
1 Kelvinator Electric Refrigerator
1 Westinghouse Electric Refrigerator
1 National Cash Register
1 Steam Table
1 Gas Range
1 Combination Grill and Gas Flats
4 Electric Fans
1 Three-Slice Toastmaster Toaster
All Light Fixtures
All dishes, crockery, silverware, cutlery, pots and pans.
The washroom next to and adjoining the diner is intended to be covered by this chattel mortgage and shall be considered to be a part and appurtenant to the diner

Chapter 6

Ohio Diners and Diner Builders

However, Ohio does not like the "diner" type of quick lunch spot extensively, records show, but has taken the cottage style to its "heart." tourists have begun to depend on this type of restaurant to supply them with meals which they desire on tour and in strange towns.

-W.S. Bittner, December 21, 1939

The quote on the previous page is from 1939. In the mid 1920s, many diner companies gave it their best shot at promoting the diner in Ohio and beyond. We are aware of four diner builders which called Ohio home between 1925 and 1935. The western New York builders knew that the Great Lakes, especially northern Ohio, held great possibilities as a market for lunch cars. Many people were traveling the improved highways of America as more highways received pavement and became wider and safer. Even Alfred Closson would have crossed the country six times by 1928. And in the northern part of Ohio, there were many industrial concerns similar to New England cities and towns that were so inviting to the lunch wagon owners. Some builders such as Raymond Richardson believed that the East was saturated with diners and that the Midwest was the best business move. History tells us that the diner manufacturers had better luck selling and placing diners in the northern third of Ohio than they did in the rest of the state.

Ward and Dickinson sent only fifteen of their first one hundred diners built to East Coast locales. In contrast, the New England and Metro New York lunch car builders had dominated the market east of the Appalachians and only sparsely infiltrated the region west of these mountains. This allowed tremendous possibilities for newer builders to enter a market less saturated with lunch cars as compared to eastern cities of similar size. Raymond Richardson was on to something, but would the citizens of the Great Lakes and Midwest accept diners?

Many Great Lakes cities had some lunch wagons, so the citizens of the Midwest were somewhat familiar with the concept. This minimal level allowed the partial acceptance of diners into the region. But a partial acceptance would still make the diner a tough sell, not only to owners, but also in attracting customers. The acceptance of the diner in the Great Lakes varied widely. In Springfield, Ohio, the cities first diner went through multiple owners in just two-plus years before leaving town. The current diner in Hillsdale, Michigan may have had many owners over the last thirty years, but

Above:
Sandusky, Ohio was home to a number of diners. No one manufacturer was able to get more than one of their diners into Sandusky. The diner in this photo seems to mirror the style of either a Brill or Dina-Car diner.

the first proprietor Joseph Leonard lasted 28 years from 1927 to 1955. Small cities such as Ashtabula, Sandusky, Medina, and Fremont in Ohio, and Pontiac and Sturgis in Michigan all had multiple diners and embraced them. Though Norwalk, Ohio, home of the Bixler Company from 1931 to 1935, may have had only one diner within the city limits, although that recognition did not make their city directories.

The year 1924 saw more than a few lunch cars enter the state from Silver Creek manufacturers, probably all from Earl Richardson. These included Galion, Ashtabula, Conneaut, Bellevue, Ravenna, Bryan, and Painesville. The next couple of years saw diners placed in more locations including Toledo, Geneva, Medina, Cleveland, Springfield, Wellington, and East Liverpool, just to name some of the verified locations. Ward and Dickinson supplied two chains in Toledo and Cleveland that both lasted no more than a year. Fortunately, individual diner owners had much better fortunes.

The Rich Dining Car Company was the first dedicated diner builder to move into Ohio, as Bixler was already in the state but was only making diners as a sideline business at the time. Raymond Richardson moved the company that his father started in Silver Creek, New York to Dayton, Ohio in the summer of 1926. The Dayton Journal reported on their move: "The Rich Dining Car Company, Inc., located in factory M-25, Barney Smith shops, Keowee Street and East Monument Avenue, manufacturers of complete restaurants on wheels, is a newcomer in Dayton manufacturing circles." The newspaper also reported that the initial workforce was twelve experienced workers. A diner was to be completed by mid August of 1926 and marked "the first dining car ever to be built in Dayton."[1]

The Rich Dining Car Company tried to do a little advertising and make a name for itself in south western Ohio. They tried to create a customer base by offering up hopes of a dependable steady job that paid the owner enough money where they could also afford the nicer things in life. One way was to create little jingles called Richograms.

[Richograms [2]]

Richograms was the title of a booklet issued by the company. Some of these little catch phrases included:

"With a Rich dining car it is
not 'quick sales and small profit',
but 'quick sales and large profit.'"

"The man working on a salary
must make a profit for his em-
ployer. Be your own boss and
take all the profit."

"A Rich car can make you rich."

Above:

The Anita Diner at 7700 Detroit Avenue in Cleveland, Ohio was probably a DinaCar, built by the Ohio Body Company, but also could have been a Brill dining car. Cleveland had approximately a dozen diners in the 1930s. In 1926 a company tired setting up a chain of ten Ward & Dickinson diners with a central commissary, but the attempt was short lived.

(Cleveland Public Library/Official City of Cleveland Photograph)

The business only lasted about one to two years before Raymond called it quits. It is believed that the company was still making wooden clad diners, although other concerns had moved to metal clad diners. Whether it was the region, the mini recession, or Raymond's inexperience in the dining car business, the diner was not appealing to potential customers and the business was over by 1928. The type of wood-clad lunch car with large wheels that Earl Richardson began to build in 1921 became obsolete. Around the same time that the Rich Dining Car Company was closing shop, a company that was building all-steel railway vehicles got into the diner building business.

The J.G. Brill Company was a noted railroad vehicle builder. The company made the decision to get into the diner manufacturing business with three of their plants in 1928. The Wason plant in Springfield, Massachusetts would supply New England, the J.G. Kuhlman plant in Cleveland, Ohio would supply the upper Midwest, and their St. Louis, Missouri plant would cover the lower Midwest. Their Wason plant was by far the most productive of the three plants. Brill dining cars seemed to be the most expensive of any diner at the time. Still, many of the diners were in business from Philadelphia up to Boston.[3] Not as many Brills made it out of the northeast.

Like many of the other companies, Brill had grand plans. The Suburbanite Economist of Chicago, Illinois announced the opening of a Brill-built diner on January 1928: "Mr. D. W. Cashin will place and operate one of the new J. G. Brill dining cars on the premises. The Brill company states that they expect to operate 60 dining cars throughout the city of Chicago."[4] It is very doubtful Brill came anywhere close to placing these 60 diners.

The Ohio Body and Blower Company's venture into the building of diners started

Above:

Bixler was selling their diners at the low end of the scale. Bixler did not ramp up the sale of their diners until 1928-1929. They became more than just a blip on the radar fron 1929 - 1933 when quite a few of their diners were placed in the lower Hudson River region of New York state. Bixler even set up a sales office in New York City.

(American Diner Heritage)

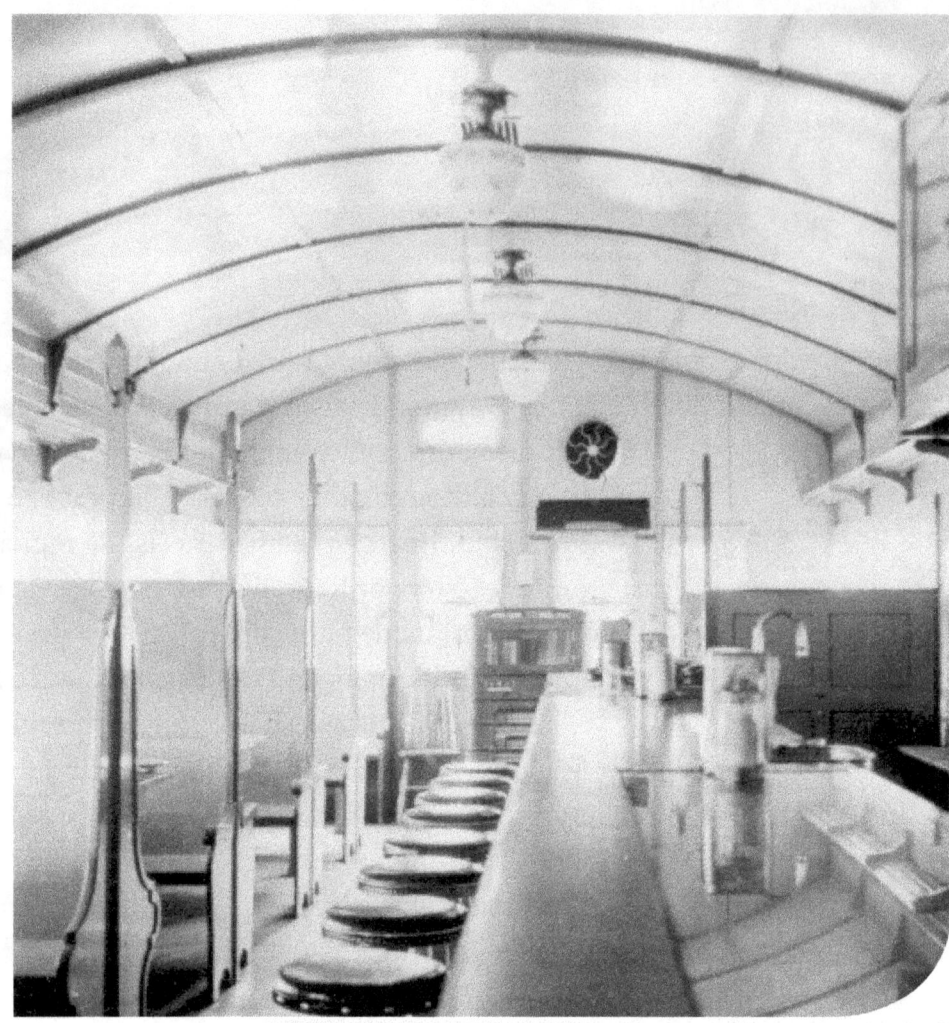

(Clark Fegraus)

(Peoria Public Library via family of Fletcher Lankton)

around 1926. Located in Cleveland, Ohio, the company started advertising what they called the "DinaCar." From drawings placed in a Youngstown newspaper, the diner looked very similar to a Brill dining car.[5] They extolled the same line that other manufacturers were using: You too can make $6,000-$12,000 profit a year with our diner.

The Ohio Body Company's main source of income was building automobile bodies for Ford. The introduction of the Model A Ford put an end to their business.[6] The company closed down in September of 1927 due to their debt issues.

Unfortunately, we do not know who built the Max Diner of Elyria and Sherrick's Diner of Ashland. The diner originally known as Max's Diner in Elyria was razed in 2004 and the former Sherrick's Diner in Ashland still exists, but has not operated for years. Both were either built by Brill or Ohio Body, that much is known.

Initially located in Fremont, Ohio, The Bixler Company seems to be the first diner manufacturer to come up with the idea of building sectional diners. The 1929 city directory for Fremont listed Frank Nagle president and Marshall Bixler as general manager. Marshall Bixler was also the general manager of the Fremont Metal Body Company, who made buses at the time.[7] The Fremont Metal Body Company started in 1921 and their factory would become the location for the manufacture of other items. The Bixler Company was listed as making, "sectional cottages, dining cars and garages." Garages were probably their most popular item as Ohio began to improve their road systems dramatically in the 1920s. Although Bixler did not start making a large impact in the diner trade until 1931, a Sandusky, Ohio newspaper blurb mentioned that the Bixler Company was placing a diner in Fremont sometime during 1925.[8]

Very little is known about Bixler while they were in Fremont. Brian Butko reported in his "Eerie Lake Erie: Dinors and Diner Manufacturers" article in the SCA News Journal, that New York piano magnate George Foster owned the Bixler Manufacturing Company.[9] Sometime in 1930, their Fremont factory was destroyed by fire and the business was moved east along Route 20 to Norwalk, Ohio. The factory in Norwalk

Preceeding Page:
The 9-W Diner in Catskill, New York proved so successful that the owner expanded their diner. The interior photo shows the booths along the windows and the high ceilings, a stark change from the other diners being built in western New York at the same time.

Below:
The Hitching Post in Peoria, Illinois is a rare Bixler that was documented to have traveled west instead of east from the Norwalk, Ohio plant. Peoria was also home to a barrel roof O'Mahony and possibly other diners.

COLONIAL HOTEL — FREMONT, OHIO

was previously used to build Chas Emerson Pianos. It was here in Norwalk where the company focused on the diner manufacturing part of the business. From 1931 to 1935, Bixler made and sold their unique diners. J. H. Shale, originally from Rochester, New York, was the foreman at the factory. Diners were shipped by rail in four-foot sections. Then, at the site, the sections were fastened together, and the diner was then placed on its foundation. This allowed, for the first time, a row a booths for four people to be placed parallel to the counter alongside the windows. (Technically, O'Mahony did build some diners with tables for four people before Bixler did. But these diners were their high end diner and were typically only shipped very short distances from their factory.) Today, every diner owner knows that booth seating is practically necessary, but at one time that was not the case. Most people sat at the counter. Owners of diners that served the traveling public came to quickly realize the importance of booth service for the families or couples that were traveling on the road.

McGrath's Diner in Pawling, New York received a blue ribbon from Bixler in April of 1935 for being the best kept-up of the 600 Bixler diners in the country.[10] That same year, Bixler's luck would turn south, but while it lasted, Bixler was very aggressive at making sure their diners were opportunities to sell new diners to new diner owners. If the 600 number is true, then Bixler had a booming business for building diners in no more than ten years time.

One of the more interesting facts is that Bixler did very well in the lower Hudson Valley, especially Westchester County—the same county that Tierney (later DeRaffele)

Above

Photos of two of the four diners that plied their trade in Fremont, Ohio in the 1930s. John Baeder states that he was told that all four diners in Fremont were trolley cars, but the photo on the right almost looks like a manufactured diner.

Trolley cars were a viable alternative to a prospective new owner. The price was right, and with shipping costs weighing in the farther west from Lake Erie, trolley car conversions became even more alluring.

(American Diner Heritage)

Below:

Al's Diner in Bono, Ohio was originally a trolley car built by the McKeen Motor Car Company of Omaha, Nebraska. The trolley car covered the Marblehead area of Ohio until it was decommissioned around 1930. Al's was a late conversion as it started as a diner around 1950 and was demolished after a fire in 1962.

(GM Andersen Photo, Krambles-Peterson Archive.)

called home. As mentioned in Gutman's American Diner Then and Now, Bixler even placed a diner right across the street from the old Tierney Plant in new Rochelle, New York.[11] Bixler also placed a diner in St. Louis, and in Peoria, Illinois, but not much is otherwise known about their luck with the Midwest market. A 1931 article in The Dayton Journal announced that Bixler diners could be placed on the rooftop of any highrise building. They made it sound like there were already a few Bixlers placed in this manner.[12] In upstate New York, Bixlers could have been found in Geneva, Lima, and two in Syracuse. Both Syracuse Bixlers still exist today. One was part of the Cameron Diner chain and sits empty on Wolf Street. The diner in Geneva is also extant, but is in storage at property owned by the City of Geneva. In 2004, the City took the diner for an urban renewal project that allowed a hotel to be built on the diner's site.

Rumor had it that Tierney was looking to start a plant in Cleveland. But there was another "supplier" of diners that has been able to be easily substantiated. Just like old trolley cars were used for lunch wagons, larger rail vehicles, especially electric trolleys and street cars were also being used for diners instead of being junked. Even the occasional box car was used as a portable restaurant, such as in Martins Ferry, Ohio. But mostly the trolley car was the prime candidate for use as a diner. By the late 1920s and into the 1930s the trolley lines were folding left and right. All the traction companies had trolleys that now had no use. Many were sold for scrap. Popular options for the trolley cars were uses as sheds or vacation shanties, but some became diners. The idea that you could get a trolley car for next to nothing

when diners were going for five to twelve thousand dollars was highly enticing to a prospective diner owner.

In his book Diners, John Baeder reported that Fremont, Ohio had four trolley-car diners.[13] Whitey's Diner, a highly remodeled trolley car, still exists today. Berta talked about an interurban trolley car diner in nearby Monroeville, Ohio that was "untouched since the day it left the tracks," when he stopped by in the 1970s. Trolley diners could be found in many places in the Great Lakes states and practically any diner found in the Dakotas may have been a trolley or railcar diner. It was far easier to take a local trolley car, maybe from urban Fargo, North Dakota, than ship a diner from back east.

It was quite easy and affordable for someone to start their own diner out of a used trolley car. An article in the July 25, 1938 edition of The Sandusky Star Journal pointed out just how affordable it was:

> A second car was sold to a man from Lorain who intends to turn his purchase into a dining car. Other prospective purchasers were from

Above: **A diner at 9016 Euclid Avenue in Cleveland, Ohio. This diner looks to be a Dina-Car, built by the Cleveland based Ohio Body Company. While not thought of as a diner city, Cleveland has had more than its fair share of diners over the years.** (Cleveland Public Library/Official City of Cleveland Photograph)

Below:

A Northern Ohio Traction and Light Company, ex 1500 Series car located on Chester Avenue and E 36th Street, Cleveland, Ohio. Note the sign in front calls it a restaurant and not a diner.

(Spencer Stewart)

> Fremont and Norwalk. It is expected that the 200 cars to be sold will be disposed of rapidly as there is much interest being shown by visitors to the car barns. Prices vary from $35 to $150. The oldest cars were purchased for transportation use about 25 years ago.
> It is estimated that a traction car can be arranged for dining car use for about $1500, exclusive of equipment. Some of the cars will probably be used for summer homes.[14]

Beyond Ohio there were some diners built. New finds always come along here and there. Small concerns in non-diner areas that built a few diners. A May 30, 1931 article from The Milwaukee Journal did just that. They announced that the Master Auto Body Company of Milwaukee, Wisconsin was going to be building six diners for the New York Coffee Pot chain:

> There's a new idea in the wind for this summer's motorists, for the breezes blowing over the miles of countryside around Milwaukee will be laden with hamburgers and onions, fried eggs and a good many other things that the hungry tourist may want when the sun stands at high noon or the hills become blue with evening shadows. The Master Auto Body Co. is busy up in its plant on Burleigh St. building six special diners for the New York Coffee Pot. Fifteen people can be seated at once in these new roadside lunchrooms and there are plenty of big open windows for those who just want to drive up and "holler" in "one up" or "two on."
> The diners are so designed that they will have seats, a counter, a kitchen range, an icebox and shelves for soft drinks, crackers, sandwiches and picnic necessities. The auto firm is also building a special trailer on which these diners will be placed and hauled to whatever roadside spot has been rented by the New York Coffee Pot.
> It is planned to have the diners open

day and night and keep them going from now until November. Hauled out on the trailer, the diner will be deposited on a specially leveled spot on the side of the road; if another spot looks better, the truck and trailer will be sent around and the diner moved on to the next place.[15]

1 Dayton Journal, Dayton, Ohio July 31, 1926
2 Dayton Daily Journal, October 25, 1926
3 Correspondence with Daniel Zilka
4 Suburban Economist, Chicago, Illinois January 17, 1928
5 Youngstown Vindicator, Youngstown, Ohio February 16, 1927
6 http://www.coachbuilt.com/bui/o/ohio/ohio.htm
7 Fremont Daily News, Fremont, Ohio December 23, 1922
8 Sandusky Star Journal, Sandusky, Ohio February 10, 1925
9 SCA News Journal, Winter 1993-1994
10 Pawling-Patterson News, Pawling, New York April 11, 1935
11 page 102, American Diner, Then and Now, Richard J.S. Gutman
12 Dayton Journal, Dayton, Ohio July 8, 1931
13 page 114, Diners, John Baeder, 5th Printing, 1988
14 Sandusky Star Journal, Sandusky, Ohio July 25, 1938
15 Milwaukee Journal, Milwaukee, Journal May 30, 1931

Above:

Edward Rosskam was working for the Farm Security Administration in 1941 when he took this photo of a home made lunch wagon in Chicago. During the depression, many entrepreneurs used whatever they could get their hands on to create a place of business.

(Library of Congress, Prints & Photographs Division, FSA/OWI Collection)

Two trolley car conversions in Ohio.

Right:

Greentown, Ohio, which is in between Akron and Canton.

Below:

Independence, Ohio, a suburb of Cleveland

(Spencer Stewart)

Menus. What is a restaurant without menus? Everyone remembers their favorite item on a menu, or a price of a meal that seems like it was much more affordable in years past. Take a trip down memory lane with a small selection of diner and lunch wagon menus.

What you will see on the next number of pages are various menus from lunch wagons and diners over the years. First is a 1916 aritcle that shows that increases have always been a part of the restaurant world.

LUNCH WAGONS TO JUMP PRICES

Proprietors of Quick Lunch Rooms of the City to Hold Meeting and Arrange a New Schedule.

The high cost of living, which is no stranger to any of us, is about to hit the homeless feeders of Gloversville right where it hurts. The proprietors of the lunch wagons and quick lunch rooms of the city are going to hold a meeting the first of next week to arrange an advance In the price of the "eats" served in the lunch houses. The devotees of the golden baked bean, the tissue paper sandwich and the asbestos pie will shortly he called upon to "come across" with more revenue for their favorite dish.

An advance in the price of the lunch wagon goodies is apparently justified and not unexpected. Everything that the lunch rooms sell, including the cost of the raw materials in all manners of prepared goods has been going up steadily for several months past, but there has been no increase in the sale prices, except in the case of pie, cheese and beans. Pies. which were formerly cut in four pieces are now cut in five, cheese sandwiches are now ten cents instead of five, and a plate of beans now cost fifteen cents, where they formerly could be bought for five or ten cents. The prices of meat sandwiches, meat dishes, eggs and many other things sold by the lunch room have not been increased heretofore, but with the prices of all food steadily advancing and no prospect of lower prices the lunch men feel that prices must now be advanced all along the line.
November 1916, Gloversville Leader Herald, Gloversville, New York.

WHITE HOUSE CAFE

If you go hungry don't blame us, because we are open night and day, and this is what we have to eat and we serve it clean and neat.

— MENU —

SANDWICHES.

Ham, Sliced	05
Ham, Chopped	05
Cheese	05
Swiss	05
Swiss, Imported	10
Limburger	10
Bean	05
Egg, Plain	05
Pork	05
Cannibal	05
Pork, Fried	10
Western	10
Ham and Egg	10
Hamburg	10
Hamburg and Egg	10
Chicken	10
Pickled Tongue	10

HOME MADE PIES.

Mince	05
Apple	05
Pumpkin	05
Chocolate	05
Berry	05
Lemon	05
Cream	05
Cocoanut	05
Custard	05
Raisin	05
Cranberry	05

MISCELLANEOUS.

Pork and Beans	05
Pork, Beans and Bread	10
Bread and Milk	10
Crackers and Milk	10
Doughnuts	05

Oysters in Season.

DRINKS.

Coffee	05
Ice Milk	05
Cocoa	05
Lemonade	05
Cordial	10

SWART & EVANS, Proprietors

Walton Reporter - August 17, 1907

The New College Diner started out as a $27,000 Ward and Dickinson diner that replaced another Ward and Dickinson diner that was only a couple of years old. Amazingly, that older diner was moved just a couple doors down the same street and was kept open as its own business.

The New College Diner was an iconic presence on West College Avenue in State College, Pennsylvania for many years. Over the years, the diner has become famous for their grilled stickies. In April 2018, it was reported that the diner was set to close. The current leasee of thirty years lamented over his rent tripling in recent years and will continue to make the grilled stickies, but do so at an off-site bakery.

(Hanover History Center)

EVENING SPECIALS

SANDWICHES

Club Sandwich	50c	Hamburger	15c
Sliced Chicken	40c	Harlem Burger	20c
Chicken Salad	25c	Cheese Burger	20c
Hot Beef—Potatoes	40c	Hot Pork—Potatoes	40c
Fried Egg	15c	Cheese	15c
Ham and Egg	30c	Boiled Ham on Bun	15c
Baked Ham on Bun	25c	Fried Ham on Bun	25c
Cold Pork	25c	Cold Beef	25c
Deviled Egg	15c	Bacon, Lettuce & Tomato	30c
Ham Steak	30c	Lettuce and Tomato	20c
Cube Steak	30c	Bacon and Egg	30c
Western	25c	Sardine	20c
Boiled Egg and Olive	20c	Ham Salad	15c
Tongue	25c	Salmon	20c
Bacon, or Bun 15c, Bread 20c		Oyster	20c

Toasted Bread or Roll 5c Extra
Lettuce and Mayonaise 5c Extra
One of the following: Onion, Pickle or Relish may be had
With the Above Sandwiches. No Charge.
Sandwiches with Everything on 5c Extra.

FROM THE GRILL

2 Eggs Fried or Scrambled	25c
1 or 2 Poached or Boiled Eggs	35c

Western Omelet	45c	Tomato Omelet	45c
Plain Omelet	45c	Cheese Omelet	45c
Bacon Omelet	45c	Jelly Omelet	45c
Ham Omelet	45c	Mushroom Omelet	45c
	Spanish Omelet	45c	

Ham and Fried Eggs or Bacon and Fried Eggs, and Potatoes 65c
Ham Steak, or order of Bacon and Potatoes 55c
Milk Toast 20c Bread and Milk 10c

Bread and Butter or Toast served with the above orders.
Beverage 5c Extra

T-bone Steak	$1.10	Cube Steak	60c
Club Steak	85c	Pork Chops	50c
Lamb Chops	60c	Hamburg Steak	45c
Veal Chops	60c	Harlam Burger Steak	50c
Calves Liver, Bacon	70c	Sausage	55c

Two Vegetables, Bread and Butter Included. Drink 5c Extra.

SORRY We Cannot Be Responsible For Lost Articles

FOUNTAIN MENU

SUNDAES

Fresh Fruit Sundaes 20c

	20c	Maple Walnut	20c
	20c	Collegian	25c
	20c	Mexican	20c
	20c	Chocolate Nut	20c
	20c	Hot Fudge	20c
	20c	Cold Fudge	20c
	20c	Banana Split	30c

Crushed Peanuts 5c extra.

DRINKS

	25c	Ginger Ale (Lrg. Bottle)	25c
	15c	Soda (Large Bottle)	25c
	15c	Lemonade	10c
	20c	Grape Juice	10c
	15c	Lemon Blend	10c
	5c	Root Beer	5c
	5c	Hot Chocolate	5c
	15c	Pineapple & Tomato Juice	10c
	10c	Postum	5c
drinks 5c; Large drinks			10c
	10c; Large		15c

CAMPBELL SOUPS

	15c	Heinz Chicken Noodle	15c
	15c	Heinz Mushroom	15c
Heinz Chicken	15c	Heinz Bean	15c
Heinz Vegetable	15c	Heinz Vegetable Beef	15c

These Soups Include Saltines, Bread and Butter 5c Extra

SPECIAL

Hot Beef or Pork Sandwiches and Potatoes 40c
Assorted Cold Vegetable Salad 40c; Special Fruit Salad 55c
Tomato Salad Shrimp Salad 50c
Assorted Cold Cuts Cole Slaw 25c
Potato Salad 30c

A Deposit Must Be Made on All Dishes Taken Out

Grand Opening
Thursday, July 13th
JEAN'S DINER
Northeast Corner Monroe and Warren
ROY RICCELLI, Proprietor.
Specializing in Extra Quality Food at Moderate Prices!
OPEN DAY AND NIGHT
— Noon and Evening Menu —

CHILI 15   HOME-MADE SOUPS 10

SANDWICHES
HAMBURGER 10	EGG 10
CHEESEBURGER 15	CHEESE 10
CANADIAN BACON ... 20	WESTERN 20
FRIED HAM 20	CHICKEN SALAD 20
TENDERLOIN STEAK . 20	HAM SALAD 15
BACON 20	LETTUCE, TOMATO ... 15

SPECIALS
BAKED HAM SANDWICH WITH POTATO SALAD ... 25
BAKED HAM WITH POTATO SALAD 30
CHICKEN SALAD WITH SLICED TOMATOES 35
HARD BOILED EGGS WITH POTATO SALAD 30
FRIED FISH WITH POTATO SALAD 30
TUNA FISH SALAD WITH SLICED TOMATOES ... 30
SALMON SALAD WITH SLICED TOMATOES 35
SHRIMP SALAD WITH SLICED TOMATOES 30

SHORT ORDERS
T-BONE STEAK 60	POTATOES, VEGETABLE, BREAD, BUTTER, COFFEE INCLUDED
PORK CHOPS—2 55	
HAMBURGER STEAK ... 40	
HAM AND EGGS 50	POTATOES, BREAD, BUTTER, COFFEE, INCLUDED
BACON AND EGGS 50	
EGGS—2—FRIED 35	
OMELETTES: HAM, BACON, CHEESE, OR JELLY ... 45	2 EGGS ANY STYLE, TOAST, COFFEE 25

BEVERAGES
COFFEE 05	CHOCOLATE MILK ... 05
MILK 05	MALTED MILK 15
COCA-COLA 05	MILK SHAKE 10

DESSERTS
SLICED PINEAPPLE . 10	CANTALOUPE 15
CANNED PEACHES ... 10	PIE 10
STEWED PRUNES 10	PIE ALAMODE 15
	CHOCOLATE SUNDAE . 10

You'll Enjoy Our Special Breakfasts.
FREE COFFEE ON OPENING DAY!

Sandusky Daily News - July 12, 1939

Jean's Diner in Sandusky, Ohio was a Ward and Dickinson that spent most of the 1930s in Defiance, Ohio. Roy A. Riccelli named the diner at the corner of Warren Avenue and Monroe Street after his daughter. In 1947, the Ward and Dickinson diner was replaced by a used O'Mahony diner which still had its porcelain enamel panels for its past incarnation, the Avenue Diner. Neil Zurcher, in one of his "One Tank Trips" articles, mentioned that the original Ward and Dickinson was sent to Marblehead where he patronized the diner in the 1960s.

Like many diners of the time, Jean's Diner was a family run business. Roy's wife, Mrs. Ciro Riccelli not only cared for the family's children, but also peeled and cut the potatoes for french fries and made the chili and soups for the diner. As the children became of age to work, they could often be seen working at the diner, doing any jobs they were capable of doing. The fruits and vegetables for the diner came from Roy's uncle, Ruggiero Riccelli who ran a local delicatessen.

Unfortunately neither diner survives today. After the Riccellis sold Jean's Diner in 1964, it went through numerous owners and was bricked over. Later on, CVS Pharmacy bought the lot and put up a store.

Sunday Dinner at the Diner

Rochester Democrat and Chronicle - May 21, 1950

Cortland Standard - November 30, 1935

Above

The Palace Diner was still growing by leaps and bounds at the time when this ad was placed in the newspaper. Just a couple of months before, a Ward and Dickinson diner was replaced with a larger O'Mahony diner. That Ward and Dickinson diner replaced a smaller Ward and Dickinson diner in October of 1930 that was only on location for a little more than three years.

Left

Dauphin's Superior Diner was the first name for today's Highland Park Diner. Around 1948 the Superior diner, built in Albion, New York, replaced a Sterling dinette model. In 1976, the diner became an Off Track Betting (OTB) parlor before Bob Malley bought the diner in 1986 and restored it to its orignal lustre.

Chapter 7

Sectional Diner Construction

Yesterday marked the opening of the new, larger Wayside Diner located at the corner of Ridge Road West and Dewey Avenue. Hundreds of friends of the proprietors, Agnes and Harry Pratt, visited the car, the newest, of its type in Western New York, to express their congratulations and several bouquets and baskets of flowers added brilliant color to the modernistic design of the interior.

The original Wayside Diner was opened by the Pratts five years ago on the same site where the new car is located. The idea of the diner caught on immediately and soon difficulties were experienced in seating the ever increasing number of customers. Knowing that the size of the car was too small, Mr. Pratt began making plans last Fall for enlargement. In order that the diner chosen would best suit the demands of their customers, Mr. and Mrs. Pratt asked the chief designer for Rochester Grills, specialists in the manufacture of deluxe dining cars, to study their situation and advise what he thought best.

The result is the new deluxe dining car opened yesterday. The beauty of design, both exterior and interior are much admired by visitors and attracts immediate attention from passersby. Entrance into the diner is gained by two large doors in the center of the car. One is somewhat astonished by the spaciousness of the interior, every foot of floor space being utilized to the best advantage. Booths for family dining are attractively decorated, and for those who prefer, a long counter with comfortable stools is provided. Refrigerator, coffee urn, sink, stove, cupboards and all kitchen equipment is of shinmg bright metal. Space for new dishes and gleaming pots and pans is provided under the counter. Steam tables and warming ovens complete the kitchen ensemble.

-Tenth Ward Courier. May 13, 1937

By the time the Bixler Company's business waned in 1935, all the eastern companies were including a row of booths in the design of their diners. The complement of booths and counter seating was now the norm in the production of diners in the eastern half of the country. With the end of Bixler imminent, it did not mean the end of their design of sectional construction. Three companies that had significant ties to upstate New York would make a scene in the Great Lakes' diner trade, although the focus of this chapter lie practically on New York state.

After Bixler's business dried up, they had to let their employees go. For our story, that meant Rochester, New York native J. H. Shale was out of a job. Shale moved back home to Rochester and obtained a position with a local furniture maker, Barnard & Simonds. While with Barnard & Simonds he was soon placed in charge of a subsidiary known as Rochester Grills. The company did not describe their product as a diner per-say. A June 30, 1935 advertisement in The New York Times noted that, "the new sectional restaurant building" was being manufactured and sold under the supervision of J.H. Shale, formerly of Bixler Mfg Co.[2] This move may have been the one that started the mini-movement of the sectional diner in central and western New York from 1935 to 1942. The sectional diner was just the latest progression in the evolution of the portable food building started by the lunch wagon.

It is possible that Rochester Grills was a secondary job for Mr. Shale, though research on Shale proves elusive. The J. H. Shale name has been associated with furniture built by Barnard & Simonds and pianos built by a Rochester concern, but neither can be verified as being the same Shale connected with Rochester Grills, as two J.H. Shales lived in Rochester at the time.

Above:
Rochester Grills used this advertisement in the classified section of newspapers around upstate New York. Many designers might cringe at the numerous fonts being used, but Rochester Grills hoped that the advertisement would stick out like a sore thumb in a section crammed with words.

Right:

The Wayside Diner replaced a five year old Ward & Dickinson diner. The replacement diner, a Rochester Grills diner, was intended to be larger and more modern. Because Rochester Grills were built in four foot sections, their width is could expanded to 14 or 16 feet. Indeed in many eyes, a Rochester Grills was more modern and spacious than a Ward & Dickinson diner. The Rochester Grills also had a barrel roof which gave the diner more height, hence more spacious to everyone. The Ward & Dickinson could have all modern equipment and compete on the equipment level, but the five year old Ward could not compete on the spacious level.

Ward & Dickinson did build two and three piece diners. They also built a 12.5 foot wide diner on occasion too. The owners could have went back for one of these larger Ward & Dickinson diners, but they chose the local concern.

LANE'S DINER, 1417 MT. HOPE AVENUE, ROCHESTER 7, NEW YORK, MONROE 9125
JACOB DE COOK, Proprietor

Previous Page Top:
Lane's Diner in Rochester, New York was an early Rochester Grills diner.
(Art Goody)

Rochester Grills was only a small-time concern. In the large city of Rochester, they probably received little if any press. Borrowing the same concepts in construction from Bixler, their diners were built in segments and shipped to the site where the diner was to be reconstructed. Often, Rochester Grills would hire local help for the reconstruction, just as Bixler did. They would still send a knowledgable person to act as foreman. They often sent John Cody of Canadice. In the 1930's news like this would always make the local news section. For example, the Wayland Register reported, "John Cody left on Monday to build a lunch car in Olean." in June of 1939 [1]. Unlike the diners built in Chautauqua County, these diners were fifteen feet wide and were shipped in four foot sections.

Another benefit of being built in segments was that this allowed for a diner to be as long as the owners' pockets were deep. The Rochester Grill in Bradford, Pennsylvania was 76 feet long. Doing the math, this would be nineteen segments![3] The 1940 newspaper announcement for the opening of the Congress Street Diner in Bradford told a little more about Rochester Grills:

> The exterior of the walls of the car are constructed of non-rust metal with a cream enamel finish, trimmed in brown. The walls, J. H. Shale of the construction pointed out, are filled with insulating material, which renders them fire and vermin proof...

Like Bixler—and by this time, diners built in New Jersey—Rochester Grills had booths along the outer wall, parallel to the counter. but instead of room for four people, six people could fit comfortably in a Rochester Grills booth. Just like the Ward & Dickinson deluxe diners, they left space for an optional kitchen, but instead of being only one hundred square feet big, the Bradford Diner had a twenty-foot by fifteen-foot kitchen which gave a total of three hundred square foot of room.

Not all Rochester Grills had a built-in kitchen. Griffeth's Swanky Diner in Syracuse did not come with a factory-built kitchen. But it did seem that Rochester Grills included men's and women's bathrooms inside their diners. This was a service started by the Tierney Dining Car Company in 1927, and was becoming more of a norm in diners.

Previous Page:
The Rochester Grills in Norwich, New York was best known as Scarcella's Diner though it was first known as McKee's Diner when this photo was taken.
(Chenango County Historical Society)

Right:

Sterling had two salesmen in central New York and found a good number of locations for their diners. The Homestead Grill opened up in Seneca Falls, New York in 1938.

Above:

Sitar's Diner is an early Sterling diner that was in Johnson City, New York. Note the transom windows, which were excluded from later Sterling diners. Sterling did a good business in central New York.

(Broome County Historical Society)

On the right is the former Crosser's Diner in Lisbon, Ohio, which is a smaller Sterling dinette model.

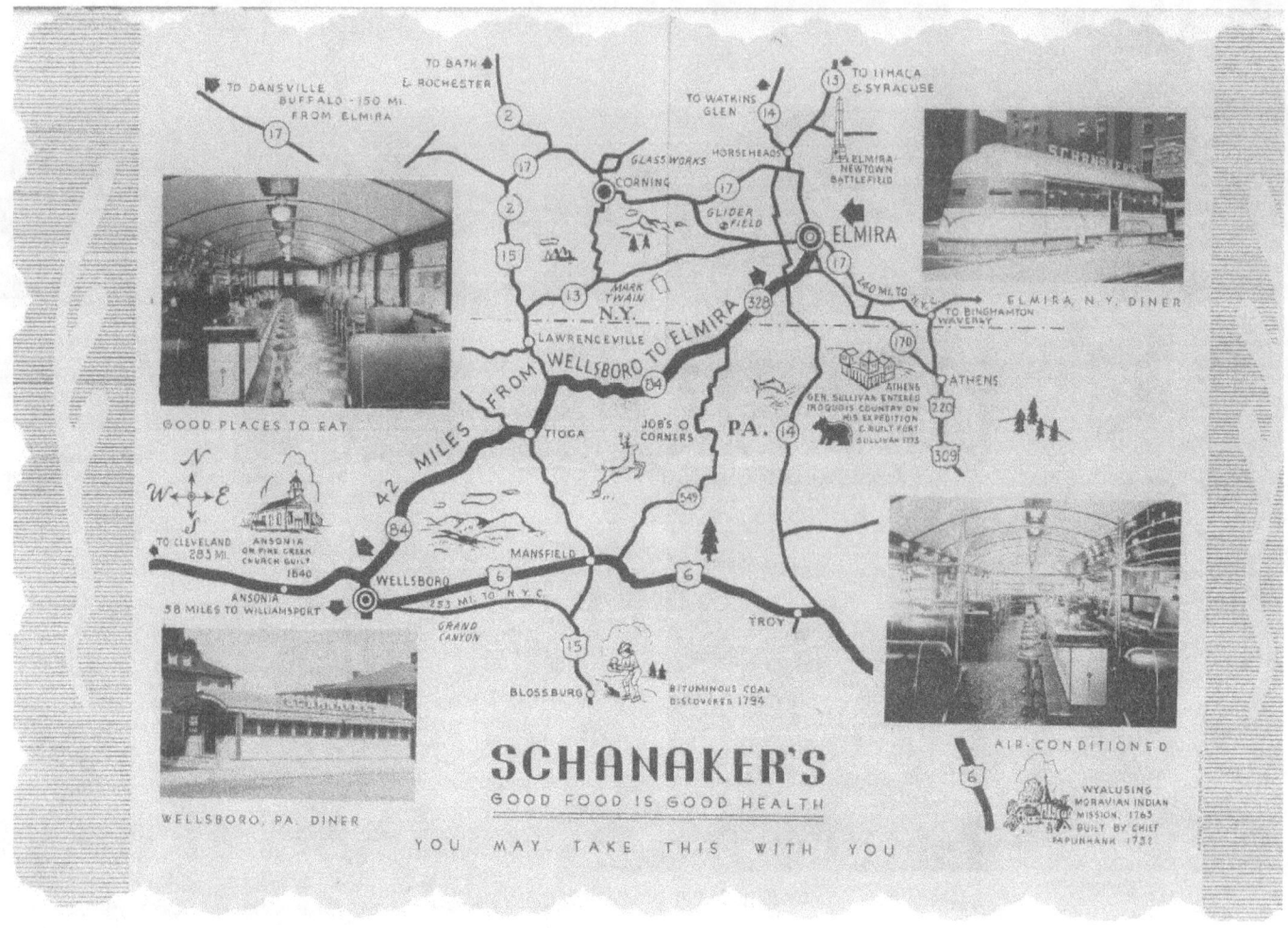

J. H. Shale, along with Louis Voelker, patented a 15-by-25-foot diner in 1938.[4] They noted that this building would be a "one man diner, seating ten." The company even ventured into portable buildings for bowling alleys and stores, similar to what Bixler did earlier. Also in 1938, Shale partnered with Frank J. Minges and Carl F. W. Kaelber to form the Loumar Corporation, whose goal was to "Deal in portable restaurant buildings."[5] The Corporation opened up the County Club Diner in Rochester, one of the larger Rochester Grills built.

Albert Herbert ran one of the early Rochester Grills in Rochester. By late 1937 he decided to start up another diner, and instead of having Rochester Grills build the new diner, he hired local contractor Joseph Entress to build a diner. Herbert's Diner at 503 Monroe Avenue in Rochester opened up May 8, 1938. The diner itself looked quite similar to a Rochester Grill with the high barrel roof and room for booths along the windows. The diner did advertise that they offered air-conditioning and mentioned that the diner would be odor-free every day of the year.[6]

Previous Page:

There were two Sterling built diners each known as Schanacher's Diner. One was in Elmira, New York and the other was in Wellsboro, Pennsylvania. The Wellsboro location still operates today as the Wellsboro Diner while the Elmira diner was taken down stream during Hurricane Agnes in 1972 and was deemed unsalvagable.

The Schanacher's seen on the right, the Elmira diner, was of a different design than your typical Sterling diner. Sterling called this model their Streamliner. One instillation of a streamliner in Pennsylvania even had part of the diner inside of a tunnel to give the feeling that the diner was actually a streamlined train car.

Rochester became a hub of sectional built diners from 1936 to 1941. A second company not actually located in Rochester would have a huge influence in the area. The Sterling Dining Car Company was an offshoot of J.D. Judkins of Merrimac, Massachusetts, maker of high-end automobile bodies. Judkins saw the dining car business as a way to keep afloat until the Depression was over. The company bought a design patent from Bertrand Harley, a Penn Yan, New York resident, and started making diners in late 1935. Harley got a commission from every diner that Sterling sold, and he also became the company's best salesman. Between Harley in Penn Yan and Anthony Tomberelli in Rochester, central and western New York was covered by impressive Sterling salesmen. Tomberelli also started a chain of three Sterling diners aptly called the Sterling Diners, centered around Rochester. Tomberelli started out in the diner business by brokering sales of Bixler diners in upstate New York, so he was familiar with the benefit of sectional diners.

Sterlings, especially their Streamliner models, were not built for the long haul. As for the engineering of Sterlings, and water infiltration, the main fault is found in an overly constructed, overly heavy roof, thin wall sections supporting the heavy roof, and poor weather seal. The windows and porcelain panels eventually allowed water to rot the walls. To be fair, Judkins built luxury coaches, not diners.

Judkins cars, like most luxury cars, were intended to be used for no more than a decade or so. In many historians' view, they built their diners with no thought given to longevity. While they were watertight when first erected on site, having seams every four feet meant there were literally hundreds of feet of seams running along the roof, walls, and floor—a recipe for leakage. For example, the type of single-pane windows with simple aluminum frames would not be

considered weather tight or efficient by modern building standards. But in the 1930s they would have been the norm. The five hand-crank end windows on a Streamliner were simply automobile window technology.[7]

Visitors of the Modern Diner in Pawtucket, Rhode Island will note it still has the scrolled crank handles. These are the same as found in a Duesenberg or Lincoln. While the Modern may look well maintained, it absolutely suffers from chronic water infiltration.

A couple of Sterlings made it to Ohio. There was a Streamliner model in Warren, and the Gateway Diner just outside of Dayton. Four Sterling diners even made it to Cleveland. But New York State was the prime spot for Sterling, outside of New England.

A few Sterlings have been disassembled within the last fifteen years. A group of diner preservationists including Colin Strayer, Kathy Stribley, and Daniel Zilka spent about ten days taking the Liberty Diner of Syracuse apart. The diner sat in the American Diner Museum's storage for a score of years before being sold to Tom Mertl in Mountain View, California, where he hopes to reconstruct it.[8] One historian says that due to the water leakage, the walls will need to be completely rebuilt in order for this diner to come back to life.

One more company would take a chance building sectional diners in central New

Above:

Four Sterling diners were once located in Cleveland, Ohio. This one was on the 9400 block of Euclid Avenue.

(Cleveland Public Library/Official City of Cleveland Photograph)

York. In 1939, a young Arthur Halladay and an older Morris Whitehouse built two diners in Watertown, New York. Recognizing the potential of the business, they began to look for a permanent place to build their diners. They chose Oswego at the Nu-Type Tool Corporation building on West First Street in 1939.[9] For over a year in 1939 and 1940, the company received good press and talked about the possibility of building three to five diners a week in the near future.

The Oswego Palladium-Times on July 29, 1939 explained how a General Diner was built.

> It is 36 feet long, 16 feet wide and seven feet high, and will accommodate 50 people. The framework is now being covered with treated wall board, and a coat of metal sheeting will be placed over this. Each diner is completely equipped with counter, stools and booths before it leaves the company plant.

Then they went on to explain how these diners were brought to their location.

> To avoid any such trouble as suffered by the legendary man who built a boat in his cellar and then couldn't get it out, the diners are built in such a way that they are easily knocked down in sections. They are transported to their places of destination on tractor trailers. When they are placed, it requires only tightening of a few bolts to reunite the sections.

Similar to Rochester Grills, the bathrooms were also placed inside of the diner.[9]

Newspaper articles continued in the Oswego Palladium-Times talking about diners sent to central New York locations like Utica, Syracuse, Cortland, and Frankfort. Some of their diners made it into the northern Adirondacks to Canton and Malone. These would be some of the last new diners to be placed in the Adirondacks.

These diners were by far the lowest costing new diner on the market, outside of

Above:

One of the first General diners built went to Maple View, New York, a small crossroads hamlet south of Watertown on US Route 11.

(Brian Butko)

Previous Page Top:

Exterior photo of the Malone Diner shows the sectional design of a General diner. They were built in the factory, knocked down and packaged on a truck. Once the truck arrives atthe destination, factory employees would reassemble the diner on location. General Diners bragged that only a few bolts needed to be tightened and the diner was together.

(Skip Goodman)

Previous Page Middle:

Interior photo of a General diner. The Malone Diner in Malone, New York was one of a number of General diners which made their way into the northern Adirondacks.

(Spencer Stewart)

Previous Page Bottom:

Denny's Diner in Syracuse, New York was a General diner. Denny's was placed in Syracuse at 515 South Geddes. Syracuse had a couple of General built diners and even hosted the company in 1942. Though it is unknown if General built any diners while located in Syracuse.

(Larry Cultrera)

the one-man Rochester Grill unit. General's standard model was priced at $5,500 and their high-end diners started at $10,000, ranging up to $16,000. Starting with three employees, they were up to fourteen employees by June of 1940, but a July 16, 1940 article possibly summed up why the company would soon end: "[D]ue to increasing business it has been necessary to enlarge the carpentry staff and officials of the company, Arthur Halladay Jr., and M. H. Whitehouse report a shortage of workmen at the present time."[10] With World War II looming ahead, every diner builder would practically shut down during the war.

Late August of 1940 was probably the peak time for the short-lived company. They had twenty employees and had just placed five diners in one week, ready to start business. They were now proclaiming that their diners could be set up on site in a mere three hours! Of course Mr. Whitehouse added, "In about a week from the time the diner has been erected it can be placed in operation." The last newspaper article concerning the company came out on September 29, 1940 and stated, "Paul Kless and Leo Osclaveta who run a chain of cabin camps in Florida," were placing an order for a diner to be sent to their Miami business.[11]

After this article, the news stopped. Nothing is known about the end of this company. A quick blurb mentioned that the company was in different quarters in Oswego in early 1941,[12] and then the next mention of this company came from a Syracuse newspaper in their classified section. A tiny advertisement in 1942 mentioned that General Diners were being built in Syracuse, but nothing else is known of this attempt.[13] After the war, Arthur Halladay showed up running a Ward & Dickinson diner known as the Amherst Diner in Buffalo before moving to Glens Falls, New York. Morris Whitehouse stayed in Syracuse where he had other concerns.

Today, there may be one or two General diners left. Frank and Mary's Diner in downtown Cortland, New York is a General which has been significantly remodeled over the years. The diner serves simple diner food twenty four hours a day. Friede's Diner in Watertown, New York is believed to be a General also. This diner is quite original, and does fit the design of a General diner. We know it was built in 1939, and local lore says it was built in Watertown.

1 Wayland Register, Wayland, New York, June 22, 1939
2 New York Times, New York City, New York June 30, 1935
3 Bradford Era, Bradford, Pennsylvania August 16, 1940
4 Design Permit 111,667 October 11, 1938 filed April 27, 1938
5 Rochester Daily Record, Rochester, New York March 2, 1939
6 Rochester Democrat and Chronicle, Rochester New York, May 8, 1938
7 emails with Colin Strayer
8 Daniel DeBolt, Mountain View Voice, Mountain View, California May 8, 2008
9 Oswego Palladium-Times, Oswego, New York July 29, 1939
10 Oswego Palladium-Times, Oswego, New York July 16, 1940
11 Oswego Palladium-Times, Oswego, New York September 29, 1940
12 Oswego Palladium-Times, Oswego, New York June 4, 1941
13 Syracuse Herald American, Syracuse, New York March 30, 1942

Next Page:
History has a msytery as to why Joseph Entress was hired to build Herbert's new diner in Rochester . Herbert's first diner was a Richester Grill. Maybe He had ideas on how a diner could be laid out, or maybe Entress gave him a better deal. Diner history has given us a number of one off builders.

Rochester's Newest, Most Modern!
HERBERT'S DINER

503 MONROE AVE.
Opposite Rowley St.

OPENS TODAY

IT'S AIR CONDITIONED! It will be comfortable and odor-free every day in the year. It will feature personally-selected quality foods, courteous, prompt service for short orders and complete luncheons and dinners with sea foods a specialty. Open day and night. Stop in the next time you are hungry! Begin a habit of dining that will give you a new conception of what a diner should be! Albert Herbert and A. C. Jefferds, proprietors, formerly of Mt. Hope Avenue, will lend their every effort to make this Rochester's outstanding diner!

The builder, Joseph Entress, is thankful for the opportunity afforded in being instrumental in offering to the public of Rochester its latest and most modern diner. "Herbert's" past reputation for serving fine foods being widely known, you can be assured that in return for your patronage you will be entirely satisfied in every way!

Equipment, Foods, Meats, Supplies Used by Herbert's Diner Furnished By The Following Well-Known Firms . . .

BARTHOLOMAY CO.
Bartholomay Quality Ice Cream Served Exclusively
555 ST. PAUL ST.   MAIN 6520

COLDWATER LUMBER CO.
All Lumber and Lumber Products Furnished By Us
COLDWATER, N. Y.   GEN. 6084-R

C. F. HAYES COMPANY
Another Complete Installation by C. F. Hayes Co. (Restaurant Equipment)
273 CENTRAL AVE.   STONE 2446

GENERAL BAKING CO.
Bond Bakers Products Served Exclusively Delivered Fresh Twice Daily
392 NORTH ST.   STONE 4700

WHITE STAR BAKERY
Complete Line of "Baked Goods You'll Like"
1467 E. MAIN ST.   CUL. 2600

MEISENZAHL'S DAIRY
Pasteurized Milk and Cream "Direct from the Farm"
HENRIETTA, N. Y.   MON. 8029-J

EMPIRE OUTDOOR ADVERTISING CO., Inc.
Neon Displays
161 HUMBOLDT ST.   CUL. 273

BOOTHBY MARKET
Fine Meats and Groceries
450 BROOKS AVE.   GEN. 3850

HEAD-MILLER, Inc.
Foods and Beverages of Value
500 WEST AVE.   GEN. 314

FEARLESS DISHWASHER Co.
Fabricators of the Equipment for Herbert's Diner
175 COLVIN ST.   GEN. 1044

EGAN FRUIT & VEGETABLE CO.
Supplies, Provisions for Hotels, Restaurants, Clubs and Institutions
140 ROSEWOOD TER.   CUL. 1566

GAR WOOD INDUSTRIES
Air Conditioning and Heating Systems
16 N. UNION ST.   STONE 3612

Coffee has always been an essential part of the diner experience. Ever since coffee has found its way into the lunch wagon, many Americans have had a strong love affair with coffee. For many years, almost from the beginning, coffee was five cents a cup. Coffee survived many years at five cents a cup. In chapter 6, a menu from 1907 shows coffee at five cents a cup, and this price stayed steady through World War II. The articles that you will read below pick up right around 1950, when things started to destabilize.

Coffee Prices Rocketing and with the Boost the Traditional 5 Cent Cup Exits

What price your cup of coffee for this morning's breakfast? Look up the answer on your grocery bill or the restaurant menu. With coffee prices now, it's a case of here today and up there tomorrow.

If you breakfast at home, it's for sure that your coffee is costing more than it used to cost. At your restaurant, it may still be served forth for the traditional nickel, or the bold-letter sign back of the counter may say "Coffee, 10c."

RISING PRICES in the wholesale coffee market are back of all this. Food merchants in Albany say that wholesale prices, which have been on the upward trend for months past, are now climbing still higher. Restaurants also have to buy coffee stocks at the higher wholesale figures.

In one chain of diners the five cent cup of coffee went up to a dime last week, and the same pries boost went into effect in restaurants in various parts of the city.

There has been no city-wide raise in the price per cup, although some restaurant proprietors, where prices now are 10 or 15 cents, said they will have to charge more if the wholesale rises continue.

ONE FOOD STORE notified its customer that a brand of coffee which a short time ago sold at 65 cents a pound would have a new price tag of 85 cents today.

An increase of seven cents a pound on a leading brand, effective Friday, boosted to 26 cents the per-pound increase during the past month. It is rumored in the trade, according to a local retailer, that the price of coffee may reach a dollar a pound before the new year. Restaurants reported the wholesale price up 15 to 30 cents a pound during the past three weeks, in addition to previous increases.

RESTAURATEURS, of course may ponder the question of upping prices a little on some food dishes 'in order to leave the price of coffee —and their customers' sunny dispositions—undisturbed. But those who were asked about this plan by The Times-Union didn't think well of it.

"We've tried that." the diner manager said. "But the customers notice the increase on

a food item just as quick as they do on the coffee. In fact, I found that we got more complaints about that than about a higher coffee price. When we raised coffee to a dime last week, we dropped the prices a nickel on several menu items, such a roast beef, ham steak and calves liver and bacon. They noticed that right away, too."
Another said he thought such a system was "not right."
"You should get the prices on the product itself, and each item should stand on its own," he declared.
FOR THE PAST YEAR or so, the wholesale price rise has been reflected in some eating places by a "minimum check" of 10 cents while the cost of a cup of coffee served with food remained five cents, in some instances this plan is continued but in others the price is now 10 cents for one cup of served with food and five cents for a second cup. Dealers said the shortage was attributed to three causes: A poor production year in Brazil; the Brazilian government's curtailment of coffee growing after an over-production season seven years ago, and the fact that coffee consumption is greater than ever before. But some expressed the opinion also that "gouging by speculators" is partly to blame.
November 14, 1949 Albany, New York, Times Union

Milk Gains Popularity As Coffee Prices Rise

It's an ill wind — for coffee distributors this time. And maybe it'll blow some good toward the dairy farmer. The recent increase in the price of coffee already has resulted in stiff consumer resistance. Housewives say they'll refuse to buy at present prices. Already too, a campaign is on foot to have coffee drinkers switch to milk. A good idea. And, if the price stays high long enough all but the most hardened coffee addict might grow accustomed to milk so that his former drink would hold no charm for him, even when the price did go down. Coffee rationing during the war taught a lot of people to drink other beverages. Maybe price rises will continue the lesson.
 Seriously speaking, the January issue of Pure Milk, organ of the Pure Milk association sees 1954 as a rough year ahead. Most Optimistic factor in the coming year is the rapidly growing population and the dairy industry's planned program of advertising, and merchandising. This is a year for planning, for watching economic corners sharply, for stepping up efficiency to get the most out of everything, for maximum yields in field crops, as well as in milk and for pulling together with fellow dairymen, says the lead editorial
January 27, 1954 Joliet, Illinois, Farmers Weekly Review

Price May Reach $1.25 next month, despite resistance.

Sales Are Off as Much As 50% at Some Points; Restaurant Men Push Milk and Tea Instead

NEW YORK, Jan. 26—Coffee prices rose in a steady spiral today with some resistance from housewives and restaurateurs. On the other hand, retailers in many localities reported that sales had increased recently as householders rushed to stock up.

Cities which reported "runs" by housewives trying to beat new price rises included Des Moines, la.; San Francisco, Minneapolis and Madison, Wis. Experts warned that the worst was yet to come, with prices possibly hitting $1.25 a pound at the end of February. They said retailers still had not passed on to their customers the latest wholesale price raises. "Too High for Me" Coffee was becoming so precious that in Chicago a gang of burglars hijacked 12,000 pounds—valued at $1 a pound— from a warehouse. Police said coffee had joined liquor and cigarettes as high-grade loot.

In Southern California, housewives were reported sending chain letters urging recipients to switch to some other beverage for a month Jo force prices down. Los Angeles housewives were talking of possible "coffeeless Wednesdays" and a mild buyers' strike was reported there. Retailers in Washington, D. C, reported some customers were switching from luxury blends to standard brands.

A radio station at Council Bluffs, la., said a telephone survey showed coffee consumption there and in nearby Omaha, Neb. is down "20% to 40%."

The station, campaigning to bring prices down, has played a jingle over the air: "I like coffee, I like tea—but coffee is too high for me."

Used as Sales Leader

The Rhode Island, Wisconsin and Iowa Restaurant Associations joined New York food retailers in urging their members to push sales of milk and tea to customers to bring coffee prices back "within reason." New York food retailers took similar action. The Rhode Island Retail Grocers Association reported that coffee sales dropped 50% there last week due to housewife resistance. Two food associations representing New York retailers issued a similar report. However, James M. O'Connor, president of the National Coffee Association, denied these reports, saying that "nobody on earth' could give an exact picture so soon.

In Boston and Des Moines, la., several stores were selling coffee at cost or taking a loss, using the commodity as a "leader" for other sales, one Des Moines retailer, for example, sold coffee at 79 cents a pound with each $3 purchase of other foodstuffs.

Coffee in This Diner Will Stay at 5 Cents a Cup

Like King Canute defying the incoming tide, Louis A. Muscato, a diner operator, today swore to stick with his 5-cent cup of coffee. Pleased but bewildered doughnut dunkers are buying 300 to 400 cups a day at that price Outside his diner at 2201 Elmwood Ave. [Buffalo, New York], near Kenmore Ave., stands a 4-by-6foot sign proclaiming, "Coffee STILL 5c." "Sure, coffee prices are too high," Mr. Muscato said this morning. "Look, this brand I buy wholesale, we use 70 to 80 pounds a week, goes up from 95 cents to an even buck tomorrow morning. So what do I do tomorrow morning? I put up another sign inside to discourage my coffee drinkers, 'Tea—Two Cups for 5c." Mr. Muscato figures he makes "maybe half a cent" on each cup of nickel coffee. Meanwhile, the Buffalo & Western New York Restaurant Association was hinting darkly that restaurants generally may go to 15 cents a cup soon as a result of the newest wholesale price rise.

"It is unreasonable to expect operators to take a loss on coffee sales indefinitely," contended Lawrence O. Belgrade, association president, after a meeting of 135 restaurateurs Monday evening. He said operators "holding the price to 10 cents" ace finding themselves in "a really-serious squeeze."

Drive-in Offers a Cup For 4 Cents, Breaks Even
LIBERAL, Kan., Jan. 26 <AP>—
Another cafe operator has taken action against the widespread increase of coffee prices from a nickel to a dime per cup, and more.

Last week Paul Park said he wouldn't boost the price because he makes $90-a-week profit on coffee in his restaurant at the nickel level. Monday Jim Lofland cut the price to 4 cents at his drive-in place. "I figured it up, Mr. Lofland said, "I can break even at 4 cents a cup. Coffee is just an accommodation for our customers."

January 26, 1954 United Press

How about a "Coffeeless Wednesday"?

Many Geneva coffee lovers say they would go along with the idea. The consensus seems to be that, with the experts predicting a price of $1.20 a pound, "something has got to be done!" Rep. Lawrence H

NOTICE!

Due to the large increase in Coffee prices, we are forced to raise Our Prices to

10¢ per cup

EFFECTIVE

Wednesday
April 1, 1953

**Model Restaurant
Central Diner
Schoony's Diner
Star Restaurant
Kandyland
Secord's Diner
Ace Restaurant
Old Home Restaurant
Cabin Court Diner**

March 25, 1963 Hancock Herald (New York)

Smith (R-Wis.) started, the ball rolling by calling for one day a week when people would not drink the beverage in an effort to clamp a lid on soaring prices.

Mike Matuzas. Proprietor of Clarke's Diner, immediately seconded him.

"Congratulations on your realistic approach to the coffee situation," read his wire to the legislator. "I had the same plan last week." he said. "I think it's a wonderful idea. Everybody likes coffee, but if they left it alone for one day it might help bring the price down."

Mr. Matuzas figured that if buyers went on a voluntary coffee strike one day a week, each restaurant on the average could save five or more pounds. This, he says, would loosen up the supply and help bring prices down. Several restaurant owners said they would go along with the idea but said that it would be up to the consumer to "lay off."

Must Serve if Asked

"We're here to serve the public." said Robert Eakins, Home Dairy Restaurant. "We're pushing other beverages like tea and cocoa, but if a customer asks for coffee, we've got to serve it"

James Legett, Club 86 thought the voluntary coffeeless day was "a good idea."

"Anything to bring

down the price," he said. "Buyers' resistance should help." "It's the only thing that will beat down the coffee price," said Wes Tuxill of Don-Wesley Inc., owners of two Geneva restaurants.

"We'd be in favor of a coffeeless Wednesday, if the people want it, but we'd have to try it if they asked for it" How about the coffee drinkers, particularly the heavy drinkers?

"Fine Idea." was the reaction of William Bergman, 499 Exchange St, who admits to at least seven cups a day. "Might be a good idea for health reasons also. I'd be in favor of it and so would my wife who drinks about five cup a day."

Is It Necessary?

On the other hand. Harris Peck. Waterloo RD 9, downtown store clerk asks: "Is it necessary?" Mr.

Peck drinks an average of eight or nine cups a day. Told it might bring down the price he said he said "Naturally anyone who drinks eight or nine cups a day wants to see the price come down."

Irnea J. Mulvey, 73 Hillcrest Ave., an eight-cup-a-day man, was definitely in favor of the coffeeless

day.

Thomas F. Gibbons, Garden Apartments, who is good for seven cups a day, prefers action by the

State Department to get Brazil to bring the coffee price down. "As far as I am concerned, you can make every day of the week coffeeless," said Harland C. Bush, 34 Seneca St "I'm down to one cup."Mr. Bush, who normally consumes about five cups every 24

hours, protested the price increase, which he claims is wholly artificial. "The Brazilians are trying to pay off their national budget by rigging the coffee price."
Could Be
Some Genevans thought it might be rough getting up Wednesday morning without the bean to support their tired eyelids. Others said. "How about when it gets cold outside? A man needs his coffee then."
The Times survey, accidentally stumbled on the last place in town (as far as we know) where a cup
of Java still goes over the counter for a nickel. "We don't sell coffee to make money on It." said Frank Picchi. Frank's Diner. 92 N. Genesee St. Mr. Picchi could see nothing wrong in the "Coffeeless Wednesday."
January 26, 1954 Geneva, New York, Daily Times

Coffee Prices Continue Slide, But 5-Cent Cup Still Missing

New York (NEA) Wholesale coffee bean prices are boiling down. A pound that cost 95 cents in April went down to 53 cents before simmering up slightly this month.
But if you think this means anything to you and your daily brew, forget all about it. You can put the five-cent cup of coffee in your memory book. Hardly any restauranteur or diner proprietor is going to pass the savings on to you.
Why should he?
In the few years since the 10-cent cup has been standard fare, there has been no decrease in America's coffee consumption. In fact, statistics show that 5,000,000 new coffee drinkers have joined the ranks since 1950.
BESIDES, STATISTICS also show that with higher prices and higher consumption, there has been no increase in the number of pounds of coffee America buys.
 The Pan American Coffee Bureau has drawn the obvious conclusion: this nation has learned how to stretch coffee. And the average American who used to drink 2.67 cups of coffee each day, now drinks 2.67 average cups of hot brown water each day.
 Two years ago, your counterman was following the Bureau's recipe of 45 cups from each pound of coffee. Today, the odds are that he's making closer to 60 cups from a pound that is dropping lower in price than it has been in three years.
AT THE EXECUTIVE office of one leading restaurant chain, however, the purchasing agent put it this way:
"Sure, prices are lower at wholesale. But we've got high operating costs and higher costs of labor. We can't drop our price back to a nickel-a-cup."

At the commissary of a chain whose coffee shops are well known coast-to-coast, a vice president said:

"Sure, prices are lower at wholesale. But nobody is lowering the cost of cream. We put cream in the coffee, don't we?"

AND FROM ONE EMPIRE of restaurants whose coffee today is so weak you can hardly get it out of the cup, comes this tentative suggestion:

"No. We're not going to lower our prices. Why not? It's none of your business."

Small restaurants are quick to admit that they have to follow the prices set by their mammoth competitors.

In some few communities – mostly in the northcentral and northwestern states – coffee is still a nickel. But for most of the nation, who has at least one coffee-break in a restaurant each day, the prices will still be a dime and the motto will still be: "It's not so good to the last drop, so leave a little in the cup."

June 18, 1955 Elmira, New York Star Gazette

Coffee Prices Simmering Down But Five-Cent Cup Is Missing

By WARD CANNEL NEW YORK (NEA) Wholesale coffee bean prices are boiling down. A pound that cost 95 cents in April went down is 53 cents before simmering up slightly this month. But if you think this means anything to you and your daily brew, forget all about it. You can put that five-cent cup of coffee in your memory book. Hardly any restaurateur or diner proprietor it going to pass the saving on to you. Why should he?

In a few years since the 10-cent cup has been standard fare, there has been no decrease in America's coffee consumption. In fact, statistics show that 5,000,000 new coffee drinkers have joined the ranks since 1950.

Besides, statistics also show that with higher prices and higher consumption, there has been no increase in the number of pounds of coffee America buys.

The Pan American Coffee Bureau has drawn the obvious conclusion: this nation has learned how to stretch coffee. And the average American who used to drink 2.67 cups of coffee each day, now drinks 2.67 average cups of hot brown water each day.

Two years ago, your counterman was following the Bureau's recipe of 45 cups from each pound of coffee. Today, the odds are that he's making closer to 60 cups from a pound that is dropping lower in price than it has been in three years.

At the executive office of one leasing restaurant chain, however, the purchasing agent put it this way: Costs Are Up

"Sure, prices are lower at wholesale. But we've got high operating costs and higher costs of labor. We can't drop our price back to a-nickel-a-cup."

At the commissary of a chain whose coffee shops are well-known coast-to-coast, a vice-president said:

"Sure, prices are lower at wholesale. But nobody is lowering the cost of cream. We put cream in the coffee, don't we?"

And from one empire of restaurants whose coffee today is so weak you can hardly get it out of the cup, comes this tentative suggestion:

"No. We're not going to lower our prices. Why not? It's none of your business."

Small restaurants are quick to admit that they have to follow the prices set by their mammoth competitors.

In some few communities — mostly in the north-central and north-western states — coffee is still a nickel. But for most of the nation. Who has at least one coffee-break in a restaurant each day? The price will still be a dime and the motto will still be: "It's not so good to the last drop, so leave a little in the cup."

July 14, 1955 Gloversville, New York Leader-Herald

Less Coffee Consumption

There has been a steady decline in per capita coffee consumption since 1962, says Marsha Mueller, University of Illinois Extension Adviser. Although retail coffee prices are now record high, the long-term downtrend in coffee consumption since 1962 is mostly explained by factors other than price.

August 11, 1977 Joliet, Illinois Farmers Weekly Review

Due to the increase of coffee prices, sugar, restaurant equipment, labor and other operating expenses, we are forced to increase our coffee price to ten cents.

TED'S DINER	134 No. Genesee St., Utica
YORKVILLE DINER	Truck Route, Yorkville
SMILEY'S DINER	274 South St., Utica
WHITESBORO DINER	Truck Route, Whitesboro
GOETZ DINER	Truck Route, Yorkville
FUSARO'S RESTAURANT	229 South St., Utica
HUNT'S POINT DINER	622 Charlotte St., Utica
CHARLOTTE ST. REST.	715 Charlotte St., Utica
ELGIN LUNCH	315 Lafayette St., Utica
PAT'S DINER	1101 Oriskany St. W., Utica
IRENE'S DINER	Truck Route, Kirkland
NEW HERMITAGE Rest.	48 Genesee St., Utica
MAIN ST. DINER	316 Main St., Utica
O.-K. LUNCH	38 Genesee St., Utica
BAGGS SQ. LUNCH	4 Whitesboro St., Utica
NORTH GENESEE DINER	No. Genesee St., Utica
~~GRAND CENTRAL HOTEL~~	
NOYES ST. DINER	825 Noyes St., Utica

November 15, 1954 Utica Daily Press (New York)

Chapter 8

After the War.
Who was Building Diners.

The restaurants have changed for the better, too, in other ways than cookery. They are modern in use of tile, glass, metal and plastics in simple lines and pleasing decorations. That's good news for the great American public which travels more and more. The vitamin-conscious and the epicure alike may wander far and yet find eating both wholesome and delightful.

-Geneva Daily Times, April 19, 1940

After World War II was over, every Great Lakes diner manufacturer was out of business. There were few options left for someone from the Great Lakes states or upper midwest looking to buy a diner. By this time, the majority of diners were large and expensive to move. A prospective owner could contact one of the East Coast based diner builders and pay a fair amount of money to have the diner transported to the midwest by truck. Or they could contact one of the Midwest concerns such as Valentine Company of Wichita, Kansas or Butler Manufacturing. After the war, some east coast diner manufacturers tried promoting tiny diners, often called dinettes, that could be easily run by one or two families. Many were perfect for the hamburger trade and did respectable in competition with the newly popular drive-ins and chains such as White Castle and White Tower. In a January 2009 article in The North Shore Magazine stated,

> Diners tried to expand to the Midwest, but Midwesterners, in love with their cars, preferred drive-ins like A&W. Chains and fast-food restaurants, especially McDonald's, became the "in" places to eat. The trend spread, even to the East Coast, where, by 1965, the diners found

Above:

East Coast diner manufacturers from time to time built smaller diners as a more affordable way into the diner business. These were moderately popular after World War II. Many of them specialized in hamburgers even more than your typical diner did.

Below:

The Indian Trailer Corporation of Chicago, Illinois decided to turn some of their trailers into food consession trailers. The trailer might be perfect for someone running an auction and would act pretty much like a lunch wagon would have acted many years ago.

themselves falling on hard times.[1]

The freedom found with cars truly exploded with the return of GIs coming back from the war. If there was any doubt about the importance of the automobile to Americans, this period in time put that to rest. The diner could have prospered in the Midwest, catering to the car culture like it did in New Jersey, but diners also had to overcome the connotations to the fast paced Eastern lifestyles. Those same fast paced styles, when related to building style changes, left the Lake Erie diner builders in the dust. Any relation of a diner to a trolley car was quickly gone from the East Coast builders by the start of the 1940s. East Coast builders were even getting away from their once popular barrel roof styled diners.

The newfound popularity of the suburbs coupled with automobiles also meant that many downtown diners began to slowly fade in popularity. America's eating habits changed after World War II and all food service businesses felt it. On the business side, getting dependable help became that much more difficult after World War II was over. Jobs of a better pay scale were easy to get for any able bodied American, so that left a dwindling pool of dependable help for restaurant owners.

In places like Metro Detroit, white enamel buildings serving hamburgers became popular in the suburbs. These buildings were meant to mimic the White Tower and White Castle chains, but had independent owners. After "cruising Woodward" or Telegraph, teenagers would stop at any of these places, or the local drive-in restaurant. Many of the buildings still exist today with names like Bates Hamburgers or Greenes Hamburgers being two of the more popular places today. Both places have a dedicated clientèle that have been patronzing the businesses for years.

Valentine looked to cash in on this culinary desire first started by the giants like White Tower and White Castle. In fact, White Tower hired the Valentine Company to build fifteen prototype buildings for them in 1950. Valentine started building enamel and metal buildings

around 1938. While they started building portable eating establishments, Valentine also branched out into similar looking buildings intended for use as liquor stores. Later they expanded into gas stations, among other types of buildings that did not share the similar Valentine diner appearance. With a few exceptions they were the only brand of diner to be found in states like Nebraska, Oklahoma and Kansas. A 1948 advertisement said theri diners could be found in thirty-eight states. After the war, Valentine started making a minor dent in the western half of the Great Lakes states. They were easy to run, and they fit in well with the hamburger and drive-in culture that was taking over the culinary palates of the car-driven society.

Valentine also tried pushing the concept of the chain, as it would mean selling more of their units. Being a one- or two-man operation, it was much easier to find help to run each small restaurant. Also having similar-looking buildings promoted the concept of the chain using what is called "place-product-packaging". One chain of Valentines was centered around Columbus, Ohio. Run by the Corwin family, they had two diners in Columbus and one each in Waverly and Delaware, Ohio. They were known as the Red Castle Diners.[2]

Many people were happy with a single unit, but Valentine did give owners the capability to put diners together to build larger buildings, and it was still cheaper to

Above Left:

An addition was placed on the left side of the Toppit Diner in Ashtabula, Ohio. The owners took the siding off the end of the diner and placed it out front to make the diner appear longer.

(Library of Congress - John Margoles Collection)

Previous Page Right:

Dimitri Drive-In of Toledo, Ohio was one of the many Valentine diners to call Ohio home. The owners did not even bother using the word diner in the name of their establishment.

(1027 Summit St. courtesy of the Toledo-Lucas County Public Library, obtained from http://images2.toledolibrary.org/)

buy a multiple-unit Valentine than it was to purchase a larger diner from an Eastern diner manufacturer. When Valentine sold multiple-unit diners, they numbered each unit individually.

One three-unit Valentine was located in Lima, Ohio. Alex Kostopulus started running units 1825, 1826, and 1827 as the Regent Grill on rented land in 1957. The diner was soon physically taken back by Valentine for failure to pay the monthly installments, causing the landowner, Louis Paulson, to sue Valentine for $1,200 in lost rent.

Other companies tried to expand into the portable restaurant business in the midwest. These companies will be expanded upon in the geekery section of this chapter, but for now, a little information is given on Butler Manufacturing:

> Butler Manufacturing of Kansas City, Missouri was another small time manufacturer of portable restaurants. They placed fourteen Band Box Diners in the St. Paul, Minneapolis area besides other parts of the midwest.
>
> Butler Manufacturing needed a sideline to its grain silo biz. After working together with Buckminster Fuller on naval housing, it found its calling; diners, prefab little boxes complete with short-order kitchen, bathroom, and space for ten customers, tops. Package up the diner and ship it on a flatbed train, plop it down on a fresh patch of cement, fasten the turnpuckles in the corners to hold the walls up and ring the dinner bell.[3]

Besides Butler, a Toledo, Ohio company tried their hand at selling small portable restaurants. This company sold their diners as kits, to be assembled by the customer.

Same Page Right:
David Hebb, a diner historian, took a number of photos of diners across the eastern part of the country. He documented this Valentine in Sun Prairie, Wisconsin.

(Sun Prairie Historical Library and Museum)

Abovee:

Butler Manufacturing built the Fort Diner in Fort Madison, Iowa. It is not known how many diners Butler ended up building, but the Fort Diner is still going strong today.

Bottom Above:

The Fort Diner (left), along with a Band Box Diner in Minneapolis, Minnesota (right) appeared in a Butler advertisement for their wayside buildings.

The Dag-wood Diner Company is the only company known for certain to have made diner kits, though it is more than likely that others did the same. Founder Albert DeCatur was in the real estate field, with Jason Coughlin as secretary who was also in the business of selling restaurant equipment. Dag-Wood brought a demonstration model to a Chicago restaurant exhibition in 1947. This diner was never meant to be used as an actual operating diner, but it was sold anyway. Donald Weiler, son of the onetime owners noted that it was sold to a man from southeast Michigan who moved it to Secor and Monroe Streets in Toledo in 1947. In 1949 the diner was sold to Bob & Jane Weiler. Donald also reiterated the fact about being a demonstration model: "That was apparent as there were many times when the roof leaked and every year a new layer of tarpaper and tar was applied." This Toledo concern, known as the "Betsy Ross Diner," lasted until a road-widening project forced the Weilers to demolish and build a larger building.[5]

The best-known Dagwood kit diner is still going stronger than ever in Ann Arbor. Starting with the Dagwood Diner name, and proclaiming Root Beer and Hamburgers on its roof, the diner's best years followed a name change to the Fleetwood Diner as it is known today. Jim Rees, an Ann Arbor historian notes, "Before 1948 the City building code required masonry for all new restaurant construction. On July 6 of that year [Donald] Reid petitioned the city for a change in the building code, and on August 2 the City Council passed an amendment that appeared to be custom written for the Dagwood. It allowed metal construction for new buildings of 1000 square feet or less and no more than a single story, but only for restaurants and stores. (A similar amendment had been passed earlier for all-metal Lustron homes.)"[6]

The Fleetwood Diner's business and popularity is so good that the owners have been able to branch out over the past decade to new locations. But the owners are still aware of the history of the original location and have fought forces of gentrification that want the original diner replaced.

Word has it that Dag-Wood folded in late 1948, before their last kit was entirely delivered to Donald Reid in Ann Arbor, Michigan. If this story is true, then the company sold a total of six kits in two years proving that either the concept was not a well received vehicle for selling fast food, or the drive-in was proving too popular in the late 1940s.

A remodeled Dag-Wood exists on the Dixie Highway in the small hamlet of Erie, Michigan that was best known as Bacarella's Diner, but today does business as an Italian restaurant. Another Dag-Wood once did business in Wyandotte and another was rumored to have made it to the Thumb of Michigan.

Lunch cars built on truck bodies had always existed, especially in the warmer southern and central states. A popular homemade diner existed in Olean, New York. Truman Creamer built a diner on wheels that caught the eye of a Kentucky resident who wrote to the local newspaper in order to get instructions on building his own lunch car.[7] A mobile home builder known as the Indian Trailer Corporation of Chicago, Illinois built a trailer they called a "Dineola," that portrayed the movable lunch wagon in the new age where travel trailers were quite popular.

After the war, two Eastern companies made extra attempts to put diners into the Great Lakes region. These companies succeeded in getting a handful of diners into the region, but they never reached the sheer numbers that diners reached on the East Coast. The Jerry O'Mahony Company had always placed a few diners here and there throughout the central part of the country. They sent Uncle Bob's Diner to Flint, Michigan, Bill's Diner was sent to Canton, Ohio, and Mickey's Diner made it to St. Paul, Minnesota. In September of 1951, the New York Times reported that O'Mahony had plans for a St. Louis manufacturing plant. It was also pointed out that O'Mahony found it profitable to ship a diner by truck no further than 300 miles. Anything farther would need to be shipped by rail.[8] Shipping by rail was not as profitable for O'Mahony as it required extra work for them.

At this time O'Mahony was only building roughly thirty diners per year. By comparison, Silk City Diners of Paterson, New Jersey was building more than 100

Top Below:

Pixie Diner in Muncie, Indiana was a favorite (or maybe infamous) place for Ball State students to go to for food.

(Ball State University and Special Collections)

Bottom Above:

This Dag-Wood diner was never intended to be sold as a operating restaurant, but was still put into operation in Toledo, Ohio as the Betsy Ross Diner. The Dag-Wood building lasted until a road widening project forced its removal. By that time, the owners decided to build a new building. (Donald Weiler)

diners a year at the time. After opening up their second factory in St. Louis, Misouri in 1952, they bragged to the New York Times that "operators in the midwest and Far West are begging for their share in this roadside business." They thought that as their potential customers moved more throughout America, more people would want to find a comfortable diner. "There are untapped markets," added President Louis F. Camardella.[9] They were also gambling against the fact that many people of the Midwest were not too keen on the more progressive lifestyles of the East Coast. Diners were often seen as an invasion of the East Coast lifestyle into the Midwest. O'Mahony was hoping that the tides were turning in their favor.

Kullman may have sent Kerr's Diner to Toledo, Ohio and also sent another diner to Seattle, Washington which Diner Magazine in July 1947 noted, "was the only one like it west of St. Paul, Minnesota." But no company was as impressive as the Mountain View Company in promoting their diners in non-traditional areas of the country, especially the Great Lakes region and Florida. Diner Magazine, a magazine dedicated to the diner trade, reported various openings of diners and in Florida thirteen of eighteen new diner openings were Mountain View diners and in the Great Lakes region thirteen of 21 were built by Mountain View.[10]

Canton-Akron was one of the big winners. They had a few Lake Erie-built diners with at least four Ward & Dickinsons, so the area residents were somewhat familiar

Above Left:
The Fleetwood Diner in Ann Arbor, Michigan is rumored to be the last Dag-Wood diner sold by the company. On a separate unrelated note, the owner had to get a special amendment to the building code to get the diner built in the city of Ann Arbor.

Above Right:
Al's Diner in Monroe, Michigan. A few diners were shipped to Michigan in the 1950s, but they were a rare breed as the drive-in and hamburger stand were the main choice for Michigan's appetite.

Below:

Mountain View sent a lone diner to Wisconsin, although they would send a number of diners to Ohio and Indiana. gordon tindall photographed it in Brookfield when it was known as Chris Eliot's Diner. The diner is rumored to be in storage in Louisville, Kentucky.

(Gordon Tindall)

with diners. A small chain was started by William Wurtz known as Bill's Diner, with two in Canton and one in Massillon. Two more diners, Smitty's Diner in Massillon and Joe's Diner in Akron, would call the area home after World War II.

Indianapolis was also another winner, especially when it came to Mountain Views. The Peter Pan and Meadowbrook Diners were accompanied by the Seven Dwarfs Diner in Wanamaker, the Oasis Diner in Plainfield and the Red Dragon Diner in Lawrence, suburbs of Indianapolis. The Pixie Diner in Muncie was a popular hangout for the students at Ball State University. The Pixie was often mentioned by David Letterman when he worked at the University's radio station.

All of these diners were built by Mountain View. Mountain View went above and beyond in their attempt to get diners into new territories. They still had to worry about shipping costs, so for now the west coast was out of bounds for the company. They did send a diner to Denver, Colorado, but even that far was cost prohibitive. They were willing to make an impact in the southern Great Lakes. In an attempt to get diners started in the region, they were willing to finance east coast diner owners to move into the region and start up new diners.

Diner Magazine did not report on every diner that was brought into the region, but they probably covered the majority. Peoria, Illinois seemed to be an outpost of diners in the Midwest. The city was home to three diners, all starting before World War II. Decatur, Illinois, though, was home to a stainless steel diner. Fort Wayne, Indiana received Dick's Diner from the east coast. Fort Wayne already had a number of diners,

many of which were street car conversions and would later receive a couple of Valentine diners. Though Dick's Diner is gone today, the diner is still fondly remembered by many residents.

Back in western New York, two last tiny attempts were made to build diners. In Silver Creek, Charles Sorge, whose brothers owned the old Richardson demonstration car, decided to build diners. On September 13, 1946, Charles filed papers with Chautauqua County to start business as the Sorge Diner Company. Besides building diners, he also offered to remodel older diners. One that Sorge did remodel was once known as the Kendall Diner, located outside of Silver Creek on a section of US Route 20 that was being bypassed. The station and the tourist camp was closed up by owner Ray Dimon. He sold the Ward and Dickinson diner to Harris Mead and Gardiner Freling, who moved it to Fredonia. There, the newly named Family Diner was remodeled on the inside "extensively" by Sorge.

Sorge probably did the same thing he did to his new diners; the ceiling would be covered with stainless steel panels—nearly the same setup as a Ward & Dickinson, but with no paint, just a shiny, easier-to-clean stainless steel. Below the windows were ceramic tiles. Both of these products were popular with many diner builders of the time in the Eastern states. The exterior looked exactly like a Ward & Dickinson, with only one major change: the famous swirled green and white glass was not always used on Sorge's model. Sorge built either three of five new diners based upon different rumors. Ones may have gone to Ashtabula, Ohio and Oil City, Pennsylvania.

Above:

Burch's Family Diner was originally known as The Chuck Wagon Diner in Gary, Indiana. The diner was the first Kentucky Fried Chicken franchise in Indiana. This diner inspired Robert Dye to buy a similar diner from the Mountain View Company and place it in Champaign, Illinois. His Chuck Wagon Diner was to become the first Kentucky Fried Chicken franchise in Illinois. You can visit that diner in Duanesburg, New York today, as it was saved and restored by Tom Ketchum.

(Steve Boksenbaum)

Above:

Jimmy Bellas Sr. brought the Meadowbrook Diner to Indianapolis in the 1950s. Mountain View influenced Bellas to come to help open up the mid-west to the possibility of the diner by financing him in his setting up the diner.

Above Inset Left:

A customer, Joey Brown, is shown interacting with Jimmy Bellas at the cashier's stand. Note the candy under the glass.

Above Inset Right:

Meadowbrook Diner is shown on location in Indianapolis with its gorgeous sign.

(James Bellas Jr.)

The other manufacturer was located in Albion, New York, a village between Buffalo and Rochester in Orleans County. They used the county name for their company, calling the concern the Orleans Manufacturing Company. The model of diner that they built was called the Superior diner and none other than Bertrand Harley was credited with the design. Three diners were built by the company, the Highland Park Diner in Rochester, New York being the lone survivor. Dauphin's Superior Diner replaced a Sterling that by 1948 had become too small. The Orleans-built diner was turned into an Off Track Betting Parlor in 1972. Local resident Bob Malley bought the gutted diner in 1985 and painstakingly restored it to its original splendor.

Another Orleans diner made its way to Haverill, Massachusetts. Diner historian Gary Thomas noted that Orleans diners were sectional diners and assembled on site. A third and final Orleans built diner was sent to Westwood, New Jersey where it became known as the Cadillac Diner. American Diner Then and Now shows a photograph of the diner before and after a 1950s styled remodeling done by a New Jersey remodeler..

1 North Shore Magazine, Boston, Massachusetts, January 2009
2 email correspondance with Mike Corwin
3 Minnesota Marvels: Roadside Attractions in the Land of Lakes, University of Minnesota Press, Minneapolis, Minnesota, Eric Dregni, 2001
4 Restaurant Management, Chicago, Illinois, Ahrens, various editions 1946-1947
5 email correspondance with Donald Weiler
6 http://www.jimrees.org/fleet/
7 Olean Times Herald, May 20, 1948
8 New York Times, September 23, 1951
9 New York Times, August 31, 1952
10 The Diner, Laurel Publications, Plainfield, Connecticut 1946-1956

Above:
Interior of a Sorge diner.

Top Right:
Newspaper advertisement placed by Sorge.

Right:
Prep work to get a Sorge diner out of a barn just outside of Silver Creek, New York where the diner was built.

(American Diner Heritage)

Orleans Manufacturing Co., Inc.
MANUFACTURERS OF SUPERIOR DINERS AND DINER EQUIPMENT
ESTABLISHED 1932

Above:

Letterhead from Orleans Manufacturing. To the best of our knowledge, they did not start building diners until after World War II.

(Gary Thomas)

Right:

The Cadillac Diner in Westwood, New Jersey. One of three Superior diners built by Orleans Manufacturing.

(Richard Gutman)

Below:

The Highland Park Diner in Rochester, New York is the lone extant example of a Superior diner, built in Albion, New York.

Above:

Daniel Zilka was given these photos from the Sorge family collection. They are believed to be photos of a Sorge built diner being put into place in Oil City, Pennsylvania. It quite possibly could be the same diner shown in the Sorge barn on the previous pages.

(American Diner Heritage)

Geekery

Perhaps someday someone will write a book on the portable structures being used as restaurants, beyond the diner. Diners started as single buildings, getting longer and wider. Companies like Bixler were the first to create segments that could be built at a factory, knocked down for shipping and then reassembled on site. The use of metal, instead of wood, made this process much easier to accomplish. It could be as simple as tightening some bolts.

In March of 1928, construction was completed on a "moveable steel building, made on an interchangeable unit plan." The designer, Lloyd W Ray, was the engineer for the White Castle Systems company. White Castle was an up and coming hamburger selling restaurant based in Wichita, Kansas. Mr. Ray spent the past two years working on this idea, which means it would have been in his mind in 1926. Ray ended up designing the building to make changing, expanding or moving the building a far easier process for any building other than a diner. All Ray had to do is have some workmen undo some bolts, unhook some panels and then reverse the process with an expanded section. The panels that Ray used were porcelain finished white enamel steel, which gave the appearance of porcelain tile. This was a change from the wood and painted steel used in many diners of the time.

Although Ray said the first building was built at a cost of $25,000, he believed that this cost could be brought down to $3000 for each building over time. Much of that original $25,000 were startup costs and attempts to find the right materials and the right process to mass produce the buildings. Not only would the similar looking buildings be quite affordable, but they would also be the start of place product packaging. This concept is something we take for granted today. But Ray and White Castle wanted the customer to see the building and know exactly what that building offered before even seeing a sign that says White Castle or even "restaurant."

White Castle was started by Walter Anderson who opened his first restaurant in a converted street car in 1916 right there in Wichita, Kansas. By the time he took the White Castle name he decided upon creating buildings that took the appearance of a castle. These early buildings were built with white bricks. A short time after Lloyd Ray developed his prototype building, White Castle started building only the modular

buildings and even covered over some of the older buildings to match Ray's design.

Arthur Valentine was another Wichita area restaurant man who looked into porcelain clad pre-fab buildings. In 1933, he hired the Metal Building Company and the Martin Perry Company of New York to build him a sectional structure clad in porcelain inside and out. Mr. Valentine started outside of Wichita, but came to town to open his grand new restaurant, someplace for a larger city like Wichita.

A third name in the pre-fab restaurant world of Wichita, Kansas was the Ablah Hotel Supply Company. In the 1920s, the company branched out into the world of prefabricated restaurants. The specific timeline of Ablah is unknown, so they could have been before or after White Castle's foray into pro-fab restaurants. It is said that sometime in the late 1920s, that Ablah built a portable lunch room for Arthur Valentine, which he placed in Hutchinson, Kansas.

Although Valentine had a different company build his porcelain clad palace in Wichita, many fortuitous things happened between Ablah and Valentine. Arthur Valentine went to work for Ablah sometime in the 1930s selling their portable restaurants. By the end of the 1930s, the owners of Ablah wanted out of the business and Arthur was all too interested in the concept not to jump at the opportunity to purchase the company. For some reason, Valentine did not continue to have the Ablah workers

Ablah Hotel Supply Company probably built this diner in conjunction with Arthur Valentine.

(American Diner Heritage)

build new portable restaurants, but instead contracted with the Hayes Equipment Manufacturing Company to make a few pre-fab restaurants for him. Hayes had previously built pre-fab metal buildings, mostly for the gasoline business. Before Arthur could really get going with the business, World War II made it difficult to procure building materials, so the rise of Arthur Valentine's diner building company would have to wait until the war was over, and the supply chains got built back up. By the time World War II was over, Hayes had called it quits, so Arthur Valentine was fully in line to make a go of the pre-fab restaurant business on his own.

Other companies used pre-fab structures for their restaurants outside of Wichita, Kansas. The Toddle House chain started in a rather roundabout kind of way. J.C. Stedman arranged to construct "nice little cottages" as a way to sell extra supplies that he had intended to sell to grocery stores. One day someone mentioned he should turn some of his buildings into restaurants and an idea was born. Stedman had the idea to move to Memphis and convince the owners of the somewhat new Britling Cafeteria to open up his restaurants and have his buildings built in Memphis. One thing led to another and Toddle House was born. Each Toddle House was built in Memphis and

Arthur Valentine worked with Hayes Equipment Manufacturing Company to have his Valentine Sandwich Shops built.

(American Diner Heritage)

Not much is known about the Hoffie National System, but this advertisement does include a drawing of one of the buildings they offered for sale.

Sparkle Hut is another little known company that did advertise a building.

It is not known if either company ever built or sold a building.

shipped to location on a flat-bed truck. Although the exterior was cottage style, the interior was quite similar to a diner of the 1920s. Just a row of stools and all the cooking was being done behind the counter. In other similarities, breakfast was key to their menu and was served all day. Hamburgers were also called, "world famous," by the company.

Another company in Memphis may have built pre-fab restaurants to accommodate expansion of their chain. The Hull Dobbs House chain had similar looking buildings to the Toddle House buildings. A Buffalo, New York 1940 building permit stated that their buildings were classified as a "metal and steel restaurant," which was consistent to how Buffalo recorded Toddle House's building permit in 1937.

Just like Hayes Equipment Manufacturing Company in Wichita, Kansas, other companies branched their business into pre-fab restaurants or other food related sidelines. Steel King started out in Milwaukee, Wisconsin in 1926 building steel garages. In 1929, Walter Junkerman, the owner, expanded his business to include roadside stands and other portable buildings. Then in the late 1940s, as the company had moved into building porcelain clad gas stations, they also built at least one porcelain clad hamburger joint.

Besides the diners that Butler Manufacturing built, they also branched off into other

This Colonial Fixture built diner was located next to a motel in Monroe, North Carolina..

wayside buildings. And they too focused on porcelain enamel sided buildings. Other companies that were mentioned to be in the portable restaurant business include: Sparkle-Hut of Michigan, Hoffie National System of Evansville, Indiana, Grauman Company of Denver, Colorado, Kay-Zee Manufacturing Company of Cleveland, Ohio, Porcelain Structures of Belleville, Illinois, Stephens Equipment Company of Kansas City, Missouri. Almost nothing is known of these companies, or if they ever built an actual building.

There were a couple of other southern businesses that did build pre-fab buildings on a small scale, but were not restaurant systems themselves. The Colonial Fixtures Company of Charlotte, North Carolina built a few boxy looking diners somewhere around 1950. The interiors had room for a counter and a number of tables to the side. The National Glass & Manufacturing Company of Fort Smith, Arkansas started building sectional restaurants which were put together on site. An advertisement for the company said their buildings are, "a Knock-Down Metal Building Manufactured Complete with Equipment and Fixtures Ready to Install on your Lot." Although the buildings did have a counter, most of the room was dedicated to tables like a typical restaurant.

National Glass built a knock down metal building to be more of a restaurant than a diner, even though they did have a counter.

Chapter 9

Decline of the Diner.

WYOMING REPORTER — SILVER SPRINGS SIGNAL — WESTERN NEW-YORKER — WYOMING COUNTY TIMES — WYOMING COUNTY GAZETTE
Thursday, July 6. 1950

BELDING DINING CAR SOLD

With the removal of the Belding dining car from Main Street, Palmyra, there passed into history one of the most famous eating places in all western New York. It was made in the Dickinson Bros, dining [Ward & Dickinson Dining Car Co.] car factory at Silver Creek and was placed here March 20th, 1927 by Mr. and Mrs. Harry Belding from Charlotte, Iowa. At that time it was modern and the very latest in dining cars. For fifteen years it was open night and day 365 days of the year, and the first year netted a business of over S20,000. For years it was a very popular eating place and served the rich and the poor alike. Truck drivers from every state in the Union made it a point to stop there and were served ham and eggs while they listened to tales of the old west from famous Cowboy Harry.

They rolled in all hours of the night tired and hungry. Often Harry let them sleep for a few hours and then called them: "It's time to get rolling, boys," and with a wave of the hand they vanished into the night. Tourists from every state and Canada and Mexico crossed its threshold at one time and another and many noted people ate there. Cowboys and rodeo people seeing the sign, Cowboy Diner never failed to stop.

Following the death of Harry Belding in 1941, his wife, Julia Belding conducted the business for several years and since then it has been rented to several different parties but since January 1st has been closed to the public. It has been moved to the Walter
Pulcini farm on the Newark road and will be used as a vegetable stand. May it have as many years as a popular vegetable stand as it did as a very famous eating place known as the Cowboy Diner and here is hoping it will bring great prosperity to the new owner.

Mrs. Julia Belding is at present making her home with Ed Dunker of Woodruff Street Silver Springs.

Ward and Dickinson's motto was, "They're built to last," but in actuality, diners were not made to last a long time. Lee Dickinson only intended for his Ward and Dickinson company to be in business for ten or fifteen years.[1] As a Sterling diner expert reported, Sterlings were not built for longevity, as they developed leaks over time. And as materials became worn and outdated, diners were looking old and tired. Even by 1940, trade magazines were reporting the usage of up to date materials like plastic. not only did materials in many diners look old, but it was not seen as up to date by the public. We can also consider sanitation. Dishwashers did not become popular until the 1950s, and many older diners simply didn't have room for a dishwasher.

Many diner companies in the east hoped that owners would trade in their old diners after 10-15 years. Of course, if it was one of their own diners being taken in for trade, the company would remodel and update the used diner into the latest look and equipment. Otherwise, the diner company may just take money off on "trade", but allow the owner to dispose of the old diner. Each company had their own policy concerning trade-ins. In Albany, when Lil's Diner, a Ward and Dickinson was replaced with a Silk City in 1940, Lillian just placed the old diner behind the new one leaving it to rot away.

Statistically, the years between 1960 & 1975 would be the worst for much of the diner scene in the Great Lakes states. The starting article concerning the Ward and Dickinson in Palmyra, New York gives part of the story. Often, when that long-time owner retired, there was someone else willing to give that 20 to 30 year old diner a chance. But many of these owners did not last long, especially given the size and condition of the outdated diner. Although Valentine thrived on the stool only diner, many of the Great Lakes smaller diners were now in cities and towns which had newer restaurants with booths and tables. These newer restaurants with booths and tables often had new

Above:

Valparaiso, Indiana. Robert Dye bought an old trolley car from Gary, Indiana and turned it into a diner, where he was famous for hamburgers. The diner was last known as Ma Cole's Luncheonette before it met its demise to the ravages of time.

(Rick Halstead)

appearances with the latest up to date materials. These newer restaurants and diners were set up in the commercial district on the edge of town, or on the latest bypass around a congested downtown. Everything about these older diners said outdated and tired. These newer Valentines were fresh, white and clean. The age of these old diners was one reason, but then, why were so many diners not replaced by new diners? The answer could be one of many reasons. In the east by the 1960s, diner builders that looked into the mid-west like Mountain View and O'Mahony were now out of business. Very few of the Mountain View diners sold in the 1950s were replacing older diners, instead they were competition for the older diners or for the fast food drive-ins. The other companies were now building large diners, ones that would have to be shipped in multiple sections. Secondly, Pat Fodero talked about the difficulty in shipping Doc's Little Gem to Syracuse, New York in 1958. With the width and general size, he could only go 40 mph on the newly built New York State Thruway. If Syracuse was a tough enough trip, companies would dread going further west. Diners were not built like the sectional diners of the age of Bixler and Rochester Grills. Each section in a newer diner was as big as an entire Bixler diner.

The new limited access Interstates were also a contributor to the demise of some diners. Highway planners were already bypassing many downtowns, as long distance travelers would spend so much time stuck in traffic passing through a city of any size, causing major traffic backups. A check of an Ohio state map today shows U S Route 20 bypassing cities like Elyria and Fremont and US Route 30 bypassing places like Wooster, Mansfield and Canton. All of these cities had diners downtown. These aforementioned diners would lose the opportunity to service the traveling crowd when its respective town was bypassed. The traveling crowd included not only out of town travelers, but also daily commuters and local citizens who were now choosing different paths to get from one place to another. On a grand scale, the Interstates only exacerbated the situation.

Above:

A rare environmental diner in the general vicinity of the Great Lakes. On the east coast, these were the norm, but in the Great Lakes, they were few. Many diner owners either let their diner be demolished or cobbled together additions and remodeled the best they could.
Shown here is Ritter's Diner in Pittsburgh, Pennsylvania.

(Mario Monti)

Above:

Steve Boksenbaum snapped these photos in the early 1980s of the former Scotty's Diner. Scotty's was a popular Pittsburgh diner chain and this one sat on Route 8 between Etna and Glenshaw, north of Pittsburgh.

(Steven Boksenbaum)

Below:

The Woodlawn Diner as it was being prepped to move off site. It was replaced shortly after World War II with a stick built restaurant that still serves customers today.

(David Ries)

Even when a diner was kept clean, with pleasurable owners, there were still many obstacles. The Electric Diner in Toronto, Ontario, Canada was a prime example.

> The Electric Diner at the foot of York St. and its two owners survive by the grace of workers nearby and by the Toronto Islanders who like to warm up with a cup of coffee before boarding the ferry home. The expressway complex has eliminated parking space and the hamburger and fish-and-chip customers have gone elsewhere. The Electric Diner is probably unique in Toronto. It stands on land owned by the Toronto Harbor Commission, which only grants a 30-day lease to the partners. Next spring could mean the end for the diner. What then? Mr. Orleski is not sure whether he and Mr. Rubinoff will bother to look for another lot.[2]

For the owners that decided to stay in the restaurant business, Kerr's Diner in Toledo, Ohio was a typical case. A 1960 article in the Toledo Blade stated, "Kerr's Diner, a downtown fixture at Jefferson Avenue and Huron Street for 21 years is moving to the suburbs. Matthew H. Kerr, owner, said his business has fallen off to the point where the move has become necessary. Once the diner's best business was in the early evening, but now "we might as well close up at 6," Mr. Kerr said. "Our only patrons are persons who work in the downtown area," he said. Downtowns became a tough place for any diner type restaurant to survive. And in the mid-west, the drive-in restaurant was flexing its muscles. Matthew Kerr knew this and planned accordingly. The article went on to state, "Drive-in facilities will be built at one end of the diner and the name of the business will be changed to Kerr's Diner and Drive-In."[3]

With the larger size of diners and multiple sections being shipped, the cost of a diner was jumping by leaps and bounds. Add to that the higher shipping costs for multiple sections, and the cost was becoming quickly prohibitive for small time operations. But even the Valentine Company was running into a lack of business as the 1950s were moving into the next decade. The company also experienced internal problems as

Arthur Valentine retired in 1951 and passed away in 1954. Ma's Coffee Pot in South Haven, Michigan may be the only rare exception. With this diner, Valentine was also moving away from their famous metal box design. They too added new, earthy toned and cost effective materials to their diners.

Then there was the type of food typically being served in a diner. On August 6, 1969, John Cunniff, Associated Press Business Analyst wrote that chain type restaurants were replacing the greasy spoon diner on the tourist trail. He said that if projections are correct, that 20,000 new units could be built in just the next two years. The majority of these new units being of the drive-in type.[4] These fast food chains like McDonalds, Burger Chef and other hamburger and root beer stands were the most significant nail in the coffin in the older diners of the Great Lakes. There was far too many choices, newer and more convenient choices, for the traveling public. Although companies like Dagwood and Valentine tried to push their models in this direction, people saw the situation just as easy to build their own buildings and buy a franchise in an established chain. The few new diners that came to the Great Lakes in the 1950s were the exception and could not touch the number of new diners that came during the late 1920s. nor could they make up for the number of diners being removed. Diners tried putting jukeboxes in to attract a younger clientèle, but the allure of cruising around in a car and driving up to the drive-in was too much for the diner, even on much of the east coast.

In the eastern Great Lakes, from about Erie, Pennsylvania east, diners began to leave their urban environments where they were formerly dominant in the minds and

Above:

Gordon Tindall snapped these photos of "The Streamliner." The photo on the right shows the diner in Elwood City, Pennsylvania. The photo on the left shows the diner when Steve Harwin was working on it in Cleveland, Ohio. The diner currently sits in storage in Duluth, Minnesota.

(Gordon Tindall)

Below:

An Off Track Betting (OTB) parlor for roughly ten years, Bob Malley fixed up the gutted diner originally known as Dauphin's Superior Diner. The diner is the last known extant example of a Superior diner, built in Albion, New York.

(Ron Dylewski)

stomachs of the residents and employees of local businesses. Urban populations in the north decreased as families moved to the suburbs and jobs all too often moved to the south, causing a double whammy to urban restaurants, especially diners dependant on business men and factory workers. Even the early hamburger chains like White Tower that set up in the early 1930s ran into similar situations.

Syracuse may be thought of as the western frontier of pro diner cities today, as they still had six diners in the city limits in 2000. To the west, Rochester and Buffalo both essentially lost all of their diners. The remaining original diner in Rochester, New York, the Highland Park Diner was turned into an Off Track Betting Parlor in the 1970s before being restored back into a diner. Buffalo's last factory built diner left somewhere around 2000 and was without a diner until the Lake Effect Diner came to town a few years later. In 2016, Buffalo also added the Swan Street Diner, a Sterling diner transplanted from Newark, New York.

The city of Detroit had serious race riots in the 1960s. Many other large cities had the same issues, but it was magnified in Detroit. By then, there was a lone S & C Coffee Car in the city, which was photographed by Time Magazine in the 1970s. Urban flight was probably the worst in Detroit, taking a majority of businesses out of the city. With diners being easily disposable, they were demolished without a thought.

The diners that did survive from the 1920s were remodeled in one way or another almost all of the time. Three concerns were paramount: increased seating for customers, upkeep and energy costs. The owner's concerns were not one of preserving history, this was not really even a thought, it was one of making money and serving their

customers. Unfortunately, preserving history would cost the owner in lost revenue. Customers were not concerned with visiting an authentic well preserved diner. Good food is what will bring the customers back. But before a new owner could worry about food, they had to often worry about disassociating themselves from a former owner. Many new owners wanted a fresh start in order to bring back old customers and aslo new customers too. And if these new owners did serve good food in an old diner, they would often find the need to upgrade to a new business location.

Money was usually not there to hire a diner manufacturer to remodel a diner, nor was there a concern to look, "diner." Again, everything goes back to the decline of the region and the decline of being diner. It just wasn't worth it, in any aspect, to keep diners going.

Three diners can give us varying looks at preservation. The Modern Diner in Wellsville, New York, a Ward and Dickinson that appeared in 1933, was remodeled sometime after World War II, the diner itself had its roof removed and was expanded so that today, one can not tell it was once an authentic Ward and Dickinson. The Coffee Cup Diner in Hillsdale, Michigan is also a Ward and Dickinson. The original diner's frame is still in place, but some of the wall on the right end has been removed so a larger addition could be placed on the back of the diner. The counter, though remodeled, is still in the same configuration. In Kenosha, Wisconsin, Frank's Diner, a 1925 O'Mahony had an addition placed on the front of the diner which sits perpendicular to the road. At Frank's, you will find the glass in the windows gone, and a row of booths along what was once the outside of the diner. Otherwise, the interior of the diner is still very much original still to this day.

The businesses that had enough money would sometimes level the old diner and

Below:

The Modern Diner in Wellsville, New York was about to be extensively remodeled and enlarged. Today, one can not tell that the current Modern Diner started out as a Ward and Dickinson diner as every wall was blown out during the remodel.

(Modern Diner - Wellsville, New York)

start over with a new building. Dewey's Diner in Buffalo, New York, the Old Hitching Post in Holland, Michigan and Domenico's Diner in Syracuse, New York all replaced their old diners at different times with a new building. Each owner believed that a diner did nothing for their business and a new building would increase business. Today, only Domenico's is still in business, but it is also the only one of the three not located downtown, and was also the last diner of the three to be demolished.

As realtors say, location, location location. So many diners were located downtown and the others that were located on major highways were finding that these same thoroughfares that brought them so much business were now being bypassed by limited access highways. In the suburbs, the hamburger joint and the drive-in took control.

Another dilemma was the retirement of a lifetime diner owner. When a lifetime diner owner would retire in the 1950's and beyond, it was very difficult to find a new owner that was willing to put in so much time to run such small diners that did not bring in great profits and were often finding themselves in questionable neighborhoods. Similar to situations in the east, most children of diner owners had the opportunity to go to college and did not desire to work long hours running their parent's worn diners. The ones that did were truly a rare and dedicated breed. Unfortunately many diners stayed closed after the long-time owner decided to retire. Other diners went through a few more years of proprietors who rarely lasted more than a year or two, until no person could be found who was interested in running a tired and worn diner.

Other downtown diners were demolished due to urban renewal or other "progress." Both diners in downtown Mansfield, Ohio were sold at auction in the 1960s to make way for new buildings. The Max Diner, a Mulholland, was run by the Dunkirk

Above:

Kirk's Diner in Cleveland, Ohio still had some appearance of a Ward and Dickinson, but was re-sided and had a new matching entryway. This type of updating was more affordable.

(Cleveland Public Library/Official City of Cleveland Photograph)

Below:

Amazingly, this Richardson diner in Bryan, Ohio made it to 1961 pretty intact. It came down only to be replaced by a parking lot.

(Bryan Times, Bryan, Ohio)

Not a train wreck, but the last of "The Dining Car" which is now making way for an addition to the Lindsey Motor Sales used car lot, is shown here. The contractor for the improvement is John Hall.

The traditional popular eating place closed last Saturday.

Dining Car Co. until it was sold to A. D. McNew in 1930. While the diner was getting ready to be auctioned off, along with its contents, Virgil Stanfield called it, "the last of a trio of popular downtown restaurants of a quarter of a century ago," in the Mansfield News Journal on March 19, 1968.[6] At it's peak, McNew had 25 employees. And while he sold the diner in 1947, the diner amazingly only had two more owners before it was sold off in 1968.

    The Ward and Dickinson in town went by the name, Shady Lawn Diner. This diner was put up for auction on May 22, 1965 by owner George Estes who already had his diner, "on skids."[7] The Shady Lawn was replaced by a building built for the Mansfield Building and Loan Association. The headline for the 1963 article on the Shady Lawn read, "New Building To Replace Landmark."[8]

    It was an emotional thing when a beloved diner was torn down. The regulars got attached to the employees and to their routines. In December of 1973, after forty-six years of continious serivce, the Lor-A-Lee Diner in Niles, Ohio was closed. People from all walks of life dined at the Lor-A-Lee, a Ward and Dickinson diner. "Mary Mangino started in 1935 and was still there when the diner closed. George Horn worked 35 years behind the counter." So it was easy for the regulars to build solid relationships with employees such as these.[9]

    Raymond Richardson remained part owner of Don Weed's Richardson diner in Wyandotte, Michigan. The dining car did business in Wyandotte for fifteen years before disappearing in January of 1941. The Wyandotte Times reported in 1954,

> It was a haven for homeless men, a meeting place for merchants and tradesmen, a rendezvous for doctors, lawyers and bankers of the town. So, too, it was frequented by bootleggers, taxi drivers, barbers, sailors, and persons of all walks of life.[10]

The paper also mentioned a similar story about the changes coming to society with "swank glass brick store fronts and smart restaurants doen in chrome and blue leather." New was more popular and made more profits, but even though diners were

Previous Page Below:

This Sterling diner started in the Eastwood section of Syracuse, New York where it was run for many years. Somewhere around the 1970s it was moved to Pulaski, New York right off the interstate. Eventually closing, the diner was left to rot away until it collapsed.

disappearing left and right, they were still viewed as landmarks for some segments of society.

The trolley car diner in Rittman, Ohio was torn down in 1957 and replaced by a new restaurant and motel. The new restaurant is known as the Heavenly Hash Diner today. Trolley car conversions of the 1920s saw an even greater decline as many were twenty to thirty years old before they spent their final years in the diner business. The Ward in Medina, New York lingered until 1985. Gert Wilde, who with her husband Harold ran the diner from 1934 to 1971. She commented in the Journal Register on November 1, 1985, "Once the pizza places and the like came in - that's when our business slowed down. We were more old fashioned."[11]

Auburn, Indiana's Ward made it to 1974, but by then, the diner had been remodeled quite a bit on the outside. Pontiac, Michigan had four diners. One diner left in the late 1940s, another in 1956 and the last two in the late 1960s. In Ashtabula, Ohio the nine diners experienced their last year in business anywhere from 1948 to 1976, with the last two diners being the Ashtabula Dinor which closed in 1971 and the Toppit Sandwich Shoppe which closed somewhere around 1976 according to city directory records. The Ashtabula Dinor was rumored to have been built by Sorge in the late 1940s, which would have replaced a Ward and Dickinson. So in some ways, it was newer than the other diners in town. The Toppit was a Valentine diner, which came to town after World War II.

Top Photo:

Mario Monti took this photo from a bus during a tour of diners in western Pennsylvania. Dick's Diner was moved to a yard in Blairsville to sit and rot away.

(Mario Monti)

Bottom Photo:

The same trolley conversion from the end of Chapter 6. This diner in Independence, Ohio shows how easy it was for a trolley conversion diner to look run down.

(Spencer Stewart)

1 "Those Were the Days", Donald Kofoed's unpublished autobiography 1991-1992
2 The Globe and Mail, Toronto, Ontario, Canada December 20, 1963
3 Toledo Blade Toledo, Ohio August 16, 1960
4 Associated Press article by John Cunniff, Watertown Daily Times, Watertown, New York, August 6, 1969
5 "Last of the White Towers" by Dick Burnhams, Burger Boy, Columbia Missouri, Vol 2 No. 6 Fall 2000
6 Mansfield News Journal, Mansfield, Ohio March 19, 1968
7 Mansfield News, Mansfield, Ohio May 22, 1965
8 Mansfield News, Mansfield, Ohio March 13,1963
9 "Dust in the Cobwebs", Grace Allison, The Times, Niles, Ohio, April 28, 2000
10 Wyandotte Times, Wyandotte, Michigan, July 8, 1954
11 Journal Register, Medina, New York, November 1, 1985

Above:

Behind that plywood sat a Valentine diner known as Tiny Tim Diner in Fort Wayne, Indiana. Unfortunately this diner did not survive all the construction in downtown Fort Wayne like Cindy's Diner did. Cindy's Diner, another Valentine, was moved twice to get out of the way of new construction and still survives and prospers today.

(Richard Gutman)

This Page:
Brought to Mansfield, Ohio in 1928, the Mulholland diner best known as Max Diner went through many changes before it met its demise in 1968. The Dunkirk Dining Car Company chose Mansfield and Marion, Ohio as two towns that they thought a diner would prosper. A. D. McNew bought the diner around 1930 and gave the diner the Max Diner name.

The middle photo shows a similar looking addition built in front of the original diner and the last two photos first show a third addition placed on top of the diner which was finally made to look like a regular building.

(Timothy Brian McKee & Kathy Ackerman)

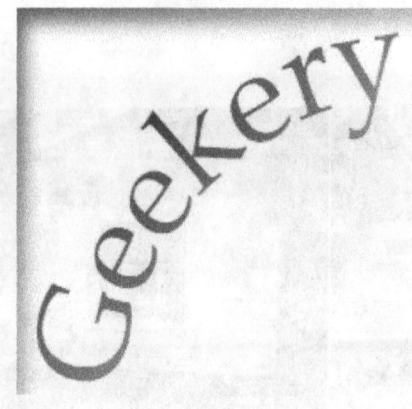

Geekery

Introduction: Conditional Sales Dockets were mandated by the state of Pennsylvania from 1925 to 1954. they were filed in the Prothonotary's Office. A docket is a legal piece of paper, so what are Conditional Sales and what are their importance to diner historians? Most diner manufacturers would sell their diners to prospective owners who did not have enough money on hand to buy the diner with cash. So most customers would buy the diner on a monthly installment plan. In order to protect their investment, diner manufacturers would file conditional sales papers in the states where either the person lived, or in the state where the diner was going to be placed. To make things more confusing to historians, there were irregularities from state to state. In New York state, conditonal sales could be filed at either the county, town or city level. there did not seem to be any rhyme or reason. In the state of Ohio, they were filed in the recorder's office. In Pennsylvania, they were filed in the Prothonotary's Office. In Pennsylvania, the Prothonotary acts like a clerk, often focusing much of their attention to Civil cases of the law.

Unfortunately, Conditonal Sales Dockets were no longer filed after 1954. They were replaced with other paperwork, but the loss of the Phrase "Conditional Sales Dockets" has meant that these records have gone into vaults, storage or maybe even thrown away as the law would allow.

The author of this book has not been to every county in the state of Pennsylvania and some counties are not able to find their records, but below is a listing of the records that the author has been able to find. In my personal opinion, these are an invaluable resource to historians that have not been used like they should be used.

Vendor is the diner company or person selling the diner and **Vendee** is the person buying the diner. Some of the vendees would put down partial payments, so the **Money still owed** is not the full price of the diner.

Armstrong County

Vendor: Ward & Dickinson
Date filed & Money still owed: 12/10/38 $4500
Vendee: William J. Short, Kittanning
Info: one "used" 40 ft #151 and equipment

Vendor: Kullman
Date filed & Money still owed: 5/10/39 $8500
Vendee: John F. Rothwell, res 486 E. High, Kittanning
Info: one dining car #170

Blair County

Vendor: Ward & Dickinson
Date filed & Money still owed: 2/8/34 $4800
Vendee: Wesley Kofoed.
Info: #170 41' 6"

Centre County

Vendor: O'Mahony
Date filed & Money still owed: 6/7/26 $5520
Vendee: Club Diner Inc
Info: serial #163-B 11x40

Vendor: Ward & Dickinson
Date filed & Money still owed: 9/5/30 $7250
Vendee: Russell W. Adanitz
Info: diner number #181

Vendor: Ward & Dickinson $10,000 48'10"
Date filed & Money still owed: 6/25/32 $10,000
Vendee: Russel W. Adanitz
Info: assigned to Lee F. Dickinson on 12/9/35 and then assigned to Edward L. Willard 2/15/36 who satisfied it the same day.

Clarion Co.

Vendor: Lee Dickinson pg 97
Date filed & Money still owed: 1/18/36 $3500
Vendee: Leslie & Mernie Cross
Info: everything listed, fire extinguisher, clock etc.

Vendor: Leslie & Mernie Cross
Date filed & Money still owed: 10/23/36 $5000
Vendee: Dr. Altom S. Giles & Elizabeth Giles
Info: known as the regular 30 foot model. Satisfied 10/20/37

Crawford County

Vendor: Charles Ward & Lee Dickinson
Date filed & Money still owed: 6/8/26 $3600
Vendee: P.L. Carey, res Meadville
Info: Diner #43

Vendor: Ward & Dickinson
Date filed & Money still owed: 10/30/1933
Vendee: John J. & Jas H. Frisk, res Meadville
Info:
$6000

Cumberland County

Vendor: Ward & Dickinson
Date filed & Money still owed: $5700
Vendee: R.F. Shetler
$5700 in remaining payments
Info: Diner #126. Payments were split up as follows:
$150 1/1/1928, then 9 months thereafter
$175 11/1/1928, then 9 months thereafter
$200 9/1/1929, then 2 months thereafter
$1850 12/1/1929
Satisfaction on 1/7/1931

"Ward" Special Dining Car #126
28 feet of marble counter tops, 12 stools, 1 electric exhaust fan, 1 hood, 1 cook stove, 1 steam table, 1 back counter, 12 screens for ventilator windows including window locks, fasteners and hooks.
1 electric fridge(Kelvinator), 1 clock, 1 twenty one foot counter, 2 built in tables and 4 booth seats, 1 dish sink, cash register and coal heater.
2 screen doors, electrical fixtures and wiring, floor linoleum, awnings, dishes, silverware, glassware, 1 hot water heater, 1 cream dispenser, 1 coffee urn, fire extinguisher.
Notary - Helen M. Dickinson

Vendor: Paterson Vehicle Company
Date filed & Money still owed: 4/1/1941 $5370
Vendee: R.F. Shetler
Info: Pike Diner #40104 14'6" by 40' US Rt 11 south side, adjoining and east of Fred and Edith Rose.

Elk County

Vendor: Ward & Dickinson #156
Date filed & Money still owed: 9/17/28 $6400
Vendee: J.R. Curry, res Ridgway
Info: 33' standard model

Vendor: Ward & Dickinson #179
Date filed & Money still owed: 10/8/28 .. satisfied 4/23/34 $6400 price named in contract
Vendee: O 7. Phelps(not sure on middle initial), res Ridgway
Info: 33' standard model

Vendor: Ward & Dickinson
Date filed & Money still owed: $4800
Vendee: Stella A. Beauseigner, res Johnsonburg
Info: none given

Erie County

Vendor: Dunkirk Dining car
Date filed & Money still owed: 11/3/1926 $4000
Vendee: William F Pollock
Info: renewed 7/9/1928

Vendor: Dunkirk Dining Car
Date filed & Money still owed: 7/21/28 $2675
Vendee: A.A. Smith
Info: assigned to Forestville bank 8/16/1932 #7205

Vendor: National Dining Car Co
Date filed & Money still owed: 4/18/1925 $3600
Vendee: Arthur Wasmund & M.L. Manning
Info: [Believed to be North East]

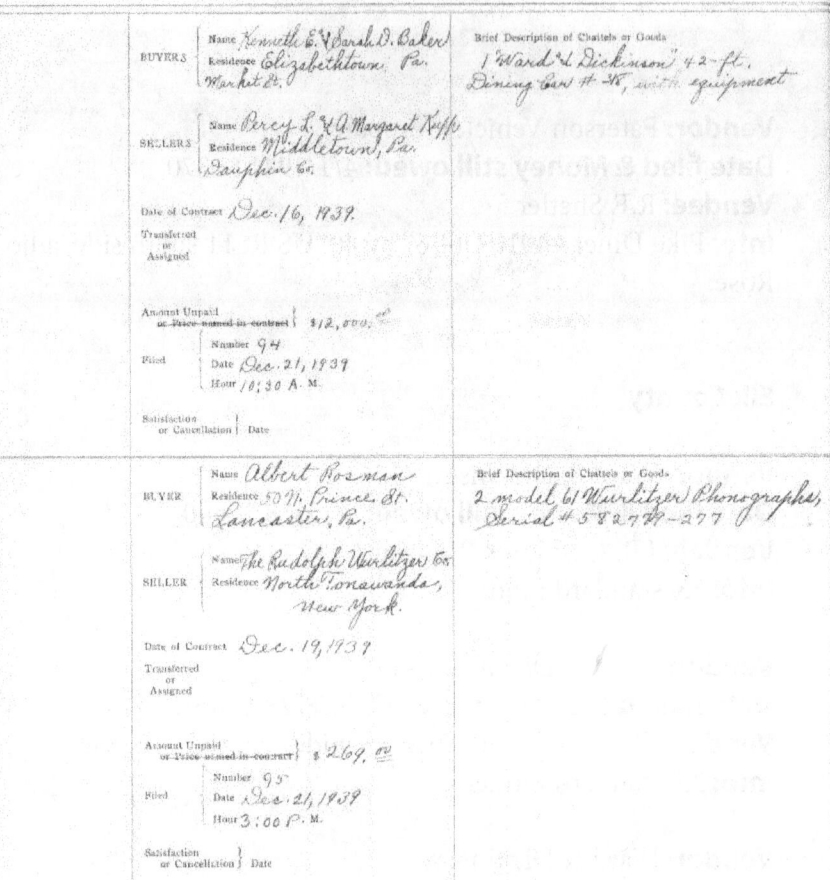

Example of a page from the Conditional Sales Docket records in Lancaster County, Pennsylvania. The top record is for a Ward and Dickinson diner that The Kupp family seemingly brokered. The family still runs a Ward and Dickinson diner in Middletown, Pennsylvania known as Kuppy's Diner.

Vendor: Wasmund Arthur
Date filed & Money still owed: 6/15/1925 $1
Vendee: Marion Manning
Info: interest in dining car

Vendor: Paterson Vehicle Co
Date filed & Money still owed: 5/11/1948 $18850
Vendee: R F MacKendrick Jr
Info: "Boston diner" satisfied 5/23/1951

Vendor: Paterson Vehicle Co
Date filed & Money still owed: 6/16/1948 $18800
Vendee: Harold E Curtis
Info: [Lawrence Park]

Vendor: Paterson Vehicle Co
Date filed & Money still owed: 7/18/1949 $19500
Vendee: R.J. Ross
Info: Satisfied 10/24/1952 [Robert Ross had diner at 3624 Peach in 1954]

Vendor: E.B. Richardson
Date filed & Money still owed: 9/4/1926 $1302 & $590.75
Vendee: George F Reinhardt

Vendor: Anthony C Seifert
Date filed & Money still owed: 9/4/1926 $1302 & $590.75
Vendee: R.G. Richardson

Vendor: George F Reinhardt
Date filed & Money still owed: 4/11/1927 $3000
Vendee: Leo W Schmidt
Info: Satisfied 11/2/1927

Vendor: Leo Schmidt
Date filed & Money still owed: 11/2/1927 $479.50
Vendee: George G Reinhardt

Vendor: Karle William
Date filed & Money still owed: 11/2/1927 $479.50
Vendee: George G Reinhardt

Vendor: Leo Reinhardt
Date filed & Money still owed: 11/22/1929 $1500
Vendee: George F Reinhardt

Vendor: Leo Reinhardt
Date filed & Money still owed: 3/17/1930 $2700
Vendee: Lawrence Cunningham

Vendor: Tierney
Date filed & Money still owed: 8/1/1926 $7250
Vendee: Leo C Reinhardt

Vendor: Tierney
Date filed & Money still owed: 6/21/1928 $502.50
Vendee: Leo C Reinhardt
Info: diner #1007

Vendor: Tierney
Date filed & Money still owed: 6/21/1928 $5819
Vendee: Leo C Reinhardt
Info: diner #2121

Vendor: Tierney
Date filed & Money still owed: 6/21/1930 $1850
Vendee: Leo C Reinhardt

Vendor: Tierney
Date filed & Money still owed: 11/11/1929 $5060
Vendee: Leo C Reinhardt
Info: Renewed $1575 11/11/1931

Vendor: Tierney
Date filed & Money still owed: 3/5/1931 $1349
Vendee: Leo & Geo Reinhardt

Vendor: Ward & Dickinson
Date filed & Money still owed:
Vendee: Louis DelPorto 6/6/27 6/6/1937 $3000 #4984 diner#53
Info: [Have never found Del Porto listed, so don't know what happened to this diner.]

Vendor: Ward & Dickinson
Date filed & Money still owed: 6/6/1927 $3000
Vendee: L.H. Youngman diner #59
Info: [Short time in Erie, quickly moved to Oil City, Penn then Waterford, NY]

Vendor: Ward & Dickinson
Date filed & Money still owed: 12/31/1927 $5500
Vendee: Val Manwaring
Info: [13th at French for only a few months. diner #78]

Vendor: Dickinson Lee & Ward Charles
Date filed & Money still owed: 6/9/1926 $4900

Vendee: A.M. Liebau
Info: [5 East 18th]

Vendor: Ward & Dickinson
Date filed & Money still owed: 3/27/1928 $1625
Vendee: A.M. Liebau diner #55
Info: [Continuation of above. diner sold to E Reynolds then B. Loper so may be below also.]

Vendor: Ward & Dickinson
Date filed & Money still owed: 7/16/1929 $7500
Vendee: E. Reynolds
Info: diner #209 [25 West 8th, sold to Hopkins] [This could be below, unsure]

Vendor: Ward & Dickinson
Date filed & Money still owed: 8/24/1929 $5100
Vendee: E. Reynolds
Info: +equipment [156 West 13th St]

Vendor: Ward & Dickinson
Date filed & Money still owed: 10/28/1929 $6300
Vendee: Mrs J.J. Schoos
Info: [710 Peach St. replaced Richardson model]

Vendor: Ward & Dickinson
Date filed & Money still owed: 3/26/1930 $460
Vendee: Mrs Gracell Hughes
Info: diner #15 [Came from Buffalo.] reconditioned

Vendor: Ward & Dickinson
Date filed & Money still owed: 2/6/1931 $6500
Vendee: R.F. MacKendrick
Info: [bought Schoos' diner.]

Vendor: Ward & Dickinson
Date filed & Money still owed: 9/30/1931 $4500
Vendee: Barbara Soper
Info: Satisfied 11/4/1938 [May be 156 West 13th St from Reynolds]

Vendor: Ward & Dickinson
Date filed & Money still owed: 10/31/1931 $6900
Vendee: Mark Hopkins #8692
Info: diner #209 [25 West 8th, moved to Westfield and called Elk Dinor in paper.]

McKean County

Vendor: Ward & Dickinson
Date filed & Money still owed: 3/28/27 $4800
Vendee: Joseph Fisher, Turtle Creek
Info: diner #48

Vendor: Ward & Dickinson
Date filed & Money still owed: 4/17/28 $3300
Vendee: Joseph C. & Mary Wasmund
Info: diner #18

Vendor: Ward & Dickinson
Date filed & Money still owed: 10/26/28 $5000
Vendee: Sylvester Falk & Leland R. Hansen, Mt. Jewett
Info: diner #3

Vendor: Ward & Dickinson
Date filed & Money still owed: 4/3/31 $8450
Vendee: Margaret Moore, Bradford
Info: diner #236

Vendor: Ward & Dickinson
Date filed & Money still owed: 5/13/35 $3790
Vendee: Margaret Moore, Bradford
Info: diner #210 41'6" w/ kitchen

CONTRACT OF CONDITIONAL SALE

THIS AGREEMENT, Made the 13th day of May, 1935, between Ward & Dickinson, Inc., a corporation organized under the laws of the State of New York, and having its principal place of business at Silver Creek, County of Chautauqua, State of New York, its successors or assigns, hereinafter called the vendor, party of the first part, and MARGARET S. MOORE, of the City of Bradford, County of McKean and State of Pennsylvania, hereinafter called the vendee, party of the second part,

WITNESSETH, the vendor, in consideration of the payments and agreements herein contained, has this day delivered to the vendee One "Ward & Dickinson" Dining Car #210, Special 41'6" with separate kitchen and equipment as follows:

    1 Electric Exhaust Fan, 1 Hood, 1 Steam Table, 1 Gasteam Radiator, 1 Grill, 1 Twin Coffee Urn, 1 Electric Refrigerator (Kelvinator), 1 Fire Extinguisher, 1 Clock, 2 Sinks, 1 Back Bar, 1 Counter with 11 Stools, 6 Built-in Tables with 12 Booth Seats, Electrical Fixtures and Wiring, 16 Transom Screens, 3 Screen Doors, Fan Thimble with cover, 1 Stack, 2 Kitchen Cupboards, 3 Cutting Boards, Awnings front side,

for the sum of Fifty-two Hundred Ninety and no/100 ($5290.00) Dollars, upon the following terms and conditions: Fifteen Hundred Dollars ($1500.00) in cash, the receipt whereof is hereby acknowledged, and the balance of $3790.00 to be paid in thirty-eight (38) monthly installments as shown by Schedule of Payments herein, at THE LIBERTY BANK OF BUFFALO, Buffalo, New York, together with interest thereon, at the rate of six percent (6%) per annum.

SCHEDULE OF PAYMENTS
(For which a series of thirty-eight notes have been given)

1 Note for $ 75.00 and interest, dated May 13, 1935, payable August 1, 1935
1 Note for $ 75.00 and interest, dated May 13, 1935, payable September 3, 1935

Above:

Margaret Moore's actual Contract of Conditional Sale. A few counties still have the actual contracts. They are arranged by number and the numbers can be found from the record in the Docket books.

Chapter 10

Diners Make a Comeback

The importance of being diner

Almost 30 years have passed since the publication of the two books that sparked the whole study of an enthusiasm for diner preservation: *Diners* by artist John Baeder and *American Diner* by Richard J.S. Gutman. Back in 1978, most people with any thoughts about it at all safely assumed that the American diner was headed for extinction, finally conquered by golden arches and orange roofs…leaving behind little more than fond memories and old postcards. Then these two books raised the status of the diner from obsolete restaurant form to unique and endangered American architectural form. Ultimately, some people sought [to] get their hands on one of the relatively numerous rundown but intact examples of the classic diner, hoping to give their acquisitions new life.

- Randy Garbin

Roadside Magazine Issue 33

If a doctor were to have examined the health of diners in the Midwest, they would have called for major surgery. But alas, no such person existed, no rescue squad was responding and no one was performing triage. The future of diners was getting darker and darker. Fortunately in the 1970s there were a couple of small glimmers of hope which would pay dividends in the future.

Whatever events we mention in this chapter are to be taken with a grain of salt. Diners are nowhere near as popular in the Midwest as they are in the Northeast. And the current positive examples of the recent past don't match the minor popularity that diners held in the Midwest in the 1920s.

Diners are more of a novelty in the Midwest today. Some are wildly successful, and others sit closed and neglected. The restaurant business is a fiercer battlefield than it was in the 1920s when the diner was often the only game in town during the nighttime hours and the fastest game in town in the daytime. Diners and lunch wagons popped up out of necessity. Today there are far too many choices for restaurant patrons, so diners are no longer at the top of most people's lists when they are seeking a meal. Perhaps with a little irony, food trucks have become very popular recently in many cities. In many ways, these truck harken back to the very earliest diners. However, instead of just serving dogs and coffee, they are now often manned by adventurous chefs who churn out all types of Asian, Mexican, Vietnamese and Thai food, along with classics like burgers and pizza.

The 1970s saw the popularity of the television show, "Happy Days." The show put a positive, wholesome spin on the decade of the 1950s, which happened to coincide with the "silver age" of the diner. Although the show focused on Al's Drive-in, (not specifically a diner as we define them) to the general public, the positive connotation went equally for the diner as it did for the drive-in.

By this time, the diner had become old enough that a few people began to study

Above:

The three books which helped to rekindle America's interest in diners. From left to right: Diners by John Baeder, American Diner by Richard J.S. Gutman and Classic Diners of the Northeast by Donald Kaplan and Alan Bellink.

Below:
The Empire Diner in Manhattan, New York is credited as being one of the diners that made "being diner" trendy again. Jack Doenias, Carl Laanes, and Richard Ruskay bought the diner in 1976 and are the ones who turned the diner's future around.

them as historical objects. Richard J.S. Gutman was a college student at Cornell University in Ithaca, New York in the 1970s. He would end up writing his thesis paper on diners and would follow this up with the seminal work on the history of diners, "American Diner," in 1979. John Baeder was an artist who was enamored with the diner. He began painting super realist images of actual diners and penned a book, "Diners," in 1978. In 1980, Donald Kaplan and Alan Bellink wrote the book, "Diners of the Northeast," which was also a very nice early arrival to the growing legion of diner aficionados.

On the metropolitan east coast, classic silver diners had already been significantly replaced by so-called "environmental" diners, starting in the early 1960s. These environmental diners would be larger restaurants covered with stone or brick. These new diners were still being built by the diner manufacturers of the glory days of the diner, but they were a different breed from the older stainless steel or porcelain enamel clad diners. While the interior footprint was still similar in some ways, more space was given to separate dining rooms in these newer diners.

Barry Levinson's 1982 film, "Diner" would really do the most to bring the diner into the minds of America. Take the positive feelings for the 1950s from "Happy Days" and mix it with the film, "Diner" and you have a recipe for a diner renaissance.

Other little things along the way helped the cause. The 1976 renovation of a dingy diner in New York City known as the Empire Diner. The diner spurred, nearly single handedly, the revival of the Chelsea neighborhood with a mix of classic American diner food, and upscale cuisine. In 1985, the Fog City Diner would be built in San Francisco to do the same thing, a mix of classic diner food and upscale cuisine.

On the museum side, Richard J. S. Gutman assisted the Henry Ford Museum in Dearborn, Michigan in acquiring Lamy's Diner, Worcester Lunch Car #789 in 1984. The diner was restored to its 1946 appearance and put in to the museum for all the visitors to view. The museum even has a restored Detroit lunch wagon in their Greenfield Village part of the

complex. Years later, other museums would take the Ford Museum's lead and purchase a diner to place in their museums.

In 1988, artist Jerry Berta of western Michigan decided to buy Uncle Bob's Diner which was wasting away in Flint, Michigan, almost ready for the scrap heap. His goal was to use the diner for an art studio. The idea worked, but this didn't stop many would-be customers from coming in and looking for hot food and a cup of coffee. Jerry didn't want to turn his diner back into a restaurant, but he did recognize the potential he had in Rockford, Michigan.

Berta went on the search for a diner where he could serve food and he found the famous Rosie's Diner, of Bounty paper towels fame, in New Jersey. Actress Nancy Walker had been cast as "Rosie" and over the years shot innumerable commercials behind the counter in that Paramount diner.

Jerry bought the diner and had it moved to his site in Michigan. The diner was an instant success. In 1992, he bought a Silk City diner from Fulton, New York in an attempt to open an upscale diner experience similar to the Empire or Fog City diners. That diner never got off the ground and after Jerry sold the complex to a local businessman, the whole diner set-up was never really a success for future operators.

All these successes led other people to purchase, move and restore diners in the Midwest. In Michigan, diners would move into Birch Run, Grand Rapids and Grand Marais, a diner brokered through Jerry himself. And in Iowa, Gordon Tindall relived the love of diners he had from his youth and bought the Clarksville Diner from outside of Princeton, New Jersey. Not only did he now own a diner, but he had it moved to Decorah, Iowa, a progressive thinking small city/college town in northeast Iowa. Tindall would go on to beautifully restore two other diners, but he was not the only person to try his hand at restoring diners.

Al Sloan and Steve Harwin also moved diners into their respective Midwestern

Above:
Lamy's Diner started out in Massachusetts from 1946 to 1984 before being bought by the Henry Ford Museum in Dearborn, Michigan. Richard J.S. Gutman assisted the museum in their three year effort to restore the diner to its original splendor.

locations. Al was living around Alpena, Michigan and moved four diners from the east coast. One diner, an O'Mahony from Wilkes Barre is doing business today on the south side of Alpena, with different owners. Of Al's three other diners, one came from outside of Port Jervis, New York which he sold to a couple from Sabina, Ohio, and the last two he still has in his possession. One of them is a Sterling Dinette from Rochester, New York and the other was the Sidetrack Café from Hudson, Massachusetts, a Worcester Lunch Car.

Steve Harwin would have a much more profound effect on diners in the Midwest. Harwin stated in Roadside Magazine that he has been involved in diners since 1985, and brokered his first deal in 1987, which he say was at a loss in order to save the diner. Steve Harwin has restored well over a dozen diners since then, many which have stayed in Midwest locations. Three of them remained in Cleveland, while others are in Sabina, Grafton and Port Clinton, Ohio; Baraboo, Lake Geneva and Delta, Wisconsin, and Harmony Corners and Canton Township, Michigan. Harwin moved one to Ottawa, Ohio, but that venture was short lived and the diner was eventually moved to New Hampshire.

Harwin is slowing down his work at restoring and selling diners today, although he is the best choice if you are looking for a ready-to-go vintage diner. In 2015, he sent the former Venus Diner of Gibsonia, Pennsylvania to Minneapolis, Minnesota. The Venus has become the Hi-Lo Diner, which is helping to rejuvenate the Longfellow, East Lake corridor with hip diner food and fancy cocktails. More importantly, it is a positive

Above:

Dinerville, as it was called, was Jerry Berta's attempt to mix art and food, all centered around diners. Not seen in this photo, but Berta even built a replica of a diner to the right of the diner closest in this photo. The Diner Store offered art and Rosie's Diner offered food.

business presence to the neighborhood.

With some minor success in building affordable "retro" styled diners by a company called Diner-Mite in Atlanta, Georgia, two Iowa men thought they could cash in on the pending diner craze in the late 1980s. Timothy Costigan and Steve Strauss decided to start a chain of diners to be named the Solid Gold Diners. They placed the first two in Columbus Junction and North Liberty, Iowa in 1989 with plans to open more if these proved to be successful. They hired Lester Timmerman and Ray Larson, previously of Commander Buildings, to build the diners. Timmerman and Larson formed DeBest Diners in Cedar Rapids, Iowa and started to build the two diners for the Solid Gold Diner chain. The Solid Gold chain was short lived and was out of business by 1995. The Columbus Junction diner was moved to Burlington, Iowa and finally landed in Sterling, Illinois. Ironically, the diner was demolished a short time ago in the name of urban renewal.

Another small concern was Mike Risko's Classic Diner venture. Risko ran hotels in the Lansing, Michigan vicinity and decided to venture into the restaurant field with new diners. He contacted an Indiana trailer builder and subcontracted to have that company essentially turn their trailer body into a diner. Risko ran the first diner he had built himself and placed the aptly named Classic Diner in a suburb of Lansing, Michigan. Plans to place a diner on the shores of Lake Michigan never materialized, but he did sell a diner to a Connecticut businessman.

In 1992, Bill Starcevic started Starlite Diners in Ormond Beach, Florida. Roadside Magazine reported in their summer 1993 issue that "Starlite is a brand-new diner manufacturer started in 1992 by Starcevic, a contractor and ardent diner-fan. Sensing the growing demand, Starcevic decided to set up shop building diners in the classic

Above:
Suzie Q's in Mason City, Iowa before the grant (left) and after the grant was received to bring the Valentine diner back to its original appearance. (right)
Suzie Q's was one of two Valentines in Mason City at one time. The other was originally owned by Lawrence Welk in what he had hoped would have been a chain of Valentine diners painted like accordians. Welk was a native of the midwest, having grown up in North Dakota.

Below:

The Solid Gold Diner as it was being demolished in Sterling, Illinois. The diner started out in Columbus Junction, Iowa in 1989 before moving to Sterling in the mid 1990s.

(Sterling and Rock Falls Historical Society)

1950s style." The diners were on the low end of the price scale in part due to Florida's pro-business benefits. Diners built in the north-east can easily cost seven figures and most of the Starlite models cost between one to two hundred thousand dollars. Starcevic also didn't use typical, now costly, 1950s diner materials. Instead of using stainless street, he used chrome. The ceiling was no longer Formica panels, now they were pressed "tin" aluminum tiles which were much more cost effective.

Starlite did a good business for about seven to nine years before things quieted down with the company. The business was sold and then bought back by Starcevic before closing up shop roughly around 2005. First selling to places like Pigeon Forge, Tennessee, Essex, Maryland, Novi, Michigan and all over Florida. They broke in to the mid-west with their contract to build for chains like Denny's Diners or Penny's Diner and through Waverly, Ohio resident Mike Corwin.

In the late 1990s, the Denny's chain decided to give their franchisees a second option for owners looking for a different type of rebranding for their buildings. Denny's offered its franchisees the opportunity to purchase a brand new diner through Starlite that was designed by Starcevic with plans accepted by Denny's. Roughly forty Denny's Diners were built and were placed all over the country. Some of the diners found their way into Minnesota, Indiana, Illinois and Ohio while a fair number also made their way into Florida or Texas. In Wisconsin Dells, Wisconsin, the owner liked the design, but thought the Starlite building was too small of a footprint, so they had a stick built replica of a Starlite built that could fool all except for the most knowledgeable diner historians.

Penny's Diners was another chain that decided to use the Starlite model. A new hotel chain, called the Oak Tree Inn was started in 1984. The hotel's concept was to give railroad men a decent option, and was set up in many railroad towns. The owners of the hotel chain also wanted a 24 hour restaurant option for their intended guests, and decided to go with the modular option. You will only

Above:

Various photographs from the Clarksville Diner that Gordon Tindall brought from near his boyhood home in Princeton Junction, New Jersey to Iowa. Tindall had the diner trucked to Decorah, Iowa where he ran it for a number a years before selling the diner to a French Television Production Company. (Gordon Tindall)

Below:

Mike Risko's Classic Diner of Delta Charter Township, a suburb of Lansing, Michigan just before its opening. Risko subcontracted with a mobile home manufacturer in Indiana to have his diners built.

be able to find a Penny's Diner next to an Oak Tree Inn. Penny's Diners are mostly located in non-diner towns from western Virginia to California. Oak Tree Inn has started building on site diners that often look very similar to the Starlite diners, since Starlite stopped making diners. Of all diners today, these Penny's Diners come the closest to giving you the feeling of being a traveler in the 1930s, looking for that one restaurant in town still ready to serve you at two in the morning, the diner. As their website announces, "Most of our hotels feature a Penny's Diner located adjacent to the property, so there are no worries if you're hungry at check-in or any other time of day or night."

Mike Corwin came from a family of diner owners. His father had four diners in central Ohio, and when he himself retired from the Police force in Waverly, Ohio, he decided to open his own diner. He contracted with Starlite to have his Diner 23 built in 2000. Through talking with people in the general vicinity who also wanted to open up a restaurant, his dealings with Starlite led to the opening of at least four other Starlite diners in southern Ohio.

Today, the mid-west may be the saving grace for the classic diner America has known and loved. Many places in the east seem to have shunned the stainless steel and smaller diners for either chains or larger stick built restaurants. While the food truck has gained popularity by leaps and bounds, the smaller sized diners have often been labeled unprofitable and undesirable. New Jersey even has a number of large diners that have been remodeled to look more like a chain restaurant than anything similar to a diner. Over the past five to ten years, the east coast has lost a fair number of classic stainless steel diners that could have been had for the price of simply moving the diners. Not that moving a diner is simple any longer, but these diners were available.

Just maybe, we hope that more people will see the overwhelming successes of the diner by a few people in the Midwest and decide that they too want to open a diner in a region

where an old time classic diner will really stand out. While a diner is still a tough business, there are success stories out there, and a few more people looking to add to that list.

Jeffrey Castree bought the former Rosie's Diner from Groton, Connecticut from Steve Harwin and placed it just outside of downtown Baraboo, right on Main Street. The diner has been nothing less than a full blown success. Harwin also sold a restored Silk City diner to a party in Sabina, Ohio that was not a successful endeavor. Within a few years, the diner in Sabina was closed, and has sat idle for what seems to be close to ten years.

A couple years before Harwin sold a diner to Castree, he sold one to Denise and Rick Shutek in 2007 which was added to the side of their restaurant building in Grafton, Ohio known as Nancy's Main Street Diner. At times it seems like the diner acts more as overflow seating to the original restaurant. But the diner is usually the part of the building that gets photographed the most. In the case of Nancy's Main Street Diner, business continues to be a popular affair.

Indiana had a number of Mountain View diners that dwindled slowly but surely over the years. In Plainfield, the Oasis Diner lingered and faced demolition. Typically the local governmental organization either has no opinion or they want the diner gone with no concern for history. The Town of Plainfield was different. They wanted to find a way to preserve the diner. When Doug Huff heard about this, he decided to look into getting involved. The prospect of saving the diner appealed to him as both a business and historical opportunity. With help from his father-in-law who was well versed in construction, he worked with the Town of Plainfield, the Diner owners and Indiana Landmarks for over three and a half years to get the diner moved to a new location. Even with all the support received, Huff still ran into a number of obstacles that might have stopped the process, but as Huff said, "…as these issues would arise, solutions would also arise and the project was able to continue to the finish by God's grace." Today, the diner is a blessing to the community and an asset for the historical National

Above:

Denise and Rick Shutek bought a Silk City diner from Steve Harwin and had it shipped to their Grafton, Ohio location. The diner has moved around a number of times, having started out in Ono or possibly Exton, Pennsylvania. After Pennsylvania, Steve Harwin obtained and rehabbed the diner before it was sold to the Log School out of Boston, Massachusetts. For a couple of years, the Log School trained at risk youth at the diner. Harwin reobtained the diner and sold it to the Shuteks.

Above:

An assortment of photographs from the rescuing of the current Spud Boy Lunch. The diner spent nearly eighty years in Wellington, Ohio where Michael Engle, Daniel Zilka (top photo) and Toni Deller worked to remove the diner from that location. A few years later, the diner was given to Gordon Tindall (lower left) who worked tirelessly to restore the diner and put it back into operation.

Road that it sits on. "Our goal is to not only tell our own story of the history of the Diner, but also allow our guests to relive their own history as well," Huff adds.

Frank's Diner in Kenosha, Wisconsin is a rare survivor from 1926. Owners in 1936 bricked in the diner and created more seating just outside the original diner. Without that extra seating, the diner may well have been demolished for lack of seating. The diner today could use five times the seating it has today! It is a huge success, owing to its multiple appearances on television and travel shows. The old grill in the diner is used solely for their famous garbage plate that consists of eggs, hash browns and whatever else you want to add to that to make it your own. The cook in charge of that station can often be seen making eight at a time, flipping and then plating each one, only to start over after a quick cleaning of the grill. The diner stayed in the Frank family until 2001when it went through a series of ownership changes. None of these ownership changes, though, have been a detriment on the business.

The other success is happening in Lanesboro, Minnesota. Gordon Tindall is running his third diner. A diminutive 20 seat diner greets customers six months of the year in the small arts community of Lanesboro. Despite this being his smallest diner, and located in a community of less than a thousand people, this diner is his biggest success. Slowly but surely people are happy they're entering the 30' by 10' Goodell built diner for breakfast. Everything is pretty good at the Spud Boy Lunch. Sadly, Gordon's knees are not what they used to be, and he has the diner for sale.

This Goodell diner is the last of its kind. The diner spent most of its days operating under various names in Wellington, Ohio until around 2002 when Michael Engle saved the diner with immense help from Daniel Zilka and Toni Deller. The diner was given to Gordon Tindall a few years later who worked on restoring the place. After working the breakfast and lunch shift at his Red Rose Diner in Towanda, Pennsylvania, Gordon would put in another six or seven hours at night working on the Goodell diner. After successfully fixing the diner up, Tindall had it shipped to Lanesboro, Minnesota where

he and his wife Val Tindall readied the place for reopening to the public in 2012.

A not as old diner, Suzie Q's Diner in Mason City, Iowa also got a nice renovation. Troy Levenhagen applied for a community grant to restore the exterior of his Valentine diner to its original condition. The Valentine with eight seats is a constant side trip for visitors coming to Mason City to see the site of the filming for The Music Man or the Frank Lloyd Wright designed Historic Park Inn.

All of these successes have helped to lead to a few more diners coming to the region. Lake Geneva, Wisconsin saw Joni's Diner open in late 2013. Joni's is the former DeCoven Diner, a 1950s O'Mahony Diner from Duncannon, Pennsylvania which spent a short time in Connecticut before coming to Wisconsin. Recently in 2015, the Hi-Lo Diner is up and running in Minneapolis. This is the former Venus Diner, a 1955 Fodero from Gibsonia, Pennsylvania picked up by Steve Harwin.

Diner-Mite, mentioned earlier in this chapter, is still making diners, and while Bill Starcevic stopped making diners in 2005, new Starlite diners can still be bought today. Don Memberg contracted with Starcevic to build Starlite diners under the name Modular Diners. Don worked for DinerMite before going out on his own. Besides brokering deals on used diners, he has built diners for the Panama Canal Zone, North Carolina and Idaho.

Above:
One of the newer Starlite diners which is currently located in Moscow, Idaho.

Above:

Penny's Diner in Low Moor, Virginia. The diner was moved from Maryland up into the mountains of Virginia to serve the patrons of the Oak Tree Inn. Nearby Clifton Forge is a CSX Rail Hub.

Below:

Another recently built Starlite model of diner. Roger's Diner sits on the campus of the Tryon International Equestrian Center in Tryon, North Carolina.

Great Lakes Diner Directory

Introduction:

Word of caution: Things change. This directory was put together in 2017 and 2018 and is by no means complete. Some of the photos are newer than others. Nearly every photo has been taken by the author, but a few, as specified, were taken by different individuals. This directory is the author's best effort to document the current diners of the Great Lakes.

Do you want to visit these diners? Do you want to eat at these diners? Please do your own research before you visit. Check on-line. As the author was working on this book, he visited a particular diner one day in early April, only to hear that the diner closed a few days later. We also have no included hours for any of the diners mentioned here.

During another day, the author intended to meet a friend at a different diner. First he checked their facebook page and noticed they were open on Wednesday evenings. So he scheduled a meeting for Wednesday evening, only to find out when they both reached the diner, it was closed for the day. After a call to the diner, we found out the diner closed on Wednesday evenings in the winter and made no effort to make a note of this change on their facebook page.

If you want to guarantee a diner is open, call them before you visit. While you are at it, check to make sure all the roads between you and the diner are open. Some states are more willing than others to close sections of road and force lengthy alternative routes.

Lastly, this list is not all inclusive. Did the author miss a diner? It is bound to happen. In a strange way, the author hopes there are more diners out there that he missed and that you the reader will tell him about them. For example, the author only heard about the diner in Mount Olive, Illinois within the past year.

IOWA

1. Dinky Diner, Decatur City
2. Fort Diner, Fort Madison
3. Suzie Q's Diner, Mason City
4. Penny's Diner, Missouri Valley
5. diner, Muscatine
6. Archie's Diner, Sioux City
7. Grand Diner, Spencer
8. diner, Spirit Lake

1. **Dinky Diner** – 104 NE 4th Street, **Decatur City** (Valentine)
   The Dinky Diner was originally the Elkhorn Diner in Ellsworth, Kansas, which opened in 1967. This variety of Valentine diner is called a Double Deluxe and is a later model Valentine. Unlike earlier Valentine diners, this model sports a counter and a number of booths.

2. **Fort Diner** – 801 Ave H., **Fort Madison** (Butler Mfg)
   The Fort Diner is a very rare Butler built diner. The diner was used in Butler's advertising so we can tell that the diner is quite original. The diner has a counter and some tables along the windows, and all the cooking is done behind the grill.

3. **Suzie Q's Diner** – 14 2nd Street NW, **Mason City** (Valentine)
   Suzie Q's is a ten stool Little Chef model Valentine diner. The diner opened up in 1948 and has been at the same spot since. Owner Troy Levenhagen has made the diner well known for its breaded pork tenderloin.

4. **Penny's Diner** – 128 South Willow Road, **Missouri Valley** (Starlite)
   This Penny's Diner, a Starlite, is made up of a single main unit and a vestibule in front. The diner is open 24 hours a day

5. **diner** – in storage, **Muscatine** (Valentine)
   This Valentine, a Little Chef model, operated in Mount Pleasant, Mount Union, Danville and Muscatine before being placed in storage at a local school.

6. **Archie's Diner** – 723 W 7th Street, **Sioux City** (1941 Kullman)
   The diner has been in Sioux city since 1949. Archie Arvin bought it in 1985 and his wife Laurie Arvin runs it on the weekends as a tribute to her late husband.

7. **Grand Diner** – 208 Grand Avenue, **Spencer** (Valentine)
   An eight stool Valentine diner that has been sided over on the outside. The innterior counter was taken out and replaced with table seating. The diner has been in town since roughly 1948.

8. **diner** – 1480 Lake Street, **Spirit Lake** (Starlite)
   This Starlite diner has been closed for a number of years. Before closing it was a Mexican restaurant for a couple of years.

1

2

3

4

5

6

7

8

MINNESOTA

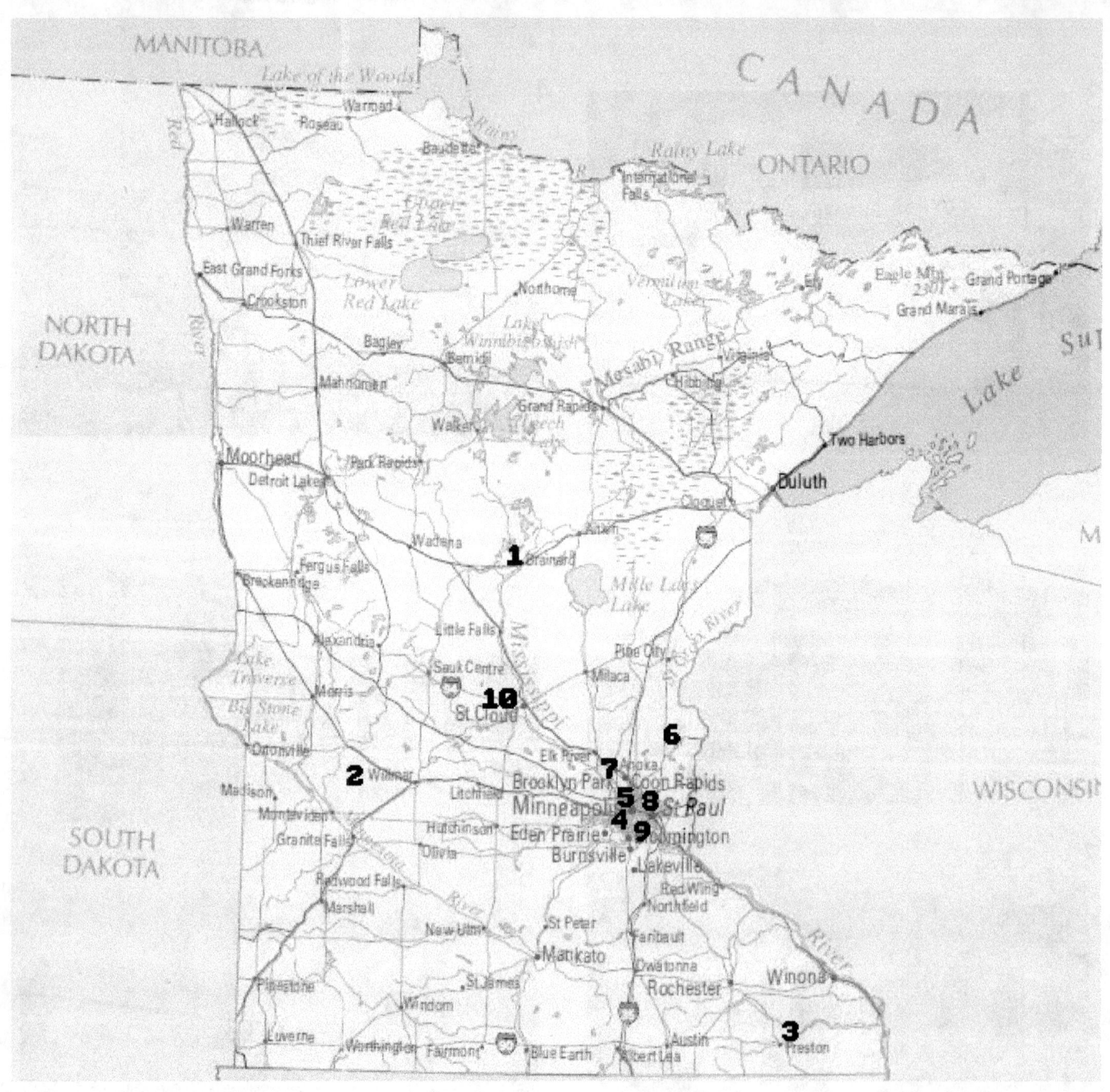

1. 371 Diner, Baxter
2. Whistle Stop, Benson
3. Spud Boy Lunch, Lanesboro
4. Hi-Lo Diner, Minneapolis
5. Band Box, Minneapolis
6. Denny's Classic Diner, North Branch
7. Denny's Classic Diner, Rogers
8. Mickey's Dining Car, St. Paul
9. Chicago's Taste Authority, St. Paul
10. Park Diner, Waite Park

1. **371 Diner** – 1175 Edgewood Drive, **Baxter** (Starlite)
   This Starlite diner is located in a summer vacation area of Minnesota. The diner is made up of three segments and a vestibule.

2. **Whistle Stop** – 1220 Atlantic Avenue, **Benson** (Railroad Car)
   The railroad car has been in Benson as a diner since 1934. It is greatly remodeled today.

3. **Spud Boy Lunch** – 105.75 Parkway Avenue N., **Lanesboro** (1927 Goodell)
   The last Goodell built diner extant. The diner spent over 70 years in Wellington, Ohio before Gordon Tindall moved it to Lanesboro. Gordon restored the diner very close to its original appearance.

4. **Hi-Lo Diner** – 4020 East Lake Street, **Minneapolis** (1957 Fodero)
   The former Venus Diner of Gibsonia, Pennsylvania which was restored by Steve Harwin before moving to Minnesota. The current owners have a slightly upscale diner menu.

5. **Band Box** – 729 South 10th Street, **Minneapolis** (Butler Mfg)
   The last of a chain of 15 Band Boxes around Minneapolis. This diner dates back to 1939. Current owners enlarged the place. During my 2014 visit, I enjoyed the hamburger.

6. **Denny's Classic Diner** – 38681 Tanger Drive, **North Branch** (Starlite)
   A Denny's restaurant housed inside a Starlite diner, located at an outlet mall.

7. **Denny's Classic Diner** – 13450 Rogers Drive, **Rogers** (Starlite)
   A Denny's restaurant located just off of I-94 in a commercial district.

8. **Mickey's Dining Car** – 36 7th Street W., **St. Paul** (1937 O'Mahony)
   A St. Paul icon. The long narrow diner, made for shipping by rail by O'Mahony is one of the most preserved O'Mahony diners anywhere, even while being open 24 hours a day, seven days a week.

9. **Chicago's Taste Authority** – 603 7th Street W., **St. Paul** (Interurban)
   The converted trolley car has not acted as a diner in a long time, but it is still a restaurant and is not that far from Mickey's Diner.

10. **Park Diner** – 1531 Division Street, **Waite Park** (Starlite)
    This Starlite diner is made up of two sections and a vestibule. The owners have been operating the diner for over twenty years. The diner sits in front of a movie theatre.

1

2

3

4

5

6

7

8

9

10

(Delia Bell)

WISCONSIN

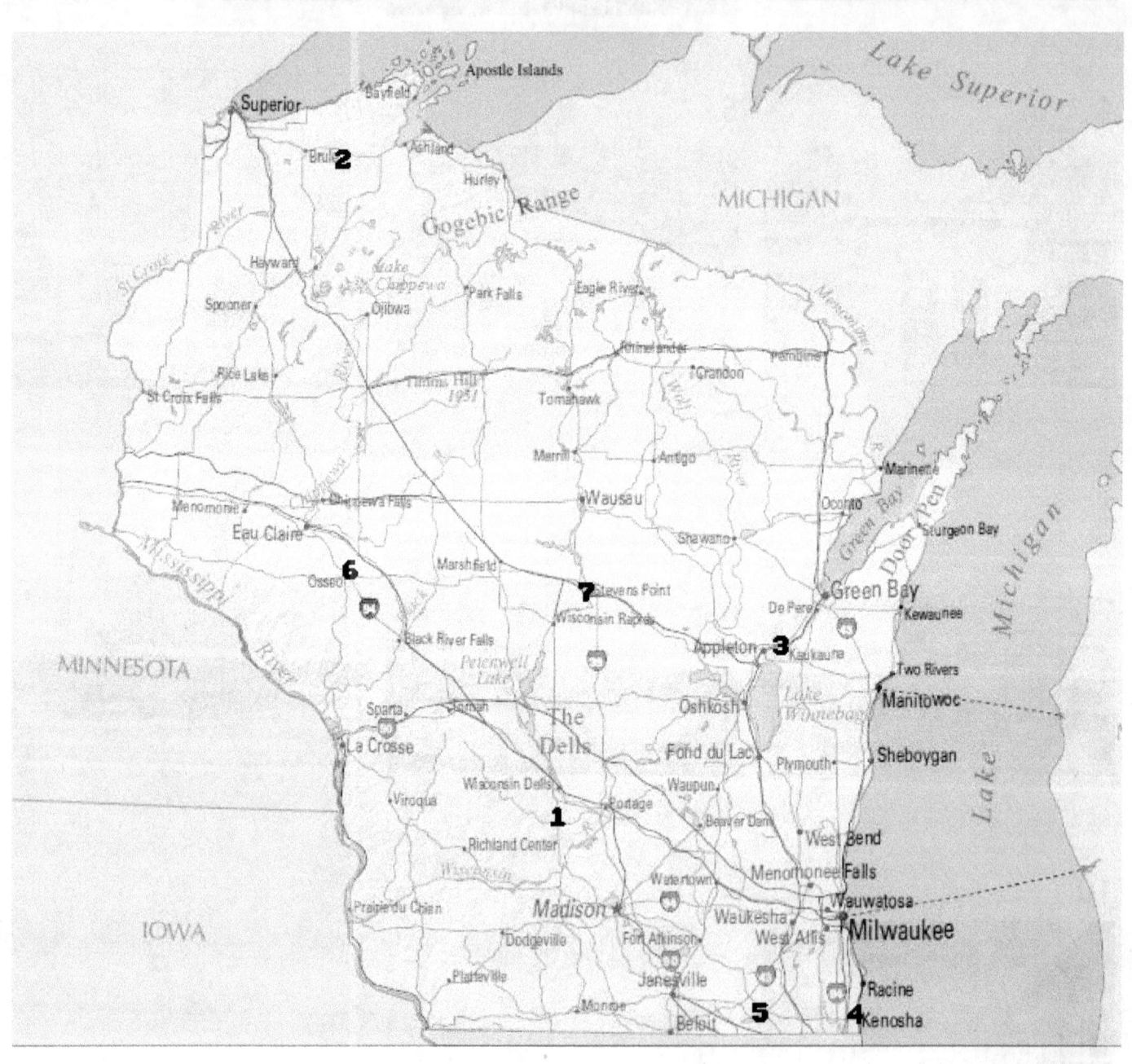

1. Broadway Diner, Baraboo
2. Delta Diner, Delta
3. diner, Kaukauna
4. Frank's Diner, Kenosha
5. Joni's Diner, Lake Geneva
6. Moe's Diner, Osseo
7. Silver Coach, Stevens Point

1. **Broadway Diner** – 304 Broadway Street, **Baraboo** (1954 Silk City)
   Steve Harwin spruced up the former Rosie's Diner from Connecticut and added a nice on-site addition for owner Jeffrey Castree. Diner has been well received by the city of Baraboo.

2. **Delta Diner** – 14385 County Highway H., **Delta** (Silk City)
   An upscale take on a diner menu in a Silk City Diner that was restored by Steve Harwin. The diner came from somewhere in New York state and prospers in northern Wisconsin.

3. **diner** – 2930 Lawe Street, **Kaukauna** (Starlite)
   A closed Starlite diner that sits right off of I-41.

4. **Frank's Diner** – 508 58th Street, **Kenosha** (1920s O'Mahony)
   An icon. A well preserved, but well used, 1920s O'Mahony diner that is constantly packed with eager customers who often order "Frank's Garbage Plate."

5. **Joni's Diner** – 111 S Wells Street, **Lake Geneva** (1954 O'Mahony)
   A recent addition to Wisconsin, the O'Mahony diner sits on the outskirts of downtown Lake Geneva, a resort town for Chicago residents. Formerly the DeCoven Diner of Pennsylvania.

6. **Moe's Diner** – 12701 10th Street, **Osseo** (Diner-Mite)
   A seasonal Diner-Mite built diner just off of I-94.

7. **Silver Coach** – 38 Park Ridge Drive, **Stevens Point** (Smith & Barney Railroad Sleeper Car)
   More of an upscale restaurant, but included because it is partially housed in a railroad car.

283

ILLINOIS

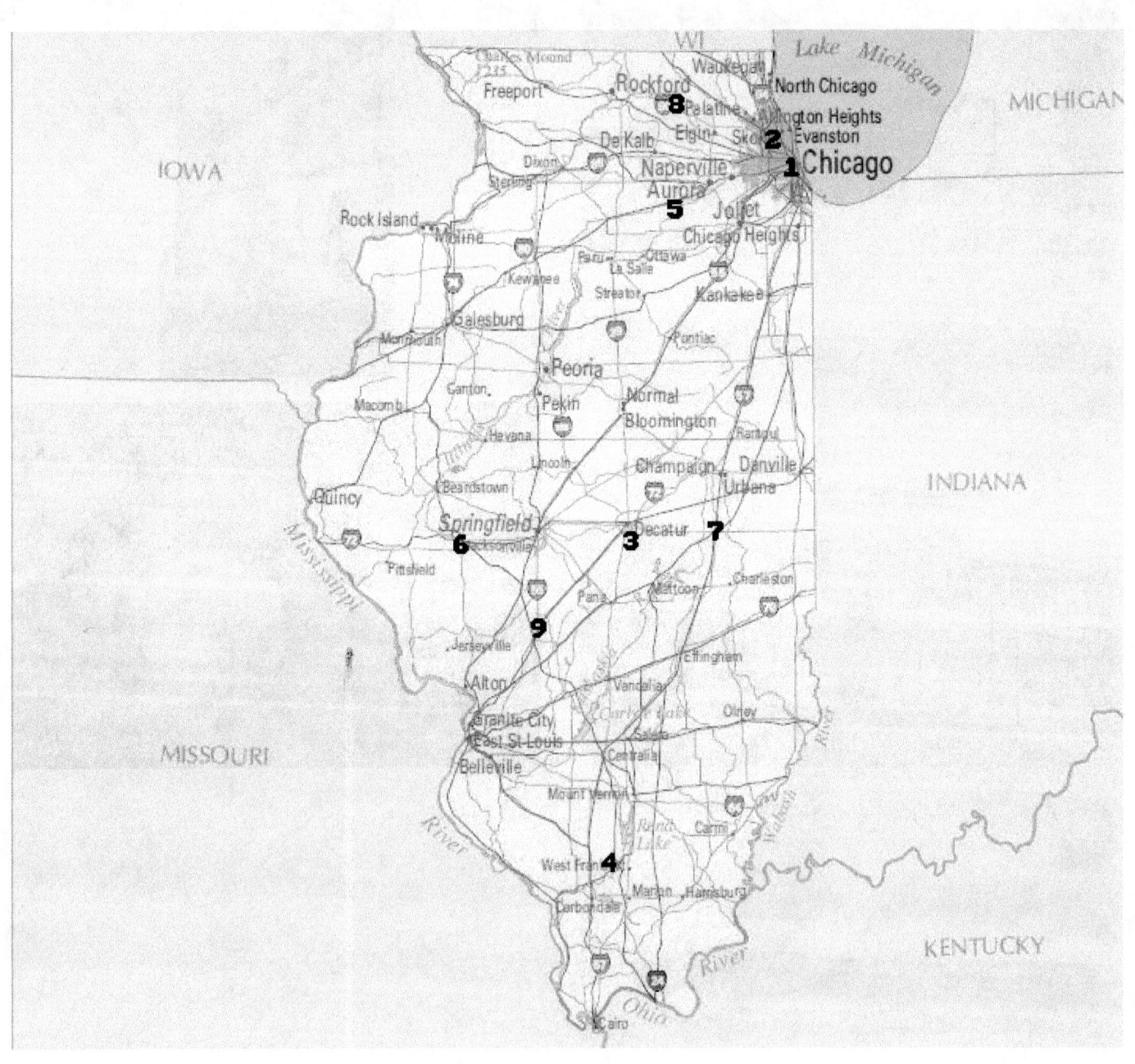

1. Tutto Italian Restaurant, Chicago
2. Diner Grill
3. Four Star Family Restaurant, Mount Zion
4. diner, Royalton
5. Kelly's Pub, Sandwich
6. diner, South Jacksonville
7. Denny's Classic Diner, Tuscola
8. diner, Union
9. Crossroads Rt 66 Diner, Mt. Olive

1. **Tutto Italian Restaurant** – 505 South Wells, **Chicago** (Converted interurban)
   An upscale Italain restaurant which is partially housed in a converted interurban car.

2. **Diner Grill** – 1635 W. Irving Park Road, **Chicago** (Formerly train car)
   The diner was housed in a highly remodeled train car up until 2017 when a devastating fire closed the location. Reopened in mid 2018. An iconic Chicago 24/7 place for food.

3. **Four Star Family Restaurant** – 1100 N State Route 121, **Mount Zion** (Starlite)
   A Starlite with a large glass block vestibule.

4. **diner** – 207 South Main, **Royalton** (Tierney)
   The closed diner sits in the former coal mining town of Royalton. The diner last saw business as a BBQ joint and is said to have come from Chicago.

5. **Bull Moose Pub & Grill** – 202 South Main Street, **Sandwich** (1893 Pullman Palace dining car)
   Originally a diner, the former railroad dining car has seen more than its share of non diner restaurants housed inside in the last twenty or so years, along with a number of remodelings.

6. **diner** – 100 Comfort Drive, **South Jacksonville** (Starlite)
   Formerly the Three Star Family Restaurant, the Starlite looks similar to the Four Star in Mt. Zion.

7. **Denny's Classic Diner** – 1104 Tuscola Boulevard, **Tuscola** (Starlite)
   A typical Denny's restaurant which sits in front of a outlet mall right off of I-57

8. **diner** – Illinois Railway Museum, 7000 Olson Road, **Union** (1934 O'Mahony)
   The diner started out in Salem, Ohio then moved to Akron, Ohio before being sold to the Illinois Railway Museum. The diner is still being restored and plans are not definite for its usage.

9. **Crossroads Rt 66 Diner** – Old Rte 66 @ Lakeview Drive, **Mt. Olive** (Valentine)
   Seems to be a two piece long Valentine diner with a rare double horseshoe counter, with what looks like a 1970s addition placed on the side.

1

(Jeff Zoline)

2

3

4

5

6

7

8

9

INDIANA

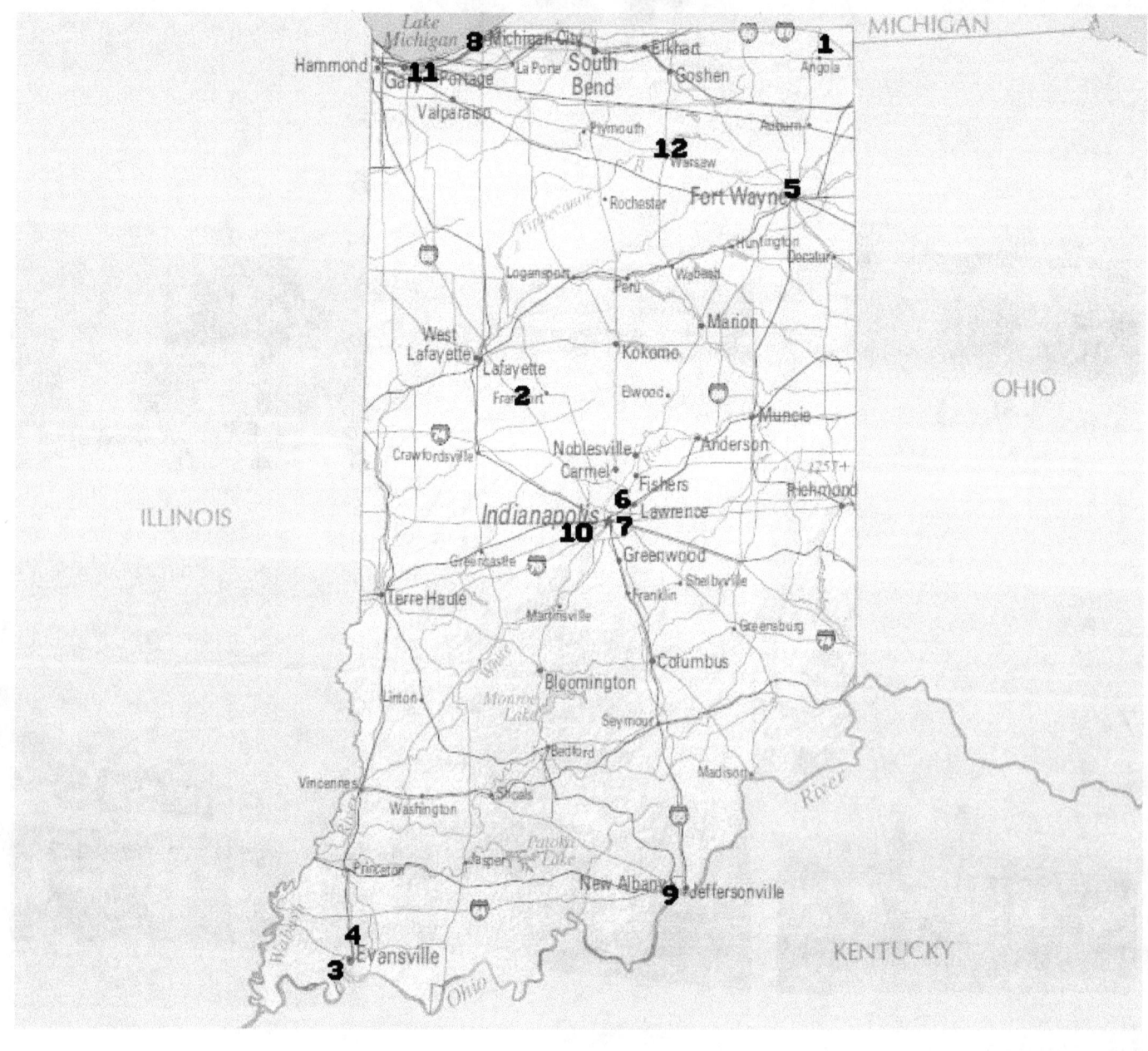

1. diner @ NATMUS, Angola
2. diner, Clarks Hill
3. Denny's Classic Diner, Evansville
4. Denny's Classic Diner, Evansville
5. Cindy's Diner, Fort Wayne
6. Subway Subs, Indianapolis
7. Sanitary Diner, Indianapolis
8. diner, Michigan City
9. Lady Tron's, New Albany
10. Oasis Diner, Plainfield
11. Schoop's, Portage
12. Schoop's, Warsaw

1. **diner @ NATMUS** – 1000 Gordon M Buehrig Place, **Auburn** (Valentine)
   This Valentine diner sat on US Rt 20 just outside of downtown Auburn for a number of years before being restored by the local car museum and placed on display inside the museum.

2. **diner** – US Route 52 @ IN Route 28, **Clarks Hill** (Mountain View)
   This Mountain View diner has not been open for years. It sits on a bypassed four lane section of US Rt 52, in front of a 1950s motel.

3. **Denny's Classic Diner** – 5212 Weston Road, **Evansville** (Starlite)
   The local Denny's operator bought two Starlites for their Evansville operation.

4. **Denny's Classic Diner** – 19501 Elphers Road, **Evansville** (Starlite)
   The local Denny's operator bought two Starlites for their Evansville operation.

5. **Cindy's Diner** – 230 West Berry Street, **Fort Wayne** (Valentine)
   Iconic Valentine diner in downtown Fort Wayne that has moved a couple of times. Longtime employee Angie Harter bought it from long time owners John and Cindy Scheele in 2016.

6. **Subway Subs** – 5151 East 38th, **Indianapolis** (Mountain View)
   Originally the Meadowbrook Diner, the current owner is still respectful to keeping the place still looking like a diner on the outside.

7. **Sanitary Diner** – Campus of Angie's List, **Indianapolis** (1937 O'Mahony)
   Not open for business, but you can still snap a photo of a Steve Harwin restoration. The diner started in Cleveland, Ohio and moved to Pennsylvania for some years before Harwin acquired it.

8. **diner** – 920 Franklin Street, **Michigan City** (Valentine)
   This double Deluxe Valentine diner is said to have opened up in 1956 and became a Barber Shop sometime in the 1970s.

9. **Lady Tron's** – 147 East Market Street, **New Albany** (Valentine)
   The Little Chef Valentine model in New Albany has received a new coat of paint that models its "retro outer space vibe" as the current owner explains it.

10. **Oasis Diner** – 405 West Main Street, **Plainfield** (1954 Mountain View)
    Iconic Mountain view diner that has seen new life on the National Road(US Rt 40) The current diner features breaded pork tenderloin and its own bakery.

11. **Schoop's** – 3285 Willow Creek Road, **Portage** (Starlite)
    This Starlite is part of a Chicagoland chain that serves hamburgers.

12. **Schoop's** – US Route 30 @ Old US Route 30, **Warsaw** (Starlite)
    This Starlite is part of a Chicagoland chain that serves hamburgers. This Starlite started as the Boston Grill in 1995 before becoming a Schoops a few years later.

1

2

3

(Gordon Tindall)

4

5

6

7

8

9

10

11

12

MICHIGAN

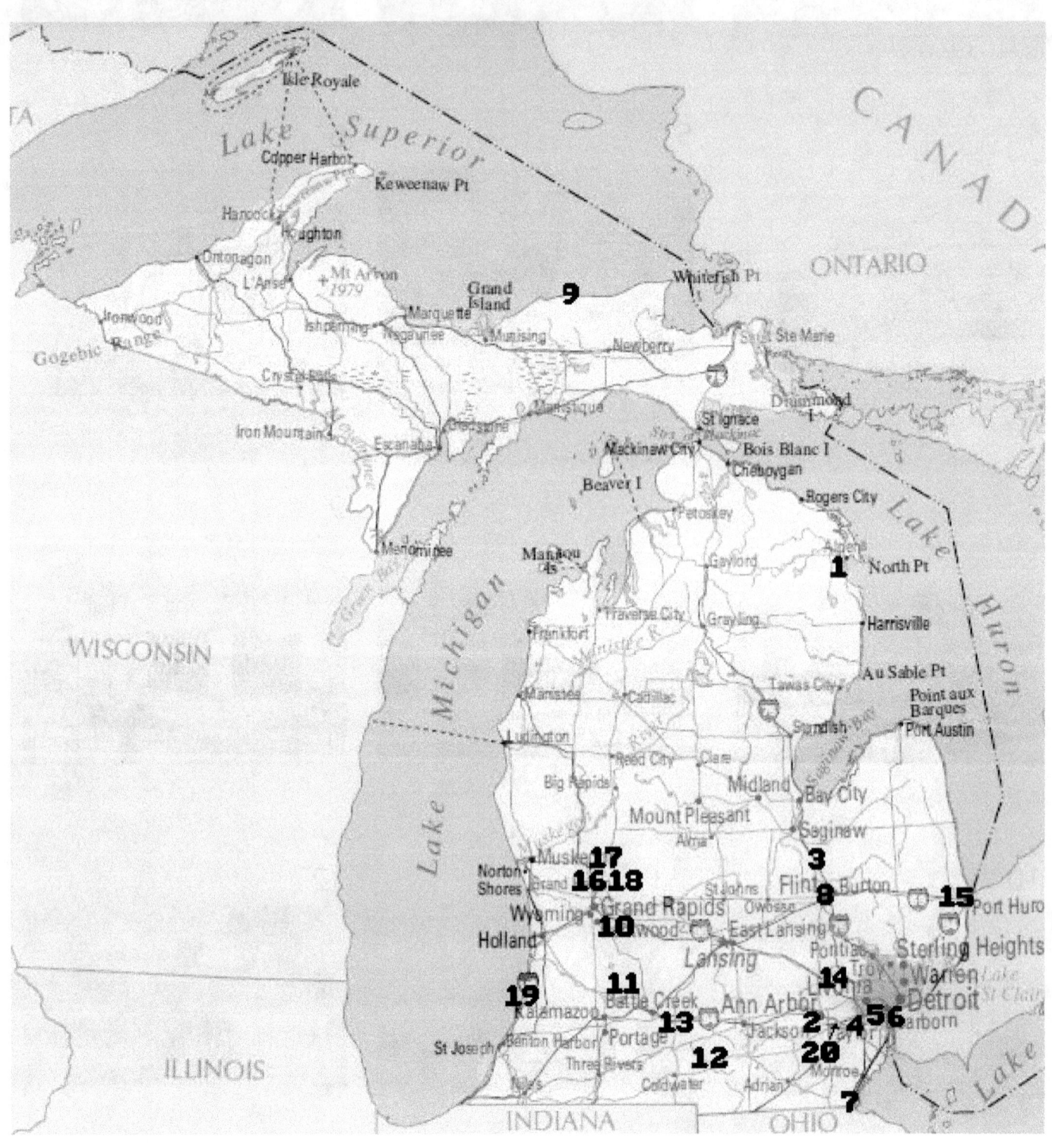

1. Nick's Southside Diner, Alpena
2. Fleetwood Diner, Ann Arbor
3. diner, Birch Run
4. Angie's Hamburger Stand, Canton
5. Lamy's Diner @ Henry Ford Museum, Dearborn
6. Owl Night Lunch Wagon @ Henry Ford Museum, Dearborn
7. JT Pizzeria and Diner, Erie
8. Classic Diner, Flint
9. West Bay Diner & Deli, West Bay
10. Pal's Diner, Grand Rapids
11. George & Sally's Blue Moon Diner @ Gilmore Car Museum, Hickory Corners
12. Coffee Cup Diner, Hillsdale
13. Denny's Classic Diner, Marshall
14. Grand Diner, Novi
15. Powers Hamburgers, Port Huron
16. diner, Rockford
17. diner, Rockford
18. Rosie's Diner, Rockford
19. Ma's Coffee Pot, South Haven
20. Blue Sky Diner, Ypsilanti

1. **Nick's Southside Diner** – 3023 US Route 23 South, **Alpena** (O'Mahony)
    1950s O'Mahony brought to Alpena by Al Sloan. Diner came from Pennsylvania.

2. **Fleetwood Diner** – 300 South Ashley Street, **Ann Arbor** (Dag-Wood)
    Some say grungy, but most say iconic. The vibe is as unique as the manufacturer. The place is filled with stickers and for many the go-to food item is the Hippie Hash.

3. **diner** – 11740 Gera Road, **Birch Run** (1955 O'Mahony)
    The O'Mahony diner came from yorkville, New York and was seemingly doing well for a number of years before languishing in the last dozen years.

4. **Angie's Hamburger Stand** – 47417 Michigan Avenue, **Canton** (Kullman)
    The stool only diner sits in front of a larger building for this hamburger stand. The diner is a well restored example of a smaller post war model of diner built in New Jersey.

5. **Lamy's Diner** @ Henry Ford Museum, **Dearborn** (1946 Worcester)
    After years of not serving food, you can now get food in Lamy's Diner. The diner was painstakingly restored to its original 1946 look by the museum and Richard Gutman.

6. **Owl Night Lunch Wagon** @ Greenfield Village @ Henry Ford Museum, **Dearborn** (lunch wagon) (photo taken 11/7/1987)
    Henry Ford used to eat at a similar lunch wagon that used to serve Detroit. When Ford started his museum, he bought the wagon when its proprietor retired. Today the wagon does not serve food.

7. **JT Pizzeria** – 9767 Dixie Highway, **Erie** (Dag-Wood)
    This remodeled Dag-Wood diner has not served diner food in roughly twenty years, but it still acts as a restaurant.

8. **Classic Diner** – 2400 Austin Parkway, **Flint** (Classic)
    Mike Risko sold his Classic Diner to a Harley dealership in Flint.

9. **West Bay Diner & Deli** – E21825 Veteran Avenue, **West Bay** (Paramount)
    Diner in a small town on the shores of Lake Superior. Jerry Berta helped owners, who are still operating the diner, find the diner which came from Pennsylvania.

10. **Pal's Diner** – 6503 28th Street SE, **Grand Rapids** (1952 Manno)
    Barry and Sam Brown moved the diner from New Jersey to Michigan in the 1990s and ran the diner for over 20 years before closing. Hopefully new owners will take over this fantastic diner.

11. **George & Sally's Blue Moon Diner** @ Gilmore Car Museum, **Hickory Corners** (1941 Silk City)
    Steve Harwin restored the diner which came from Meriden, Connecticut. The diner serves food seasonally in the car museum that also has a restored old time gas station.

12. **Coffee Cup Diner** – 73 North Broad Street, **Hillsdale** (1927 Ward & Dickinson)
    The diner has been bricked over, remodeled and enlarged over the years, but it still holds the charm of a small diner. Current owner serves some Thai dishes along with diner favorites.

1

2

3

4

5

6

(Larry Cultrera)

7

8

9

10

11

12

13. **Denny's Classic Diner** – 15250 Old US Route 27, **Marshall** (Starlite)
    A Denny's restaurant housed inside a Starlite diner, located just off I-94.

14. **Grand Diner** – 48730 Grand River Boulevard, **Novi** (Starlite)
    One of the first Starlites built in 1994.

15. **Powers Hamburgers** – 1209 Military Street, **Port Huron** (Starlite)
    Powers Hamburgers was a well known hamburger stand in Port Huron. Ownered replaced the old building with a Starlite and have since sold the business to new owners.

16. **diner** – 4500 14 Mile Road, **Rockford** (1952 Silk City)
    Former Garden of Eatin from Fulton, New York. Last diner added to Diner-Land

17. **diner** – 4500 14 Mile Road, **Rockford** (O'Mahony)
    Former Uncle Bob's Diner from Flint. First diner added to Diner-Land by Jerry Berta. Used as an art studio and store by Jerry and his wife.

18. **Rosie's Diner** – 4500 14 Mile Road, **Rockford** (1946 Paramount)
    The diner where food was once served at Diner-Land. Rosie's came from New Jersey and was best known as the diner where Bountry paper towel commercials were filmed.

19. **Ma's Coffee Pot** – Exit 18 of Interstate 196, **South Haven** (Valentine)
    Late model Double Deluxe Valentine diner that served as a truck stop diner off of I-196

20. **Blue Sky Diner** – 1340 Ecourse Road, **Ypsilanti** (Mahony)
    Very few original pieces are left in this popular restaurant. Believed to be reported in Diner Magazine as Gay's Diner, bought by Evelyn Gay.

13

14

15

16

17

18

19

20

OHIO

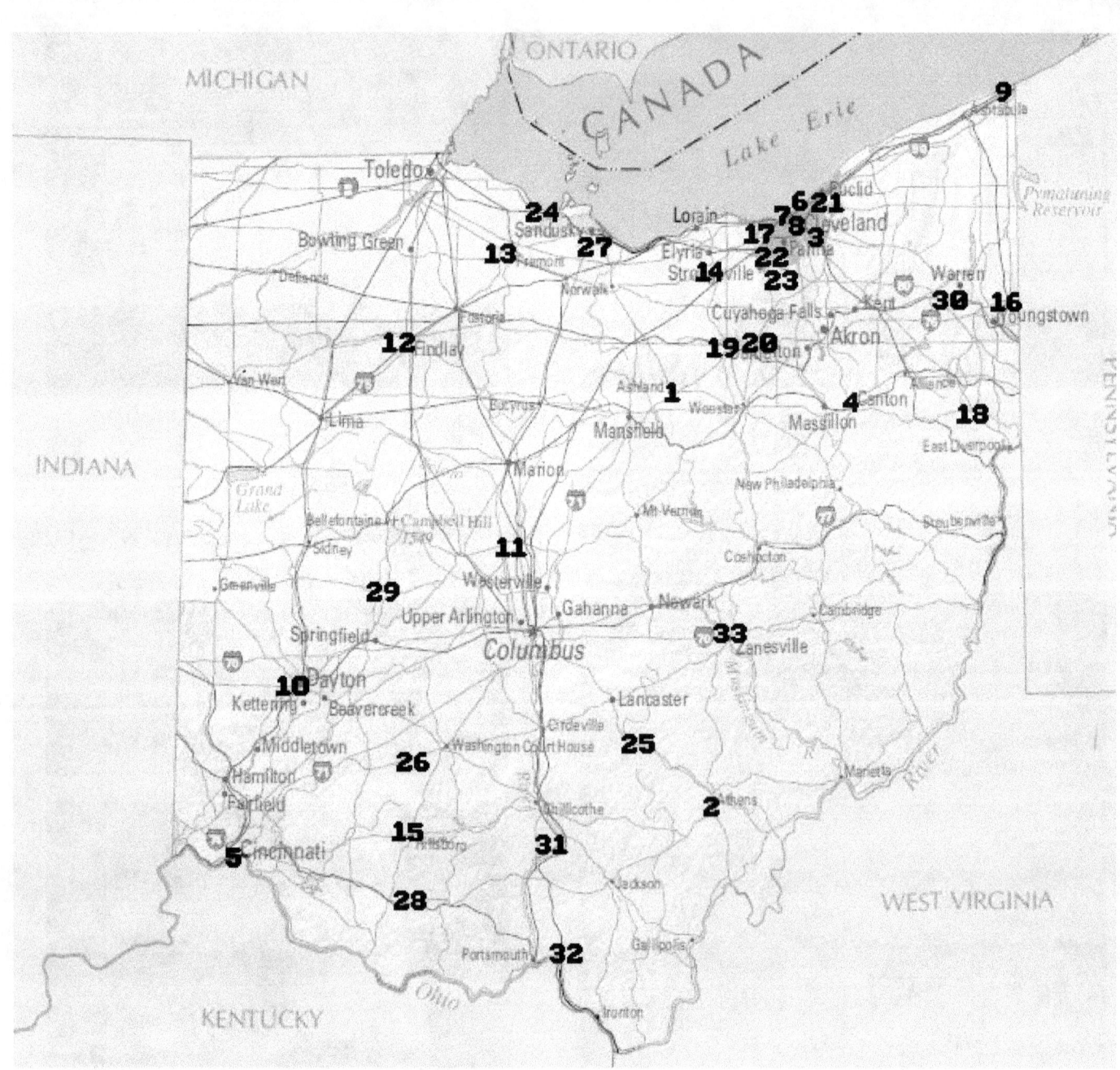

1. diner, Ashland
2. Court Street Diner, Athens
3. Harley Diner, Bedford Heights
4. LA City Diner, Canton
5. diner, Cincinnati
6. The Den by Dennys, Cleveland
7. Diner on 55, Cleveland
8. diner, Cleveland Heights
9. State Street Diner, Conneaut
10. Pearl Nightclub, Dayton
11. diner, Delaware
12. Denny's Classic Diner, Findlay
13. Whitey's Diner, Fremont
14. Nancy's Main Street Diner, Grafton
15. Classic's Diner, Hillsboro
16. Emerald Diner, Hubbard
17. John's Diner, Lakewood
18. Steel Trolley Diner, Lisbon
19. Cups Café, Medina
20. Denny's Classic Diner, Medina
21. Annabelle's Diner, Mentor
22. Charlie's Restaurant, Parma
23. State Road Tavern, Parma
24. Tin Goose Diner, Port Clinton
25. Sandy Sues Silver Diner, Rockbridge
26. diner, Sabina
27. Jolly Donut, Sandusky
28. Cruiser's Diner, Seaman
29. Rock 'N Robin Diner, Urbana
30. Agree's Auto Sales, Warren
31. Diner 23, Waverly
32. Toro Loco, Wheelersburg
33. Denny's Classic Diner, Zanesville

1. **diner** – 269 South Street, **Ashland** (Brill or Dina-Car)
   Diner has been used for other purposes for many years.

2. **Court Street Diner** – 18 North Court Street, **Athens** (Starlite)
   Two piece Starlite diner situationed in downtown Athens has become a popular part of the city.

3. **Harley Diner** – 23105 Aurora Road, **Bedford Heights** (1946 Worcester)
   This diner came from Rochester, New Hampshire and is used for seating and storage for a larger restaurant inside the Harley Dealership. restoration was done by employees and customers.

4. **LA City Diner** – 920 West Tuscarawus Street, **Canton** (1959 Kullman)
   This Kullman with large picture windows sits on an old stretch of the Lincoln highway in front of a motel.

5. **diner** – 1203 Sycamore Street, **Cincinnati** (Mountain View)
   This diner came from Massillon

6. **The Den by Dennys** – 11377 Bellflower, **Cleveland** (Diner-Mite)
   This Diner-Mite was placed on the campus of Case Western and was taken over by Denny's some time ago.

7. **Diner on 55** – 1328 E 55th, **Cleveland** (Diner-Mite)
   Popular breakfast and lunch place housed in a Diner-Mite diner.

8. **diner** – 1975 Lee Road, **Cleveland Heights** (1949 O'Mahony)
   Steve Harwin restored an O'Mahony and a Mountain View diner and sold them to an owner who placed them side by side in Cleveland Heights. That effort failed. Both diners were gutted by future owners and the Mountain View was the victim of a fire. The diner standing may or may not be used for special events.

9. **State Street Diner** – 251 State Street, **Conneaut** (unknown make)
   Very little is left of the original diner which houses the counter at this popular restaurant.

10. **diner/Nightclub** – 101 South Street, **Dayton** (Mountain View)
    Diner has housed a nightclub for roughly twenty years before being bought by new owners and closed.

11. **diner** – 755 US 23 North, **Delaware** (Starlite)
    Different looking Starlite first opened up in Columbus before becoming Famous Jacks at this location for a number of years.

12. **Denny's Classic Diner** –1051 Interstate Court, **Findlay** (Starlite)
    Franchisee for Denny's was very proud to have been able to purchase a Starlite diner. This three piece and vestibule Starlite can be found off of I-75.

1

2

3

4

5

6

7

8

9

10

11

12

13. **Whitey's Diner** – 216 East State Street, **Fremont** (Interurban?)
    Long time diner known for big portions food wise. Interurban part of building almost completeley remodeled.

14. **Nancy's Main Street Diner** – 426 Main Street, **Grafton** (1946 Silk City)
    Steve Harwin restored this Silk City diner that has been in Pennsylvania and Massachusetts. Diner almost acts as overflow seating in this popular diner.

15. **Classic's Diner** – 1581 North High Street, **Hillsboro** (Starlite)
    This Starlite diner is located on the northern outskirts of Hillsboro and has been going quietly for twenty or so years.

16. **Emerald Diner** – 825 North Main Street, **Hubbard** (O'Mahony)
    Actually a 1939 diner updated by O'Mahony in the 1950s while in Connecticut. diner had a fire a number of years ago and was repaired by recent owners.

17. **John's Diner** – 18260 Detroit Avenue, **Lakewood** (Worcester)
    A Worcester lunch car which has been in Ohio all of its life. Has become an important part of the Lakewood community. Diner is very original iside, but has addition room for more customers.

18. **Steel Trolley Diner** – 132 East Lincoln Way, **Lisbon** (1955 O'Mahony)
    The diner came from Salem in 1979. The owners have pushed it towards being a tourist destination and featuring their quirky burgers. The diner is very original.

19. **Cups Café** – 128 North Court Street, **Medina** (O'Mahony)
    This long time O'Mahony in downtown Medina is now part of a non-profit community cafe for teenagers.

20. **Denny's Classic Diner** – 3105 Medina Road, **Medina** (Starlite)
    A Starlite Denny's located right off of I-71.

21. **Annabelle's Diner** – 8637 Twinbrook Road, **Mentor** (Mountain View)
    Diner came from Euclid where it was part of the Kenny Kings local restaurant chain. Unsure about their hours of operation.

22. **Charlie's Restaurant** – 2102 Brookpark Road, **Parma** (Valentine)
    Popular hot dog joint on a commercial strip of Parma. Valentine is not recognizable, but people still flock to the restaurant for its hot dogs and hamburgers, though they also serve other menu items.

23. **State Road Tavern** – 5221 State Road, **Parma** (1961 Swingle)
    Farthest west environmental diner delivered, but remodeled beyond diner recognition.

24. **Tin Goose Diner** – 3515 East State Road, **Port Clinton** (1951 O'Mahony)
    Beautiful diner with nice on-site matching addition housed as at museum, but still acting as a restaurant. Diner came from Jim Thorpe, Pennsylvania.

13

(Frank Goebel)

14

15

16

17

18

19

20

21

22

23

24

25. **Sandy Sues Silver Diner** – 26784 US Route 33, **Rockbridge** (Frey-Moss)
    The diner, built by one of Diner-Mite's subcontractors, is located in a touristy part of Ohio, nicknamed, "Southeastern Ohio's Scenic Wonderland." The diner sits in front of a touristy market.

26. **diner** – 303 West Washington Street, **Sabina** (Silk City)
    Steve Harwin restored this Silk City diner that came from the town of Greenville, New York, outside of Port Jervis. The diner has been closed for what seems like ten years.

27. **Jolly Donut** – 2815 Milan Road, **Sandusky** (Mountain View)
    Originally Miranda's Diner. Look at the floor by the front door for verification. The exterior is bricked over, but nice inside. Food is dependable and diner and donuts are popular among locals.

28. **Cruiser's Diner** – 155 Stern Drive, **Seaman** (Starlite)
    This Starlite diner was placed on the Appalachian Highway in an edge of town commercial district.

29. **Rock 'N Robin Diner** – 1010 Scioto Street, **Urbana** (Diner-Mite)
    Diner has been there for twenty-three years according to current owner.

30. **Agree's Auto Sales** – 4126 Youngstown Road, **Warren** (1964 DeRaffele)
    Space-age googie styled diner that is now used as part of an auto sales lot.

31. **Diner 23** – 300 West Emmitt Avenue, **Waverly** (Starlite)
    Mike Corwin, former cop bought diner from Starlite around twenty years ago and has kept the diner going strong since then.

32. **Toro Loco** – 8630 Ohio River Road, **Wheelersburg** (Starlite)
    First owner did not last long. Then diner bought by Mexican restaurant who has been housed inside the diner for a number of years.

33. **Denny's Classic Diner** – 10 Airport Road, **Zanesville** (Starlite)
    A Denny's housed inside of a Starlite. Diner historian John Shoaf talked up Starlite diners so much that the franchisee decided to buy a Starlite. He was very happy with his purchase.

25

26

27

28

29

30

31

32

33

PENNSYLVANIA

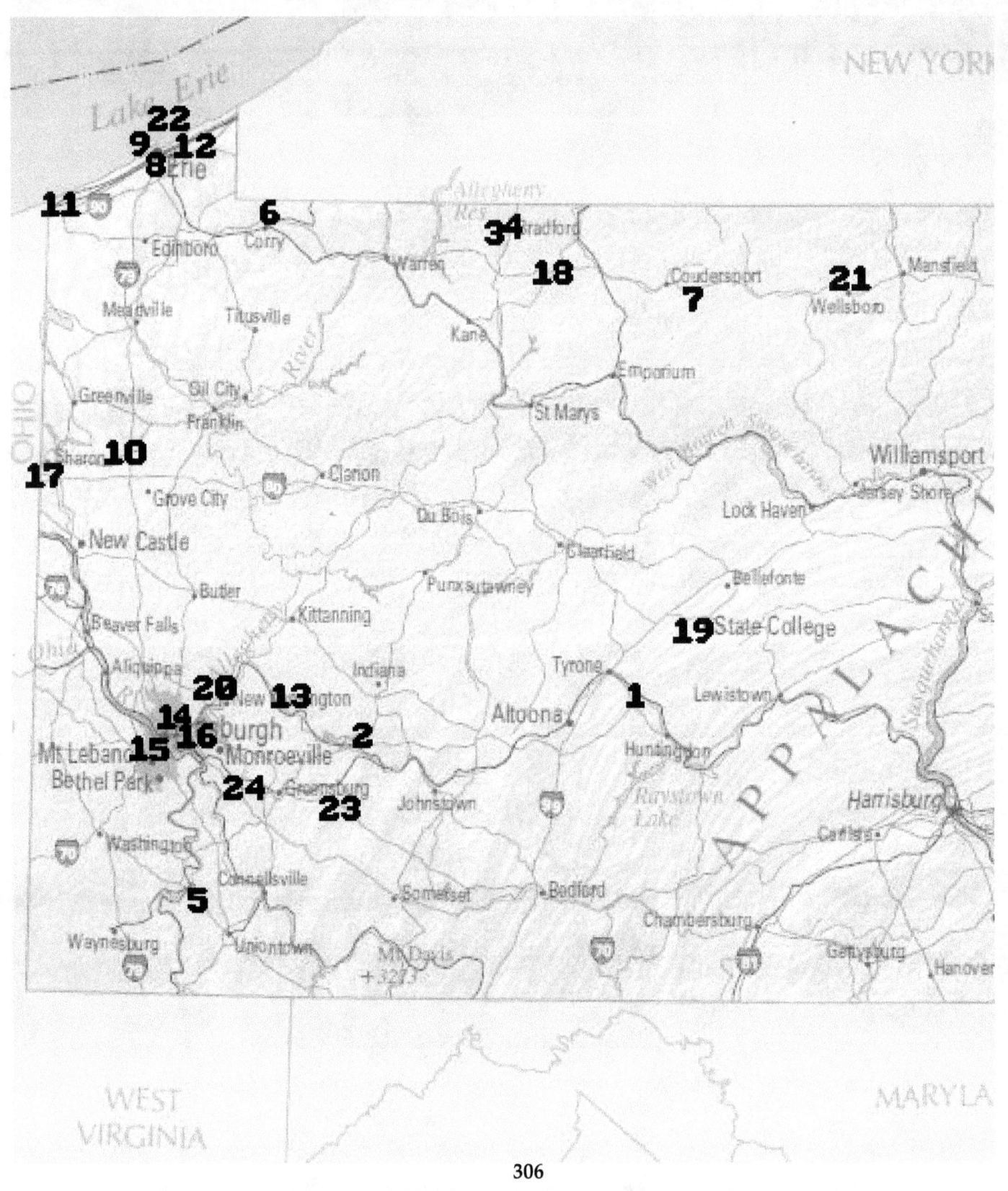

1. Diner 22, Alexandria
2. Dean's Diner, Blairsville
3. diner, Bradford
4. diner, Bradford
5. Route 40 Classic Diner, Brownsville
6. Gigi's Route 6 Diner, Corry
7. Fezz's Diner, Coudersport
8. Haggerty's Bar, Erie
9. Sally's Diner, Erie
10. Aunt Ginny's Diner, Fredonia
11. Girard Dinor, Girard
12. Park Dinor, Lawrence Park
13. Yak Diner, North Apollo
14. Ritter's Diner, Pittsburgh
15. Johnny's Diner, Pittsburgh
16. Peppi's, Pittsburgh
17. Donna's Diner, Sharon
18. diner, Smethport
19. Baby's Burgers and Shakes, State College
20. Gatto's, Tarentum
21. Wellsboro Diner, Wellsboro
22. Russ's Dinor, Wesleyville
23. diner @ Lincoln Highway Heritage Center
24. diner, Irwin

1. **Diner 22** – 5094 William Penn Highway, **Alexandria** (1919 Railroad Mail Car)
    This is the third location for the former mailcar now turned diner. Looks nothing like a railcar from the outside, but inside is preserved. The restaurant also has an attached kitchen and dining room.

2. **Dean's Diner** – 2175 US-22, **Blairsville** (Fodero)
    Three generations of Deans ran diners in this region. This Fodero was the biggest and the last. Now in new hands, it still welcomes visitors to the very original diner on the busy william Penn Highway.

3. **diner** – 12 Congress Street, **Bradford** (Rochester Grills)
    This Rochester Grills replaced an older diner at this location. It has not been a diner in a long time. It previously housed a florist and a non-profit kitchen.

4. **diner** – 431 East Main Street, **Bradford** (Ward & Dickinson)
    Margaret Moore was the original owner. This diner has not been a diner in a number of years and has been remodeled greatly over the years.

5. **Route 40 Classic Diner** – 6229 National Pike, **Brownsville** (Starlite)
    This Starlite came from Mattoon, Illinois and currently sits on the old alignment of the National Pike. Owner wanted a diner to place close by to neighboring Drive-In movie theater.

6. **Gig's Route 6 Diner** – 344 East Columbus Street, **Corry** (Swingle)
    A transitional Swingle diner with large picture windows, it originally sat in Huntingdon. This nice looking diner now sits on the popular U.S. Route 6 on the edge of Corry.

7. **Fezz's Diner** – 9 Ice Mine Road, **Coudersport** (1954 Silk City)
    This very nice Silk City diner used to sit in Bethlehem where it replaced an older diner. Owner wanted a diner to anchor his small commercial plaza on the outskirts of Coudersport.

8. **Haggerty's Bar** – 1930 West 26th Street, **Erie** (Silk City)
    Started out as the Boston Diner at a different location in Erie. Diner is now overflow seating in a biker bar.

9. **Sally's Diner** – 25 Peninsula Drive, **Erie** (Mountain View)
    Diner started out as Serro's in Irwin then moved to Butler where it was known as Morgan's Eastland Diner before becoming part of a seasonal food operation on Presque Isle.

10. **Aunt Ginny's Diner** – 149 State Rte 4024, **Fredonia** (1910 Interurban)
    The Interurban has been mostly gutted and expanded over the years, but at least this small town has a restaurant open again.

11. **Girard Dinor** – 222 West Main Street, **Girard** (1913)
    Mystery shrouds who built this barrel roof lunch wagon. The ceiling is still there but the place has been expanded with extra seating and a kitchen over the years.

12. **Park Dinor** – 4019 Main Street, **Lawrence Park** (Silk City)
    On the National Register of Historic Places. This Silk City is in impeccable shape and serves the former company town of Lawrence Park, which was formed to serve General Electric employees.

1

(Glenn Wells)

2

3

4

5

6

7

8

9

10

11

12

13. **Yak Diner** – River Road, **North Apollo** (O'Mahony)
    Former Gateway Diner, just east of Monroeville before being sold of its contents and becoming a video store in Vandergrift. Debbie Pugsley and friends saved the diner and reopened it to the public.

14. **Ritter's Diner** – 5221 Baum Boulevard, **Pittsburgh** (1976 Fodero)
    A rare environmental styled diner in the Great Lakes region. Ritter's has become a silent icon in the life of Pittsburgh, especially as it is open twenty-four hours a day.

15. **Johnny's Diner** – 1900 Woodville Road, **Pittsburgh** (Tierney)
    A much remodeled and expanded old barrel roof diner that serves the hilly district of Pittsburgh called the West End.

16. **Peppi's** – 7619 Penn Avenue, **Pittsburgh** (National)
    This diner was originally owned by the Ritter family and was next a part of the locally popular Scotty's Diner chain. Today, it is a branch of Peppi's, which brands itself as an "Old Tyme Sandwich Shoppe"

17. **Donna's Diner** – 10 West State Street, **Sharon** (Starlite)
    A Starlite diner placed right along the Shenango River in downtown Sharon.

18. **diner** – 423 West Main Street, **Smethport** (locally built)
    A local concern was hired to build a diner in the 1930s that looked very similar to many other diners being built in western New York at the time.

19. **Baby's Burgers and Shakes** – 131 South Garner Street, **State College** (Silk City)
    A late model Silk City diner with a metal roof added to the top.

20. **Gatto's Cycle Diner** – 139 East 6th Street, **Tarentum** (1946 O'Mahony)
    The diner opened up in Butler where it ran for many years. The diner was saved from the scrap pile by the owner of Gatto's Cycle Shop, Geroge Gatto. The diner does serve breakfast and lunch.

21. **Wellsboro Diner** – 19 Main Street, **Wellsboro** (1938 Sterling)
    This well preserved Sterling diner with factory built kitchen, (look around back!) still serves downtown Wellsboro and the many tourists that come through town to get away from it all.

22. **Russ's Dinor** – 2902 Buffalo Road, **Wesleyville** (replacement)
    While not a factory built diner, the restaurant replaced a Mulholland diner and has a footprint of a 1950s diner. This old time restaurant serves its community well.

23. **Serro's Diner** – 3435 State Route 30 East, **Latrobe** (O'Mahony)
    The first of the Serro's Diners that were in operation, it has been restored by the people at the Lincoln Highway Experience in Latrobe where they plan to open the diner to the public.

24. **diner** – 220 Main Street, **Irwin** (DeRaffele)
    The first Ritter's Diner on Baum Boulevard was first moved to downtown Pittsburgh for many years before recently moving to Irwin where the hopes are to use it alongside the Lamp Theater.

13

14

(Mario Monti)

15

(Steve Boksenbaum)

16

17

18

19

20

21

22

23

(Brian Butko)

24

NEW YORK

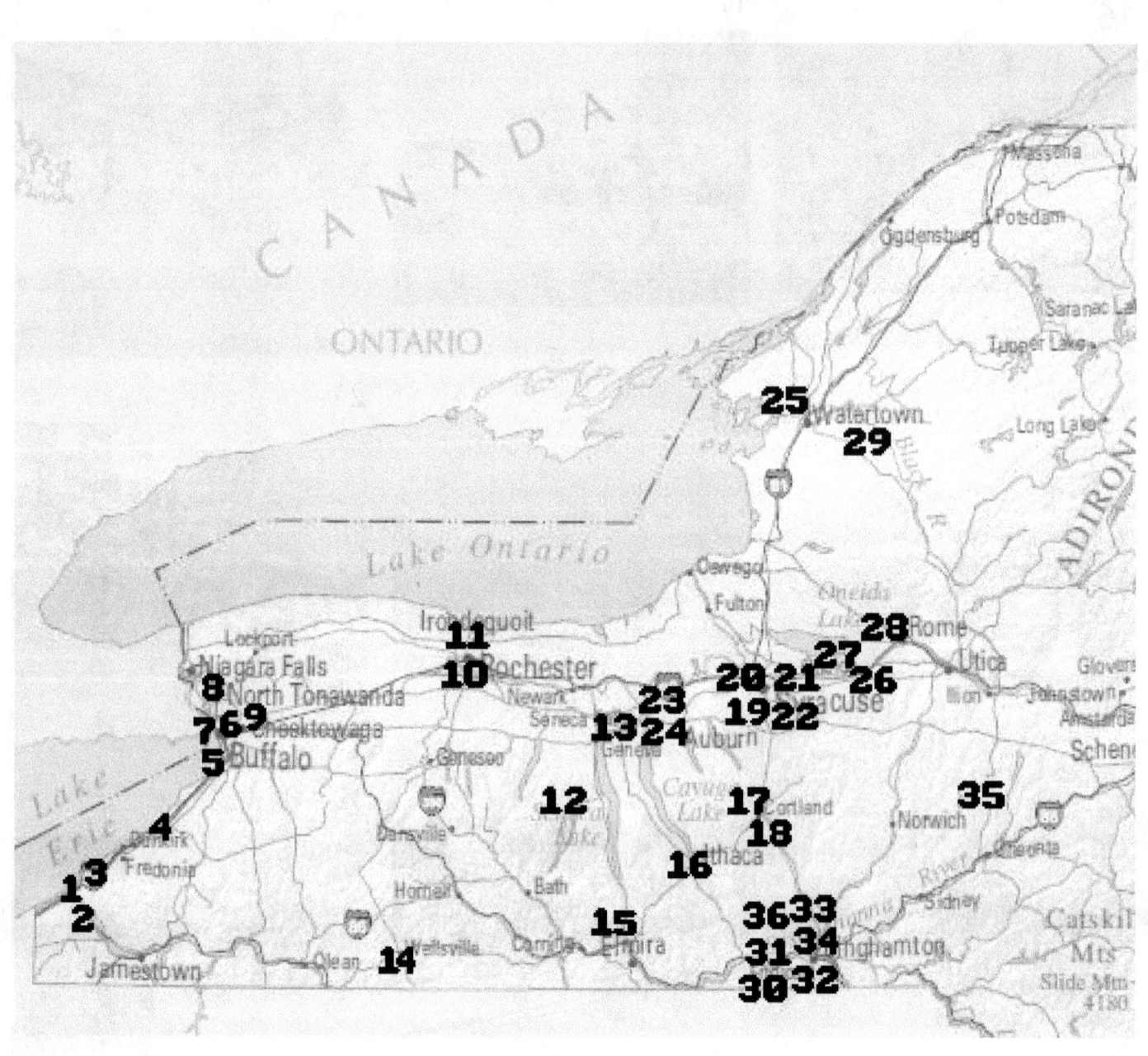

1. Westfield Main Diner, Westfield
2. Mayville Diner, Mayville
3. Green Arch, Brocton
4. diner, Silver Creek
5. Woodlawn Diner, Woodlawn
6. Lake Effect Diner, Buffalo
7. Swan Street Diner, Buffalo
8. Soup Lady @ 412 Diner, North Tonawanda
9. Smokin Little Diner, Depew
10. Highland Park Diner, Rochester
11. Bill Grey's Strong Museum, Rochester
12. Penn Yan Diner, Penn Yan
13. Connie's Diner, Waterloo
14. Modern Diner, Wellsville
15. The Diner, Horseheads
16. State Diner, Ithaca
17. Frank & Mary's Diner, Cortland
18. diner, Polkville
19. Gem Diner, Syracuse
20. JR Diner, Syracuse
21. Redwood Diner, Syracuse
22. Miss Syracuse Diner, Syracuse
23. Auburn Diner, Auburn
24. Hunter's Dinerante, Auburn
25. Friede's Restaurant, Watertown
26. Morey's Diner, Oneida
27. diner, Canastota
28. Eddie's Paramount Diner, Rome
29. Lloyd's of Lowville, Lowville
30. Skylark Diner, Vestal
31. Boulevard Diner, Endwell
32. Danny's Diner, Binghamton
33. The Spot, Binghamton
34. Red Oak Diner, Binghamton
35. T's Diner, New Berlin
36. Red Robin Diner, Johnson City
37. Miss Batavia Diner, Batavia

1. **Westfield Main Diner** – 40 East Main Street, **Westfield** (Ward & Dickinson)
   Probably the oldest Ward & Dickinson diner extant. Diner has been remodeled over the years and includes two additions. Owners restored original neon sign a couple of years ago.

2. **Mayville Diner** – 7 West Chautauqua Street, **Mayville** (Sorge)
   Very little is left of the last Sorge diner extant.

3. **Green Arch** – 41 West Main Street, **Brocton** (Mulholland)
   The last extant Mulholland diner is one of their 1931 models that sported a graceful curved barrel roof. The body of the diner is original, but much has been added on, including a larger dining room.

4. **diner** – 172 Central Avenue, **Silver Creek** (Ward & Dickinson)
   Originally Lown's Diner, placed in front of the factory in 1938, this diner was best known as Steve's Diner when it sat just outside of town. The diner was restored by former historian Louis Pelleter.

5. **Woodlawn Diner** – 3200 Lake Shore Road, **Woodlawn** (replacement)
   Long standing restaurant in Woodlawn. The current building replaced a Sharpe diner.

6. **Lake Effect Diner** – 3165 Main Street, **Buffalo** (Mountain View)
   The diner came from Wayne, Pennsylvania where it was last a chinese restuarant. Tucker Curtin brought the diner in and serves updated diner food on Main Street.

7. **Swan Street Diner** – 700 Swan Street, **Buffalo** (Sterling)
   The former Newark Diner was moved to Buffalo where it was freshened up after years of use. The menu features updated diner food. Diner is part of a plan to rejuvenate the Larkinville neighborhood.

8. **Soup Lady @ 412 Diner** – 412 Oliver Street, **North Tonawanda** (O'Mahony)
   This O'Mahony has seen plenty of owners and remodelings over the years, but still includes a number of original features. The current owner will serve food, but focuses on her soups which you can buy frozen.

9. **Smokin Little Diner** – 4870 Broadway, **Depew** (Silk City)
   Housed in a nice circa 1954 Silk City diner, the restaurant serves diner food and their popular BBQ. One part of the counter was removed for extra seating many years ago.

10. **Highland Park Diner** – 960 South Clinton Avenue, **Rochester** (Orleans)
    Bob Malley brought this diner back to its original glory. The last Orleans Superior diner extant. The restaurant serves an updated diner menu.

11. **Bill Gray's Diner @ Strong Museum** – 1 Manhattan Square Drive, **Rochester** (Fodero)
    A local chain housed in a diner that was located north of Williamsport, Pennsylvania on US Rt 15. The diner is inside the Strong Museum of Play. Typical Bill Gray's menu.

12. **Penn Yan Diner** – 131 East Elm Street, **Penn Yan** (1925 Richardson)
    Dean Smith helped to transition the diner to the current owners who have really turned things up a notch with a nice menu. Last extant Richardson is very authentic and sports a 1930s addition.

1

2

3

(Marybelle Beigh)

4

5

6

7

8

9

10

11

12

13. **Connie's Diner** – 205 East Main Street, **Waterloo** (1965 Manno or DeRaffele)
    Rare 1960s diner in western New York. Diner is well preserved with a lot of added 1950s memorabilia inside the diner. Diner is well patronized and a popular destination.

14. **Modern Diner** – 73 North Main Street, **Wellsville** (replacement)
    Nothing is left of the original diner, but the spirit of the restaurant is going just as strong as it ever has.

15. **The Diner** – 59 Old Ithaca Road, **Horseheads** (Silk City)
    The diner survived Hurricane Agnes while in Elmira and moved to Horseheads shortly afterwards. Diner has had some alterations over its recent past but still is quite original.

16. **State Diner** – 428 West State Street, **Ithaca** (replacement)
    There was a Mulholland and possibly a Sterling on this site in years past. Diner was remodeled many times over the years and suffered a fire a few years ago. Popular local restaurant.

17. **Frank & Mary's Diner** – 10 Port Watson Street, **Cortland** (1940 General)
    The last verified General diner extant has been remodeled over the years, but the footprint of the diner is still evident. Cooking still done on grill out front.

18. **diner** – 3823 US-11, **Polkville** (Kullman)
    This Kullman, on the outskirts of Cortland, right off of an exit of I-81 has been closed for a number of years and used to sit very close to a double Silk City diner where they both prospered for years.

19. **Gem Diner** – 832 Spencer Street, **Syracuse** (Fodero)
    Well known and popular diner in Syracuse. The original diner was expanded with a nice addition.

20. **JR Diner** – 1208 Wolf Street, **Syracuse** (Rochester Grills)
    Once part of the Cameron Diner chain, the diner feels like a neighborhood diner, even though it sits in an industrial type neighborhood. Diner shell is original, but has had updatings over the years.

21. **Redwood Diner** – 121 East Manlius Street, **Syracuse** (Ward & Dickinson)
    The shell of the Ward and Dickinson is recognizable, but it has been remodeled over the years. Breakfast and lunch place with added dining room. Unsure how long it has been at location.

22. **JJ's Miss Syracuse Diner** – 258 East Water Street, **Syracuse** (Bixler)
    Long time downtown Syracuse stalwart, being located right next door to Syracuse City Hall. Remodeled over the years, the shell and heart of the diner is still there.

23. **Auburn Diner** – 64 Columbus Street, **Auburn** (Bixler)
    This Bixler diner has been in Auburn all of its life. Previously located next to the jail, the diner had a fire and was shut down for a long time until current owner renovated and reopened diner.

24. **Hunter's Dinerante** – 18 Genesee Street, **Auburn** (1951 O'Mahony)
    Fourth diner on this location. Diner is uniquely cantilevered over Owasco Creek. Well preserved 1950s diner survived some hard times to shine today. Once owned by V.P. Joe Biden's father-in-law.

13

14

15

16

17

18

19

20

21

(Mike Mastracco)

22

23

24

25. **Friede's Restaurant** – 455 Court Street, **Watertown** (General or locally built)
    Diner was either locally built or first diner built by General. Rumored to be haunted. Retains the feel of the original diner.

26. **Morey's Diner** – 119 Phelps Street, **Oneida** (Ward & Dickinson)
    Diner was saved from the scrap heap by former cop Lynn Morey. Very well preserved. Typically serves only breakfast.

27. **diner** – 523 North Main Street, **Canastota** (Silk City)
    Diner has been remodeled on the inside a fair amount. Came from Syracuse where it was the Pelican Diner.

28. **Eddie's Paramount Diner** – 414 West Dominick Street, **Rome** (O'Mahony)
    Venerable spot for food in Rome. Diner shows some wear, but is very original. They serve some honest old time blue plate specials for lunch and dinner.

29. **Lloyd's of Lowville** – 7405 South State Street, **Lowville** (locally built)
    Built by a local contractor around 1940.

30. **Skylark Diner** – 248 Vestal Parkway East, **Vestal** (O'Mahony)
    1950s diner with added on dining room section. Outside is covered over, but interior is mostly original. Twenty-four hour popular joint.

31. **Boulevard Diner** – 3140 Watson Boulevard, **Endwell** (Rochester Grills)
    Diner has been at this spot over 50 years, has been added on to multiple times. Original diner is moderately original on the inside. Popular local diner.

32. **Danny's Diner** – 151 Main Street, **Binghamton** (Sterling)
    Moderately original diner that is truly a neighborhood diner.

33. **The Spot** – 1062 Front Street, **Binghamton** (1973 Kullman)
    Environmental Kullman diner which is mostly original for its style. Replaced a roadside stand. Like most diners of this style, it has an extensive menu.

34. **Red Oak Diner** – 305 Front Street, **Binghamton** (1976 Swingle)
    Environmental Swingle with terra-cotta roof shingles. Diner is original to its time period, which is becoming a rarity. Like The Spot, there is a large seating capacity as the Red Oak can seat 200 people.

35. **T's Diner** – 5709 NY-8, **New Berlin** (Kullman)
    Diner came from Oneonta in the 1970s. Before that is a mystery. Quite original diner inside and out only with new roof added to exterior.

36. **Red Robin Diner** – 268 Main Street, **Johnson City** (Mountain View)
    Diner sits in downtown Johnson City. Moved here from nearby location around 1958.

37. **Miss Batavia Diner** – 566 East Main Street, **Batavia** (Replacement)
    After explosion, diner was replaced by on-site building. Still a fixture of the community.

25

26

27

28

29

30

31

32

33

34

35

36

Index

Symbols

9-W Diner 167

A

Abbott, Sherman 29
Akin, James F. 31
Albany, New York 197
Albion, New York 218
Alpena, Michigan 259
Al's Diner 169, 214
Altoona, Pennsylvania 153
Amherst Diner 194
Anita Diner 164
Ann Arbor, Michigan 212, 214
Arlington, Massachusetts 218
Ashland, Ohio 167
Ashtabula Dinor 240
Ashtabula, Ohio 154, 216, 218, 240
Auburn, New York 107, 115
Austin, Will 18

B

Bacarella's Diner 212
Baeder, John 168, 170, 257
Bailey Diner 75
Bain, James H. 61
Balling, Leon F 147
Ballston Spa, New York 98
Bancroft Dining Car 54
Band Box Diner 210
Baraboo, Wisconsin 259
Basloe, Joseph 29
Bath, New York 149
Belding, Mr. and Mrs. Harry 229
Bellas, Jimmy 216, 217
Bellefontaine, Ohio 102
Bellevue, Ohio 71, 143, 159
Bellink, Alan 256, 257
Berta, Jerry 258, 259
Bethlehem, Pennsylvania 113
Betsy Ross Diner 94, 211, 213
B-G Sandwich Shops 109
Bickerton, Harvey 29
Bill's Diner 212, 215
Birdsey, Elmer 94
Bixler Manufacturing 167, 182
Bixler, Marshall 167
Blairsville, Pennsylvania 94
Blanding, Ernest W. 96
Blanding, Wilbur E. 74, 94
Boksenbaum, Steve 232
Bono, Ohio 169
Boston, Massachusetts 265
Bosworth, Mr. B. H. 15
Boyles, F.T. 50
Bradford, Pennsylvania 185
Bradford Sales Company 153
Brigham, O.W. 24
J.G. Brill Company 165
Britting, Howard G. 142
Brocton, New York 140
Brooklyn 142
Bryan, Ohio 71, 103, 238
Buck, A. H. 109
Buckley, Thomas 14, 17, 29
Buffalo, New York 17, 26, 32, 72, 75, 91, 97, 99, 102, 109, 110, 116, 117, 120, 121, 122, 123, 135, 140, 142, 153, 154, 155, 194, 199, 218, 235, 237
Burlington, Iowa 260
Burnham, C.W. 51
Burns, Thomas 29
Bush, G. W. 115
Butko, Brian 167
Butler Manufacturing 210

C

Cadillac Diner 218
Camardella, Louis F. 214
Cameron, Alexander 137
Cameron Diner 169
Campau, Mr. 150
Canandaigua, New York 112
Canton, Ohio 212, 215
Canton Township, Michigan 259
Carey, Philip L. 154
Carriage Monthly 30, 40
Carroll Diner 115
Cashin, Mr. D. W. 165
Castree, Jeffrey 264
Catskill, New York 167
Cease's Diner 136, 138
Cecil's Trackside Diner 149
Cees, E.A. 136
Champaign, Illinois 26
Charleston, West Virginia 112
Chautauqua Lunch Car Company 47
Cheney and Brown Carriage Works 30
Chicago, Illinois 20, 109, 111, 165, 172, 207, 212
Chris Eliot's Diner 215
Cincinnati, Ohio 102
Cindy's Diner 242
Clarence, New York 104, 143, 148
Clarksville Diner 258, 262
Classic Diner 260, 263
Clees, Henry 135
Cleveland, Ohio 102, 164, 165, 170, 171, 237, 259
Closson, Albert H. 20, 40–61, 71
Closson Lunch Wagon Company

38–56
Clute, Howard 71, 103, 110
Clute's Diner 145
Cody, John 185
Coffee Cup Diner 236
Colburn, Miss Lucile 51
Colquhoun, John 27
Columbia, Missouri 147
Columbus Junction, Iowa 260, 261
Columbus, Ohio 24
Command, Judge Edward 27
Congress Street Diner 185
Conneaut, Ohio 64
Cortland, New York 98, 156, 179, 194
Corwin, Mike 263
Costigan, Timothy 260
Coughlin, Jason 211
County Club Diner 188
Court House Diner 149
Crawford, Jesse 154
Creamer, Truman 212
Crosser's Diner 187
Cross, Leslie and Mernie 154
Cunniff, John 234

D

Dag-Wood diner kits 211, 213, 214
Dann, Mr. C. A. 150
Dauphin's Superior Diner 179, 218, 235
David Letterman 215
Dawson, Art 45, 49
Dayton, Ohio 134, 163
Dearborn, Michigan 257, 258
DeBest Diners 260
DeCatur, Albert 211
Decatur, Illinois 215
Decorah, Iowa 258, 262
DeCoven Diner 268

Deller, Toni 149, 266, 267
Delta, Wisconsin 259
Denny's Diner 193
Denver, Colorado 215
Detroit, Michigan 26, 235
Dewey's Diner 237
Dickinson, C.B. 50
Dickinson, Howard 94
Dickinson, Lee 74, 91, 99, 110, 113, 114, 115, 230
Dickinson, William 110
Dick's Diner 215
Dimitri Drive-In 208
Dimon, Ray 216
Diner 23 263
Diner-Mite 260, 268
Dinette Diner 149, 150, 151
Dining Car Sales Corporation 109
Doenias, Jack 257
Domenico's Diner 237
Draves, William A. 140
Duncannon, Pennsylvania 268
Dunkirk Dining Car Company 103, 136, 237, 243
Dunkirk, New York 136, 138

E

Eakins, Robert 200
East Aurora, New York 72
East Liverpool, Ohio 140
East Rochester, New York 142
Electric Diner 233
Electric Diners 109, 111
Elite Diner 140
Ellis Omnibus and Cab Company 30, 40
Elmira, New York 10, 11, 32, 115, 125, 189, 202
Elwood City, Pennsylvania 96

Elyria 167
Empire Diner 257
Empire State Diner 140
Engle, Michael 149, 266, 267
Entress, Joseph 188
Erie, Michigan 212
Erie, Pennsylvania 110, 136
Estes, George 239

F

Fairmount Diner 114
Fitzpatrick, Dr. 72
Fleetwood Diner 214
Flint, Michigan 212, 258
Fodero, Pat 231
Fog City Diner 257
Ford, Henry 27
Fort Diner 210
Fort Madison, Iowa 210
Fort Wayne, Indiana 215, 242
Foster, George 167
Fowler, G.E. 71
Fox, Ernest 71
Frank and Mary's Diner 194
Frank's Diner 236, 267
Freling, Gardiner 216
Fremont Metal Body Company 152, 167
Fremont, Ohio 167, 168
Fuller, Charley 41
Fulton, New York 258

G

Gaebler's Club Diner 147
Galloway, R.P. 71
Gardner, William J. 31, 35
General Diners 193, 194
Geneva, New York 169, 201
Gibsonia, Pennsylvania 259, 268

Gillson, Wallace 136
Glens Falls, New York 40, 45, 48
Gloversville, New York 174, 203
Goodell Hardware 146, 149
Goodrich, Wilson 31
Gorman, Wildridge H. 31, 35
Grafton, Ohio 259, 265
Greentown, Ohio 173
Gregory, George 153
Griffeth's Swanky Diner 185
Grimsby, Ontario Canada 109
Gross, Robert J. 136
Groton, Connecticut 264
Guedelhoffer Company 31
Gutman, Richard J.S. 10, 257, 258

H

Haigh, Anna 114
Halbritter, Louis 30
Halladay, Arthur 191, 194
Hall, F.A. 51
Hamburg, New York 65
Hamel, Ephraim 15
Hamilton, Ohio 104
Hamilton, Ontario 109
Hamister, Winnie 103
Hammond, C.G. 136
Hammond, Indiana 103
Hancock, New York 199
Hanna, Mr. R.H. 17
Harley, Bertrand 189, 218
Harmony Corners, Michigan 259
Harwin, Steve 258, 259, 265
Hazel, Hon. John R. 52
Heavenly Hash Diner 240
Hebb, David 209
Heider, John L. 142
Henry Ford Museum 257, 258
Herbert, Albert 188

Herbert's Diner 188
Herkimer, New York 29
Highland Park Diner 179, 220, 235
Hillsdale, Michigan 162, 236
Hi-Lo Diner 259, 268
Hitching Post 167
Holland, Michigan 237
Homestead Grill 186
Horn, George 239
Howard, Estelle and Clive 98
Hudson, Massachusetts 259
Huff, Doug 264

I

Independence, Ohio 173, 241
Indiana, Pennsylvania 94
Indianapolis, Indiana 31, 215
Indian Trailer Corporation 207, 212
Irving, New York 108
Ithaca, New York 114

J

Joe's Diner 215
Johnson City, New York 187
Johnson, Percy 111
Joliet, Illinois 197, 203
Joni's Diner 268
Judkins, J.D. 189

K

Kaelber, Carl F. W. 188
Kaplan, Donald 257
Kendall Diner 107, 216
Kenosha, Wisconsin 236, 267
Kerr, Matthew H. 233
Kerr's Diner 214, 233
Kingston, New York 159
Kirk's Diner 237
Kless, Paul 193

Knapp, C. Warren 136
Kofoed, Berthel 74, 91, 111, 114
Kofoed, Donald 95, 115
Kostopulus, Alex 209
Kramer, Arthur 153
Kullman Dining Car Company 214
Kuppy's Diner 248
Kurtz, Harold 111

L

Laanes, Carl 257
Lake Effect Diner 235
Lake Geneva, Wisconsin 259, 268
Lamy's Diner 256, 257, 258
Lanesboro, Minnesota 146, 149, 267
Lane's Diner 185
Larson, Ray 260
Lawrence, Indiana 215
LeRoy, New York 103
Levinson, Barry 257
Liberal, Kansas 199
Liberty Diner 190
Liberty Dining Car Company 142, 147
Lima, Ohio 209
Lisbon, Ohio 187
Lor-A-Lee Diner 239
Love, Robert M. 15
Low, Andrew 12
Low Moor, Virginia 269
Lown, Jack 114

M

Madison, Wisconsin 54
Malley, Bob 179, 218, 235
Malone Diner 193
Malone, New York 193
Mangino, Mary 239
Manhattan, New York 257

Mansfield, Ohio 136, 237, 243
Marion, Ohio 137
Martin, Roscoe B. 136
Martins Ferry, Ohio 169
Martonis, Vince 99, 120, 149
Marvin, William H. 136
Ma's Coffee Pot 234
Mason City, Iowa 260, 268
Massena, New York 41
Massillon, Ohio 215
Master Auto Body Company 171
Matuzas, Mike 200
Max Diner 167, 237, 243
May's Diner 151
Mayville, New York 137
McCraig, Robert 94
McGrath's Diner 168
McKeen Motor Car Company 169
McKee's Diner 185
McKendrick, Robert 103, 110, 136
McNew, A. D. 239, 243
Mead, Harris 216
Meadowbrook Diner 215, 217
Meadville, Pennsylvania 50, 154
Medina, Ohio 74, 147
Memberg, Don 268
Merrimac, Massachusetts 189
Mertl, Tom 190
Meyer, Howard 142
Mickey's Diner 212
Mickle., Harry L. 61
Miles, "Crab" 17, 18
Milford, New Hampshire 148
Miller Blum Lunch Company 30
Milwaukee, Wisconsin 171
Minges, Frank J. 188
Minneapolis, Minnesota 210, 259
Modern Diner 190, 236
Modular Diners 268
Monroe, Michigan 214

Monroeville, Ohio 170
Montreal, Quebec, Canada 31
Moore Diner 111, 113
Moore, Margaret 253
Moore, Walter 113
Morey, D.J. 50
Moscow, Idaho 268
Mountain View, California 190
Mountain View Diners 214, 215
Moyer, F.C. 50
Mulholland Company 135–140
Muncie, Indiana 213
Muscato, Louis A. 199
Myers, Lyle 107

N

Nagle, Frank 167
Nancy's Main Street Diner 264
National Dining Car Company 145, 148
Neebuhr, Sheldon 64
Newark, New York 235
New College Diner 176
New York City 41, 150, 165
New York Coffee Pot 171
Niles, Ohio 239
North East, Pennsylvania 154
North Liberty, Iowa 260
North Tonawanda, New York 148, 149, 150
Norwalk, Ohio 163, 167
Norwich, New York 185
Null's Diner 147

O

Oakland, California 103
Oak Tree Inn 261
Oasis Diner 215, 264
Ogdensburg, New York 14, 17, 30, 31, 32, 33, 35, 123, 128
Ohio Body Company 164, 165, 170
Ohio Dining Car Company of Cleveland 102
Oil City, Pennsylvania 216
Old Hitching Post 237
Olean, New York 17, 18, 32, 136, 140, 142, 155, 185, 212, 218
Omaha, Nebraska 169
Jerry O'Mahony Dining Car Company 65, 212
O'Mahony, Jerry 45
Ono, Pennsylvania 265
Orleans Manufacturing Company 218
Osclaveta, Leo 193
Oswego, New York 191, 194
Ottawa, Ohio 259

P

Pace Restaurant Corp 112
Palace Diner 179
Palmyra, New York 230
Parmelee, Foster 110
Paul, Neil 143
Paulson, Louis 209
Pawling, New York 168
Pawtucket, Rhode Island 190
Peletter, Louis 114
Penn Yan Diner 135
Penn Yan, New York 135, 189
Penny's Diners 263, 269
Peoria, Illinois 167, 215
Peter Pan Diner 215
Phoenix, Mr. E.V.D. 51, 52
Picchi, Frank 201
Pickup, Jim 140
Pittsburgh, Pennsylvania. 231
Pixie Diner 213
Plainfield, Indiana 215

Plattsburgh, New York 15, 17
Plum, Walter 95
Plymouth, Pennsylvania 153
Pontiac, Michigan 240
Port Clinton, Ohio 259
Port Jervis, New York 259
Portville, New York 154
Princeton Junction, New Jersey 262
Princeton, New Jersey 258
Providence, Rhode Island 110, 112
Pulaski, New York 239

Q

Quarrier Diner 112

R

Racine, Wisconsin 52
Ravenna, Ohio 71
Reading, Pennsylvania 111, 113
Record, Walter 136
Red Arrow Diner 148
Red Castle Diners 208
Red Dragon Diner 215
Red Rose Diner 267
Rees, Jim 211
Regent Grill 209
Reid, Donald 211, 212
Restaurant World's Fair 109
Riccelli, Roy A. 178
Richardson, Earl 68–74, 134
Richardson, Elmer & Aletta 115
Richardson, Franklin 115
Richardson, Gertrude 114
Richardson, Harry 115
Richardson, Merle 134
Richardson, Raymond 115, 134, 162, 239
Rich Dining Car Company 134, 163, 165, 238

Ripley, New York 154
Risko, Mike 260, 263
Ritter's Diner 231
Rittman, Ohio 240
Roadside Magazine 259
Rob Roy's Dinette 182
Rochester Grills 181–184, 185, 188
Rochester, New York 23, 24, 25, 103, 168, 179, 185, 188, 220, 235, 259
Roger's Diner 269
Rosie's Diner 258, 264
Rosskam, Edward 172
Ruskay, Richard 257
Russell, Guy 154

S

Sabina, Ohio 259, 264
Salt Lake City 29
Sanderl, A.B. 24
Sandusky, Ohio 150, 151, 162, 178, 257
Saratoga Springs, New York 42
Scarcella's Diner 185
S & C Coffee Car 235
Schanacher's Diner 189
Schwartz, Ray 136
Schweikert, Sidney 75
Scott, Walter 10, 14
Scotty's Diner 232
Scrimger, Andrew 27
Seattle, Washington 214
Seneca Falls, New York 186
Seven Dwarfs Diner 215
Shady Lawn Diner 239
Shale, J. Harry 168, 182, 188
Sharpe, Dr. J. J. 72, 75, 148, 149
Sherrick's Diner 167
Shutek, Denise and Rick 265

Silver Creek Dining Car Company 148
Silver Creek, New York 68, 69, 71, 145, 148, 163, 219
Sitar's Diner 187
Sloan, Al 258
Smethport, Pennsylvania 154
Smith, Henry 148
Smitty's Diner 215
Solid Gold Diners 260, 261
Sorge, Charles 216
Sorge Diner Company 216, 240
South Haven, Michigan 234
Spillman Engineering Company 149–152
Springfield, Massachusetts 165
Springfield, Ohio 162
Spud Boy Lunch 266
Stanfield, Virgil 239
Starcevic, Bill 268
Starkweather, C. V. 150
Starlite Diners 268
State College, Pennsylvania 114, 176
State Grill 142
Sterling Dining Cars 179, 186, 187, 189, 190, 259
Sterling, Illinois 260, 261
Sterling, Paul 154
Steve's Diner 114
Stewart, Spencer 150
St. Louis, Missouri 165, 214
St. Paul, Minnesota 12, 13, 14, 209, 212, 214
Strauss, Steve 260
Strayer, Colin 190
Stribley, Kathy 190
Sun Prairie, Wisconsin 209
Sunset Bay Diner 108
Suzie Q 260, 268
Swan Street Diner 235

Syracuse, New York 25, 28, 96, 114, 185, 190, 193, 194, 237, 239

T

Tefft, John 154
Thomas, Gary 218
Tiffany, Mr. Edward L. 45
Timmerman, Lester 260
Tindall, Gordon 146, 149, 258, 266, 267, 268
Tiny Tim Diner 242
Toledo Dining Car Company 102
Toledo, Ohio 94, 208, 209, 211, 214
Tomberelli, Anthony 189
Toppit Diner 208
Toronto, Ontario, Canada 109, 111, 233
Towanda, Pennsylvania 267
Tryon, North Carolina 269
Twin Diner 112

U

Uncle Bob's Diner 212, 258
Utica, New York 203

V

Valentine, Arthur 234
Valentine Manufacturing 207, 208, 209, 240, 242, 260, 268
Venus Diner 259, 268
Voelker, Louis 188

W

Walton, New York 175
Wanamaker, Indiana 215
Ward and Dickinson Dining Car Company 71, 74, 88–126, 134, 153, 162, 176, 178, 179, 216, 230, 236, 237, 239
Ward, Charles 74, 91, 96, 99, 104, 142, 147
Warren, Pennsylvania 115
Warsaw, New York 76
Watertown, New York 191, 194
Waverly, Ohio 263
Wayside Diner 183
Weed, Don 239
Weiler, Bob & Jane 211
Weiler, Donald 211
Welch, Dr. Charles 45
Welch, Edgar T. 47
Wellington, Ohio 146, 149, 266, 267
Wellsboro, Pennsylvania 189
Wellsville, New York 236
Westfield, New York 46, 54, 68
Westwood, New Jersey 218
Whitehall, New York 43, 45
Whitehouse, Morris 191, 194
White Tower 207
Whitey's Diner 170
Whitney, Charles 24
Wilde, Gert 240
Wilkes Barre, Pennsylvania 52
Williamsport, Pennsylvania 113
Wilson, L.A. 134
Wilson, Mathew P. 136
Woodlawn Diner 232
Woodlawn, New York 75
Worcester Lunch Car Company 259
Worcester, Massachusetts 24
Wurtz, William 215
Wyandotte, Michigan 239

Y

Yonk, Clement 71, 103
Youngsville, Pennsylvania 115

Z

Zelienople, Pennsylvania 146, 149
Zilka, Daniel 45, 149, 190, 266, 267
Zounakos, Louis 17
Zurcher, Neil 178

Artwork

Besides all the people that assisted me with technical knowledge, there were artists who imparted their artwork and creativity in this book.

Rick Ivansek - Advanced Grafix - http://www.ag-werks.com/
Valentine graphic at the start of Chapter 8. Rick provides everything from design and concept creation to finished marketing products.

Wendy Nooney - Nooney Art Designs - http://www.nooneyart.com/
Map in Geekery section of Chapter 3. Wendy operates a design studio located in upstate New York that specializes in creating artistic, completely custom, hand made wedding invitations and stationery.

Allen Pinney - https://allenpinney.company/
Posters and more. Freelance graphic designer and creative consultant.

Val Tindall - https://blackcrowgallery.com/
Featuring wearable, functional and decorative arts and crafts.

More Information

Michael Engle maintains http://www.nydiners.com/
American Diner Heritage can be found at http://www.americandinermuseum.org/
Larry Cultrera maintains https://dinerhotline.wordpress.com/
Spencer Stewart maintains https://dinerhunter.com/
Wesli Dymoke maintains https://www.dinerville.info/
Glenn Wells maintains http://www.roadsidefans.com/

Non-Diner information:
Randy Garbin maintains https://www.walkablejenkintown.com/
Ron Dylewski operates https://www.overeasyseo.com/

www.ingramcontent.com/pod-product-compliance
Lightning Source LLC
Chambersburg PA
CBHW081207170426
43198CB00018B/2877